Logic,
Programming
and Prolog

# Logic, Programming and Prolog

**ULF NILSSON**

and

**JAN MAŁUSZYŃSKI**

*Linköping University, Sweden*

JOHN WILEY & SONS

Chichester · New York · Brisbane · Toronto · Singapore

*Other Wiley Editorial Offices*

John Wiley & Sons, Inc., 605 Third Avenue,
New York, NY 10158-0012, USA

Jacaranda Wiley Ltd, G.P.O. Box 859, Brisbane,
Queensland 4001, Australia

John Wiley & Sons (Canada) Ltd, 22 Worcester Road,
Rexdale, Ontario M9W 1L1, Canada

John Wiley & Sons (SEA) Pte Ltd, 37 Jalan Pemimpin    05-04,
Block B, Union Industrial Building, Singapore 2057

*British Library Cataloguing in Publication Data available*

ISBN 0 471 92625 6

Printed in Great Britain by Courier International, Tiptree, Essex

# Contents

# Preface

During the recent five years the interest in logic programming and the programming language Prolog has grown substantially and the field has expanded to such extent that it is now difficult to keep up-to-date with all new advances. The sudden popularity of logic programming languages also provoked a large number of textbooks — within this time-period the number of monographs on logic programming and Prolog has increased from only a couple to several tens. These books usually fall into one of the following two categories:

- books which provide a *theoretical basis* for logic programming, and

- books which describe how to write programs in Prolog (sometimes even in particular Prolog systems).

## Objectives

The main objective for writing yet another textbook on these topics is to provide an intuitive account of *both* the foundations of logic programming and some simple programming techniques in the programming language Prolog. It is *not* primarily intended to be a theoretical handbook on logic programming. Nor is it intended to be a book on advanced Prolog programming. In both cases there are more suitable books around. Because of the diversity of the field there is of course a risk that nothing substantial is said about anything. We have tried to compensate for this risk by limiting our attention to (what we think are) the most important areas of logic programming and by providing the interested reader with pointers containing suggestions for further reading. As a consequence of this:

- the theoretical presentation is limited to well-established results and some of the most elaborate theorems are stated only with hints or pointers to their proofs;

- most of the program examples are small (toy?) programs whose prime aim is to illustrate the principal use of logic programming and to inspire the reader to apply similar techniques when writing "real" logic programs.

# Prerequisites

Like many other monographs, this book emerged out of lecture notes which finally stabilized after several years of teaching. It has been used as introductory reading in the logic programming course for third year undergraduate students mainly from the computer science curriculum at Linköping University. To take full benefit from the book, introductory courses in logic and discrete mathematics are recommended. Some basic knowledge in automata theory may be helpful but is not strictly necessary.

# Organization

The book is divided into three parts:

- Foundations;

- Programming in Logic;

- Alternative Logic Programming Schemes.

The first part deals with the logical aspects of logic programming and tries to provide a logical understanding of the programming language Prolog. Logic programs consist of logical formulas and computation is the process of deduction or proof construction. This makes logic programming fundamentally different from most other programming languages, largely a consequence of the fact that logic is considerably much older than electronic computers and not restricted to the view of computation associated with the traditional Von Neumann machine. The main difference between logic programming and modern programming languages is the *declarative* nature of logic. A program written in, for instance, Fortran can, in general, not be understood without taking *operational* considerations into account. That is, the Fortran-program cannot be understood without knowing *how* it is going to be executed. Logic on the other hand *can* be understood without any notion of evaluation or execution in mind. Logic formulas are propositions about some domain of discourse and each formula is always true or false in this world. One of the most important aims of this book is to emphasize this distinction between logic programs and programs written in traditional programming languages.

Chapter 1 contains a recapitulation of notions basic to logic in general. Readers who are already well acquainted with predicate logic can without problem omit this chapter. The chapter discusses concepts related both to model- and proof-theory of predicate logic including notions like *language, interpretation, model, logical consequence, logical inference, soundness* and *completeness*. The final section introduces the concept of *substitution* which is needed in subsequent chapters.

Chapter 2 introduces the restricted language of *definite programs* and discusses the model-theoretic consequences of restricting the language. By considering only definite programs it suffices to limit attention to so-called *Herbrand interpretations* making the model-theoretic treatment of the language much simpler than for the case of full predicate logic.

The operational semantics of definite programs is described in Chapter 3. The starting point is the notion of *unification*. A unification algorithm is provided and proved correct. Some of its properties are discussed. The unification algorithm is the basis for *SLD-resolution* which is the only inference rule needed for definite programs. Soundness and completeness of this rule are discussed.

The use of *negation* in logic programming is discussed in Chapter 4. It introduces the *negation-as-failure* rule used to implement negation in most Prolog systems and also provides a logical justification of the rule by extending the user's program with additional axioms. Thereafter definite programs are generalized to *normal* and *stratified* programs. The resulting proof-technique of this language is called *SLDNF-resolution* and is a result of combining SLD-resolution with the negation-as-failure rule. Results concerning soundness of both the negation-as-failure rule and SLDNF-resolution are discussed.

The final chapter of Part I introduces two notions available in existing Prolog systems. *Cut* is introduced as a mechanism for reducing the overhead of Prolog computations. The main objective of this section is to illustrate the effect of cut and to point out cases when its use is motivated, but also to point out cases when *not* to use cut, being one of the most common sources of errors. The conclusion is that cut should be used with great care and only when one has a thorough understanding of the principal ideas of logic programming. As a consequence, cut is not used in subsequent chapters. The second section of Chapter 5 discusses the use of predefined *arithmetic* predicates in Prolog and provides a logical explanation for them.

The second part of the book is devoted to some simple, but yet powerful, programming techniques in Prolog. The goal is not to study implementation-specific details of different Prolog systems nor is it our aim to develop real-size or highly optimized programs. The intention is rather to emphasize two basic principles which are important to appreciate before one starts considering writing "real" programs:

- logic programs are used to describe *relations*, and

- logic programs have both a declarative and an operational meaning. In order to write good programs it is important to keep both aspects in mind.

Part II of the book is divided into several chapters which relate logic programming to different fields of computer science while trying to emphasize these two points.

Chapter 6 describes logic programming from a *database* point of view. It is shown how logic programs can be used, in a coherent way, as a framework for representing relational databases and for retrieving information out of them. The chapter also contains some extensions to traditional databases. For instance, the ability to define infinite relations and the use of structured data.

Chapter 7 proceeds by describing how to define relations between *recursive data-structures* illustrated in the case of *lists*. The objective is to study how recursive data-structures give rise to recursive programs which can be defined in a uniform way by means of inductive definitions. The second part of the chapter defines an alternative representation of lists and describes advantages and disadvantages of this new representation.

Chapter 8 introduces the notion of *meta-* and *object*-language and illustrates how to use logic programs for describing SLD-resolution. The ability to do this in a simple way facilitates some very powerful programming techniques. The chapter also introduces some (controversial) built-in predicates available in most Prolog implementations.

Chapter 9 provides a continuation of Chapter 8. It demonstrates how to extend an interpreters from Chapter 8 into a simple *expert-system* shell. The resulting program can be used as a starting point for developing a full-scale expert system.

Historically one of the main objectives for implementing Prolog was its application for natural language processing. Chapter 10 demonstrates Prolog's ability to describe grammars. First different ways of recognizing strings in context free languages by means of logic programs are discussed. Thereafter larger classes of languages are considered. The last two sections introduce the notion of *Definite Clause Grammars* (DCGs) commonly used for describing both natural and artificial languages in Prolog.

The last chapter of Part II of the book elaborates on results from Chapter 6. The chapter demonstrates simple techniques for solving search-problems in state-transition graphs and raises some of the difficulties which are inherently associated with such problems.

The final part of the book is intended to give a brief introduction to some extensions of the logic programming paradigm. All three chapters deal with areas of active research. The objective is to raise the basic ideas and intuition which underlie these fields of research. It is our hope that the chapters will provide the reader with a foundation for further studies in one or more of these areas.

Chapter 12 describes a class of languages commonly called *concurrent logic programming languages*. The underlying execution model of these languages is based on concurrent execution and it allows for some interesting new applications of logic programming, like simulation and systems for controlling processes. The presentation concentrates on the characteristic principles of this class of languages, in particular on the mechanisms used to enforce *synchronization* between parallel processes and the notion of *don't care nondeterminism*.

The two final chapters can be seen as attempts to combine logic programming with *functional* programming. Chapter 13 introduces the use of *equations* for this purpose. The notion of *E-unification* (unification modulo a set $E$ of equations) is introduced and properties of $E$-unification algorithms are discussed. Finally it is shown how to generalize the notion of SLD-resolution to incorporate $E$-unification instead of "ordinary" unification.

The final chapter of Part III concerns the use of *constraints* in logic programming. The constraint logic programming scheme has attracted many people because of its generality, elegance and expressive strength. A rigorous semantical framework is available for the scheme but we prefer to illustrate the underlying principles via some simple examples.

In addition the book contains two appendices. The first of them provides bibliographical remarks to most of the chapters of the book including suggestions for further reading. The second appendix contains solutions and hints for some of the exercises which are available in the main text.

# Acknowledgements

The authors would like to thank a number of persons for their involvement in the course of writing this book. We are particularly indebted to students who lived through draft versions of the book and provided us with invaluable feedback. We also thank Staffan Bonnier, Wlodzimierz Drabent, Gu Xinli, Jalal Maleki, Mirka Miłkowska, Simin Nadjm-Tehrani, Torbjörn Näslund and Linda Smith who devoted much of their time reading parts of the manuscript. Needless to say, the remaining flaws are to be attributed to the authors.

Our deepest gratitude also to Rosemary Altoft, managing editor at John Wiley, and the anonymous referees whose comments influenced the final structure and contents of the book.

Finally we should mention that the material presented in this book is closely related to our research interests. We gratefully acknowledge the financial support of our research projects by the Swedish National Board for Technical Development and by Linköping University.

Linköping, Sweden                                                                ULF NILSSON
June 1989                                                                    JAN MAŁUSZYŃSKI

# Part I

# Foundations

# Chapter 1

# Preliminaries

## 1.1 Logic Formulas

When describing some state of affairs in the real world we often use *declarative*[1] sentences like:

(1) "Every mother loves her children"

(2) "Mary is a mother and Tom is Mary's child"

By applying some general rules of reasoning such descriptions can be used to draw new conclusions. For example, knowing (1) and (2) it is possible to conclude that:

(3) "Mary loves Tom"

A closer inspection reveals that (1) and (2) describe some *universe* of persons and some *relations* between these individuals — like "... is a mother", "... is a child of ..." or the relation "... loves ..." — which may or may not hold between the persons.[2] This example reflects the principal idea of *logic programming* — to describe possibly infinite relations on objects and to apply the programming system in order to draw conclusions like (3).

---

[1]The notion of declarative sentence has its roots in linguistics. A declarative sentence is a complete expression of natural language which is either true or false, as opposed to e.g. imperative or interrogative sentences (commands and questions). Only declarative sentences can be expressed in predicate logic.

[2]Some people would probably argue that "being a mother" is not a relation but rather a property. However, for practical reasons properties will be called relations and so will statements which relate more than two objects (like "... is the sum of ... and ...").

However, for a computer to deal with sentences like (1), (2) and (3) the *syntax* of the sentences must be precisely defined. What is even more important, the rules of reasoning — like the one which permits inferring (3) from (1) and (2) — must be carefully formalized. Fortunately most of these concepts are already studied by logicians. This chapter recapitulates some of the concepts which are used as a formal basis for further discussions in the rest of this book.

The first concept considered is that of *logic formulas* which provide a formalized syntax for writing sentences like (1), (2) and (3). Such sentences refer to *individuals* in some *world* and to *relations* between those individuals. Therefore the starting point is an assumption about the alphabet of the language. It must include:

- symbols for denoting individuals (e.g. the symbol *tom* may be used to denote the person Tom of our example). Such symbols will be called *constants*;

- symbols for denoting relations (like *loves, mother, child_of*). Such symbols are called *predicate symbols*.

Every predicate symbol has an associated natural number, called its arity. The relation named by an $n$-ary predicate symbol is a set of $n$-tuples of individuals; in the example above the predicate symbol *loves* denotes a set of pairs of persons, including the pair Mary and Tom, denoted by the constants *mary* and *tom*.

With the alphabet of constants, predicate symbols and some auxiliary characters, sentences of natural language like "Mary loves Tom" can be formalized as formulas like *loves(mary, tom)*.

The formal language should also provide the possibility of expressing sentences like (1) which refers to *all* elements of the described "world". This sentence says that "for all individuals X and Y, if X is a mother and Y is a child of X then X loves Y". For this, the language of logic introduces the symbol of *universal quantifier* "∀" ( to be read "for every" or "for all") and the alphabet of *variables*. A variable is a symbol that refers to an unspecified individual, like X and Y above. Now the sentences (1), (2) and (3) can be formalized accordingly:

(1')  $\forall X\,(\forall Y\,((mother(X) \wedge child\_of(Y, X)) \rightarrow loves(X, Y)))$

(2')  $mother(mary) \wedge child\_of(tom, mary)$

(3')  $loves(mary, tom)$

The symbols "∧" and "→" are examples of *logical connectives* which are used to combine logic formulas — "∧" reads "and" and is called *conjunction* whereas "→" is called *implication* and corresponds to the "if-then" construction above. Parentheses are used to disambiguate the language whenever necessary. Another connective which will be used frequently is that for expressing negation. It is denoted by "¬" (with reading "not"). For example the sentence "Tom does not love Mary" can be formalized as the formula:

$\neg loves(tom, mary)$

In what follows the symbol "∃" is sometimes used. It is called the *existential quantifier* and it reads "there exists". It makes it possible to express the fact that in the world under consideration there exists at least one individual which is in a certain relation with some other individuals. For example the sentence "Mary has a child" can be formalized as the formula:

$\exists X\ child\_of(X, mary)$

On occasion the logical connectives "∨" and "↔" are used. They formalize the connectives "or" and "if and only if" ("iff").

So far individuals have been represented only by constants. However it is often the case that in the world under consideration, some "individuals" are "composed objects". For instance, in some world it may be necessary to discuss relations between families as well as relations between persons. In this case it would be desirable to refer to a given family by a construction composed of the constants identifying the members of the family (actually what is needed is a *function* that constructs a family from its members). The language of logic offers means of solving this problem. It is assumed that its alphabet contains symbols called *functors* that represent functions over object domains. Every functor has assigned a natural number called its arity, which determines the number of arguments of the function. The constants can be seen as 0-ary functors. Assume now that there is a ternary[3] functor *family*, a binary functor *child* and a constant *none*. The family consisting of the parents Bill and Mary and children Tom and Alice can now be represented by the construction:

$family(bill, mary, child(tom, child(alice, none)))$

Such a construction is called a *compound term*.

The above informal discussion based on examples of simple declarative sentences gives motivation for introducing basic constructs of the language of symbolic logic. The kind of logic used here is called *predicate logic*. Next a formal

---

[3]Usually the terms *unary*, *binary* and *ternary* are used instead of 1-ary, 2-ary and 3-ary.

definition of this language is given. For the moment we specify only the form of allowed sentences, while the meaning of the language will be discussed separately. Thus the definition covers only the *syntax* of the language separated from its *semantics*.

From the syntactic point of view sentences are finite sequences of primitive symbols. Therefore the first thing to be defined is the *alphabet* of the language — it consists of the following classes of symbols:

- *variables* which will be written as identifiers beginning with capital letters. Examples of variables are $X, Xs, Y, X_7, \ldots$;

- *constants* which are integers or identifiers beginning with lower-case letters. Examples of constants are $x, alf, none, 17, \ldots$;

- *functors* which are identifiers beginning with lower-case letters and with an associated arity $> 0$. To emphasize the arity $n$ of a functor $f$ it is sometimes written in the form $f/n$;

- *predicate symbols* which are identifiers starting with lower-case letters and with an associated arity $\geq 0$. The notation $p/n$ is used also for predicate symbols;

- *logical connectives* which are $\wedge$ (conjunction), $\neg$ (negation), $\leftrightarrow$ (logical equivalence), $\rightarrow$ (implication) and $\vee$ (disjunction);

- *quantifiers* — $\forall$ (universal) and $\exists$ (existential);

- *auxiliary* symbols like parentheses and commas.

No syntactic distinction will be imposed between constants, functors and predicate symbols. It will be clear from the context what is intended. Notice also that the sets of functors and predicate symbols may contain identical identifiers with different arities. Constants are sometimes viewed as functors of arity 0. In general we shall try to use a syntax which is similar to that of the programming language *Prolog*.

Sentences of natural language consist of words where objects of the described world are represented by nouns. In the formalized language of predicate logic objects will be represented by strings called *terms* whose syntax is defined as follows:

**Definition 1.1 (Terms)** The set $\mathsf{T}$ of *terms* over a given alphabet $\mathsf{A}$ is the smallest set such that:

- any constant in $A$ is in $T$;

- any variable in $A$ is in $T$;

- if $f$ is an $n$-ary functor in $A$ and $t_1, \ldots, t_n \in T$ then $f(t_1, \ldots, t_n) \in T$.

∎

In natural language only certain combinations of words are meaningful sentences. The counterpart of sentences in predicate logic are special constructs built from terms. These are called *formulas* or well-formed formulas (wff) and their syntax is defined as follows:

**Definition 1.2 (Formulas)** Let $T$ be the set of terms over the alphabet $A$. The set $F$ of *wff* (wrt[4] $A$) is the smallest set such that:

- if $p$ is an $n$-ary predicate symbol and $t_1, \ldots, t_n \in T$ then $p(t_1, \ldots, t_n) \in F$;

- if $F$ and $G \in F$ then so are $(\neg F)$, $(F \wedge G)$, $(F \vee G)$, $(F \rightarrow G)$ and $(F \leftrightarrow G)$;

- if $F \in F$ and $X$ is a variable then $(\forall X F)$ and $(\exists X F) \in F$.

∎

Formulas of the form $p(t_1, \ldots, t_n)$ are called *atomic formulas* (or simply *atoms*). In order to use a syntax similar to that of Prolog, formulas in the form $(F \rightarrow G)$ are instead written in the form $(G \leftarrow F)$. To simplify the notation parentheses will be removed whenever possible. For this it will be assumed that the connectives have a binding-order where $\neg$, $\forall$ and $\exists$ bind stronger than $\vee$, which in turn binds stronger than $\wedge$ followed by $\rightarrow$ and finally $\leftrightarrow$. For instance, $(a \leftarrow ((\neg b) \wedge c))$ will be simplified into $a \leftarrow \neg b \wedge c$. Sometimes binary functors and predicate symbols are written in infix notation between their arguments.

Let $F$ be a formula. An occurrence of the variable $X$ in $F$ is said to be *bound* either if the occurrence follows directly after a quantifier or if it appears inside the subformula which follows directly after "$\forall X$" or "$\exists X$". Otherwise the occurrence is said to be *free*. A formula with no free occurrences of variables is said to be *closed*. A formula/term which contains no variables is called *ground*.

Let $X_1, \ldots, X_n$ be all variables that occur free in a formula $F$. The closed formula of the form $\forall X_1(\ldots(\forall X_n F)\ldots)$ is called the *universal closure* of $F$ and is denoted $\forall F$. Similarly, $\exists F$ designates the *existential closure* of $F$.

---

[4]With respect to.

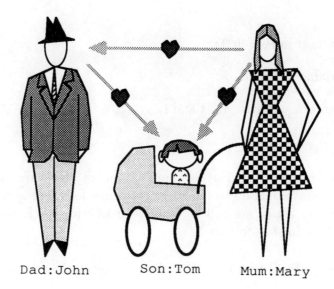

Dad:John            Son:Tom            Mum:Mary

Figure 1.1:  A family structure

## 1.2   Semantics of Formulas

The previous section introduced the language of formulas as a formalization of a class of declarative statements of natural language. Such sentences refer to some "world" and may be true or false in this world. The meaning of a logic formula is also defined relative to an "abstract world" called an (algebraic) *structure* and is also either true or false. In other words, to define the meaning of formulas, the formal connection between the formal language and a structure must be established. This section discusses the notions underlying this idea.

As stated above declarative statements refer to individuals, and concern relations and functions on individuals. Thus the mathematical abstraction of the "world", called a structure, is a nonempty set of individuals (called the *domain*) with a number of relations and functions defined on this domain. For example the structure referred to by the sentences (1), (2) and (3) may be an abstraction of the world shown in Figure 1.1. Its domain consists of three individuals — Mary, John and Tom. Moreover, three relations will be considered on this set: a unary relation, "... is a mother", and two binary relations, "... is a child of ..." and "... loves ...". For the sake of simplicity it is assumed that there are no functions in the structure.

The building blocks of the language of formulas are constants, functors and predicate symbols. The link between the language and the structure is established as follows:

**Definition 1.3 (Interpretation)** An interpretation $\Im$ of an alphabet $A$ is a nonempty domain $D$ (sometimes denoted $|\Im|$) and a mapping that associates:

- each constant $c \in A$ with an element $c_\Im \in D$;

- each $n$-ary functor $f \in A$ with a function $f_\Im : D^n \to D$;

- each $n$-ary predicate symbol $p \in A$ with a relation $p_\Im \subseteq D^n (= \underbrace{D \times \cdots \times D}_{n})$.

■

The interpretation of constants, functors and predicate symbols provides a basis for assigning truth values to formulas of the language. The meaning of a formula will be defined as a function on meanings of its components. First the meaning of terms will be defined since they are components of formulas. Since terms may contain variables the auxiliary notion of *valuation* is needed. A valuation is a mapping from variables of the alphabet to the domain of an interpretation. Thus, it is a function which assigns objects of an interpretation to variables of the language.

**Definition 1.4 (Semantics of terms)** Let $\Im$ be an interpretation, $\varphi$ a valuation and $t$ a term. Then the *meaning* $\overline{\varphi}_\Im(t)$ of $t$ is an element in $|\Im|$ defined as follows:

- if $t$ is a constant $c$ then $\overline{\varphi}_\Im(t) := c_\Im$;

- if $t$ is a variable $X$ then $\overline{\varphi}_\Im(t) := \varphi(X)$;

- if $t$ is of the form $f(t_1, \ldots, t_n)$, then $\overline{\varphi}_\Im(t) := f_\Im(\overline{\varphi}_\Im(t_1), \ldots, \overline{\varphi}_\Im(t_n))$.

When no ambiguity may arise the subscript of $\overline{\varphi}_\Im$ is dropped. ■

Notice that the meaning of a compound term is obtained by applying the function denoted by its main functor to the meanings of its principal subterms, which are obtained by recursive application of this definition.

**Example 1.5** Consider a language which includes the constant *zero*, the unary functor $s$ and the binary functor *plus*. Assume that the domain of $\Im$ is the set of the natural numbers ($\mathbb{N}$) and that:

$$
\begin{aligned}
zero_\Im &:= 0 \\
s_\Im(x) &:= 1 + x \\
plus_\Im(x, y) &:= x + y
\end{aligned}
$$

That is, *zero* denotes the *natural number* 0, *s* denotes the successor function and *plus* denotes the addition function. For the interpretation $\Im$ and a valuation $\varphi$ such that $\varphi(X) := 0$ the meaning of the term $plus(s(zero), X)$ is obtained as follows:

$$
\begin{aligned}
\overline{\varphi}(plus(s(zero), X)) &= \overline{\varphi}(s(zero)) + \overline{\varphi}(X) \\
&= (1 + \overline{\varphi}(zero)) + \varphi(X) \\
&= (1 + 0) + 0 \\
&= 1
\end{aligned}
$$

∎

The meaning of a formula is a truth value. The meaning depends on the components of the formula which are either (sub-) formulas or terms. As a consequence the meanings of formulas also rely on valuations. In the following definition the notation $\models_\Im^\varphi Q$ is used as a shorthand for the statement "$Q$ is true in $\Im$ wrt $\varphi$" and $\not\models_\Im^\varphi Q$ is to be read "$Q$ is false in $\Im$ wrt $\varphi$".

**Definition 1.6 (Semantics of wff's)** Let $\Im$ be an interpretation, $\varphi$ a valuation and $Q$ a formula. The meaning of $Q$ in $\Im$ wrt $\varphi$ is defined as follows:

- $\models_\Im^\varphi p(t_1, \ldots, t_n)$ iff $\langle \overline{\varphi}(t_1), \ldots, \overline{\varphi}(t_n) \rangle \in p_\Im$;

- $\models_\Im^\varphi (\neg F)$ iff $\not\models_\Im^\varphi F$;

- $\models_\Im^\varphi (F \wedge G)$ iff $\models_\Im^\varphi F$ and $\models_\Im^\varphi G$;

- $\models_\Im^\varphi (F \vee G)$ iff $\models_\Im^\varphi F$ or $\models_\Im^\varphi G$ (or both);

- $\models_\Im^\varphi (F \rightarrow G)$ iff $\not\models_\Im^\varphi F$ or $\models_\Im^\varphi G$;

- $\models_\Im^\varphi (F \leftrightarrow G)$ iff $\models_\Im^\varphi (F \rightarrow G)$ and $\models_\Im^\varphi (G \rightarrow F)$;

- $\models_\Im^\varphi (\forall X F)$ iff $\models_\Im^\sigma F$ for all $\sigma$ such that $\sigma(Y) = \varphi(Y)$ for every $Y \neq X$.

- $\models_\Im^\varphi (\exists X F)$ iff $\models_\Im^\sigma F$ for some $\sigma$ such that $\sigma(Y) = \varphi(Y)$ for every $Y \neq X$.

∎

The semantics of formulas as defined above relies on the auxiliary concept of *valuation* that associates variables of the formula with elements of the domain of the interpretation. It is easy to see that the truth value of a closed formula depends only on the interpretation. It is therefore common practice in logic programming to consider all formulas as being implicitly universally quantified, that is whenever there are free occurrences of variables in a formula its universal closure is considered instead. Since the valuation is of no importance for closed formulas it will be omitted when considering the meaning of such formulas.

**Example 1.7** Consider Example 1.5 again. Assume that the language contains also the predicate symbol $p$ and that:

$$p_\Im := \{\langle 1 \rangle, \langle 3 \rangle, \langle 5 \rangle, \langle 7 \rangle, \ldots\}$$

Then the meaning of the formula $p(zero) \land p(s(zero))$ in the interpretation $\Im$ is determined as follows:

$$
\begin{aligned}
\models_\Im p(zero) \land p(s(zero)) \quad &\text{iff} \quad \models_\Im p(zero) \text{ and } \models_\Im p(s(zero)) \\
&\text{iff} \quad \langle \overline{\varphi}(zero) \rangle \in p_\Im \text{ and } \langle \overline{\varphi}(s(zero)) \rangle \in p_\Im \\
&\text{iff} \quad \langle \overline{\varphi}(zero) \rangle \in p_\Im \text{ and } \langle 1 + \overline{\varphi}(zero) \rangle \in p_\Im \\
&\text{iff} \quad \langle 0 \rangle \in p_\Im \text{ and } \langle 1 \rangle \in p_\Im
\end{aligned}
$$

Now $\langle 1 \rangle \in p_\Im$ but $\langle 0 \rangle \notin p_\Im$ so the whole formula is false in $\Im$. ∎

**Example 1.8** Consider the interpretation $\Im$ that assigns:

- the persons Tom, John and Mary of the structure in Figure 1.1 to the constants *tom*, *john* and *mary*;

- the relations "... is a mother", "... is a child of ..." and "... loves ..." of the structure in Figure 1.1 to the predicate symbols *mother*/1, *child_of*/2 and *loves*/2.

Using the definition above it is easy to show that the meaning of the formula:

$$\forall X \, \exists Y \; loves(X, Y)$$

is false in $\Im$ (since Tom does not love anyone), while the meaning of formula:

$$\exists X \, \forall Y \; \neg loves(Y, X)$$

is true in $\Im$ (since Mary is not loved by anyone). ∎

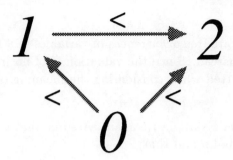

**Figure 1.2: An alternative structure**

## 1.3   Models and Logical Consequence

The motivation for introducing the language of formulas was to give a tool for describing "worlds" — that is, algebraic structures. Given a set of closed formulas P and an interpretation $\Im$ it is natural to ask whether the formulas of P give a proper account of this world. This is the case if all formulas of P are true in $\Im$.

**Definition 1.9 (Model)** An interpretation $\Im$ is said to be a *model* of P iff every formula of P is true in $\Im$. ∎

Clearly P has infinitely many interpretations. However, it may happen that none of them is a model of P. A trivial example is any P that includes the formula $(F \wedge \neg F)$ where $F$ is an arbitrary (closed) formula. Such sets of formulas are called *unsatisfiable*. When using formulas for describing "worlds" it is necessary to make sure that every description produced is *satisfiable* (that is, has at least one model), and in particular that the world being described is a model of P.

Generally, a satisfiable set of formulas has (infinitely) many models. This means that the formulas which properly describe a particular "world" of interest at the same time describe many other worlds.

**Example 1.10** Figure 1.2 shows another structure which can be used as a model of the formulas (1') and (2') of Section 1.1 which were originally used to describe the world of Figure 1.1. In order to be a model the constants *tom*, *john* and *mary* are assigned the natural numbers 0, 1 and 2 respectively — the predicate symbols *loves*, *child_of* and *mother* are interpreted as the relations greater-than, less-than and even. ∎

Our intention is to use the description of the world of interest to obtain more information about this world. This new information is to be represented by new formulas not explicitly included in the original description. An example is the formula (3') which is obtained from (1') and (2'). In other words, for a given set P of formulas other formulas (say $F$) which are also true in the world described by P are searched for. Unfortunately, P itself has many models and does not uniquely identify the "intended model" which was described by P. Therefore it must be required that $F$ is true in every model of P to guarantee that it is also true in the particular world of interest. This leads to the fundamental concept of *logical consequence*.

**Definition 1.11 (Logical consequence)** Let P be a set of closed formulas. A closed formula $F$ is called a logical consequence of P (to be denoted $P \models F$) iff $F$ is true in every model of P. ∎

**Example 1.12** To illustrate this notion by an example it is shown that (3') is a logical consequence of (1') and (2'). Let $\Im$ be an arbitrary interpretation. If $\Im$ is a model of (1') and (2') then:

(a) $\models_\Im \forall X (\forall Y ((mother(X) \wedge child\_of(Y,X)) \rightarrow loves(X,Y)))$

(b) $\models_\Im mother(mary) \wedge child\_of(tom, mary)$

For (a) to be true it is necessary that:

(c) $\models_\Im^\varphi mother(X) \wedge child\_of(Y,X) \rightarrow loves(X,Y)$

for any valuation $\varphi$ — specifically for $\varphi(X) =$ Mary and $\varphi(Y) =$ Tom. However, since these individuals are denoted by the constants *mary* and *tom* it must also hold that:

(d) $\models_\Im mother(mary) \wedge child\_of(tom, mary) \rightarrow loves(mary, tom)$

Finally, for this to hold it follows that $loves(mary, tom)$ must be true in $\Im$ (by Definition 1.6 and since (b) holds by assumption). Hence, any model of (1') and (2') is also a model of (3'). ∎

This example shows that it may be rather difficult to prove that a formula is a logical consequence of a set of formulas. The reason is that one has to use the semantics of the language of formulas and to deal with all models of the formulas.

One possible way to prove $P \models F$ is to show that $\neg F$ is false in every model of P, or put alternatively, that the set of formulas $P \cup \{\neg F\}$ is unsatisfiable (has no model). The proof of the following proposition is left as an exercise.

**Proposition 1.13 (Unsatisfiability)** Let P be a set of closed formulas and $F$ a closed formula. Then $P \models F$ iff $P \cup \{\neg F\}$ is unsatisfiable.                   ∎

It is often straightforward to show that a formula $F$ is not a logical consequence of the set P of formulas. For this, it suffices to give a model of P which is not a model of $F$.

**Example 1.14** Let P be the formulas:

(1')   $\forall X(p(X) \vee q(X) \leftarrow r(X))$
(2')   $r(a) \wedge r(b)$

To prove that $p(a)$ is not a logical consequence of P it suffices to consider an interpretation $\Im$ where $|\Im|$ is the set consisting of the two persons "Adam" and "Eve" and where:

- $a := \text{Adam}, b := \text{Eve}$;

- $p_\Im := \{\langle \text{Eve} \rangle\}$ (the property of being female);

- $q_\Im := \{\langle \text{Adam} \rangle\}$ (the property of being male);

- $r_\Im := \{\langle \text{Adam} \rangle, \langle \text{Eve} \rangle\}$ (the property of being a person).

Clearly, (1') is true in $\Im$ since "any person is either female or male". Similarly (2') is true since "both Adam and Eve are persons". However, $p(a)$ is false in $\Im$ since Adam is not a female.                                                    ∎

Another important concept based on the semantics of formulas is the notion of *logical equivalence*.

**Definition 1.15 (Logical equivalence)** Two formulas $F$ and $G$ are said to be logically equivalent (denoted $F \equiv G$) iff $F$ and $G$ have the same truth value for all interpretations $\Im$ and valuations $\sigma$.                                            ∎

Next a number of well-known facts concerning equivalences of formulas are given. Let $F$ and $G$ be arbitrary formulas and $H(X)$ a formula with zero or more free occurrences of $X$. Then:

$$
\begin{array}{rcl}
\neg\neg F & \equiv & F \\
F \rightarrow G & \equiv & \neg F \vee G \\
F \rightarrow G & \equiv & \neg G \rightarrow \neg F \\
F \leftrightarrow G & \equiv & (F \rightarrow G) \wedge (G \rightarrow F) \\
\neg(F \vee G) & \equiv & \neg F \wedge \neg G \qquad \text{DeMorgans's law} \\
\neg(F \wedge G) & \equiv & \neg F \vee \neg G \qquad \text{DeMorgans's law} \\
\neg\forall X H(X) & \equiv & \exists X \neg H(X) \qquad \text{DeMorgans's law} \\
\neg\exists X H(X) & \equiv & \forall X \neg H(X) \qquad \text{DeMorgans's law}
\end{array}
$$

and if there are no free occurrences of $X$ in $F$ then:

$$\forall X(F \vee H(X)) \equiv F \vee \forall X H(X)$$

Proofs of these equivalences are left as an exercise to the reader.

## 1.4  Logical Inference

In Section 1.1 the sentence (3) was obtained by reasoning about the sentences (1) and (2). The language was then formalized and the sentences were expressed as the logical formulas (1'), (2') and (3'). With this formalization, reasoning can be seen as a process of manipulation of formulas, which from a given set of formulas, like (1') and(2'), called the *premises*, produces a new formula called the *conclusion*, for instance (3'). One of the objectives of the symbolic logic is to formalize "reasoning principles" as formal re-write rules that can be used to generate new formulas from given ones. These rules are called *inference rules*. It is required that the inference rules correspond to correct ways of reasoning — whenever the premises are true in any world under consideration, any conclusion obtained by application of an inference rule should also be true in this world. In other words it is required that the inference rules produce only logical consequences of the premises to which they can be applied. An inference rule satisfying this requirement is said to be *sound*.

Among well-known inference rules of predicate logic the following are frequently used:

- *Modus ponens* or elimination rule for implication: This rule says that whenever formulas of the form $F$ and $(F \rightarrow G)$ are concluded from a set of premises $G$ can be inferred. This rule is often presented as follows:

$$\frac{F \quad F \rightarrow G}{G} \quad (\rightarrow E)$$

- Elimination rule for universal quantifier: This rule says that whenever a formula of the form $(\forall X F)$ is concluded from the premises a new formula can be concluded by replacing all free occurrences of $X$ in $F$ by some term $t$ which is *free for* $X$ (that is, all variables in $t$ remain free when $X$ is replaced by $t$: for details see e.g. [171] page 68). This rule is often presented as follows:

$$\frac{\forall X F}{F\{X/t\}} \quad (\forall E)$$

- Introduction rule for conjunction: This rule states that if formulas $F$ and $G$ are concluded from the premises then the conclusion $F \wedge G$ can be inferred. This is often stated as follows:

$$\frac{F \quad G}{F \wedge G} \quad (\wedge \text{I})$$

Soundness of these rules can be proved directly from the definition of the semantics of the language of formulas.

Their use can be illustrated by considering the example above. The premises are:

(1') $\forall X\, (\forall Y\, (mother(X) \wedge child\_of(Y, X) \rightarrow loves(X, Y)))$

(2') $mother(mary) \wedge child\_of(tom, mary)$

Elimination of the universal quantifier in (1') yields:

(1a) $\forall Y\, (mother(mary) \wedge child\_of(Y, mary) \rightarrow loves(mary, Y))$

Elimination of the universal quantifier in (1a) yields:

(1b) $mother(mary) \wedge child\_of(tom, mary) \rightarrow loves(mary, tom)$

Finally *modus ponens* applied to (2') and (1b) yields:

(3') $loves(mary, tom)$

Thus the conclusion (3') has been produced in a formal way by application of the inference rules. The example illustrates the concept of *derivability*. As observed, (3') is obtained from (1') and (2') not directly but in a number of inference steps, each of them adding a new formula to the initial set of premises. Any formula $F$ that can be obtained in that way from a given set P of premises is said to be *derivable* from P. This is denoted by $P \vdash F$. If the inference rules are sound it follows that whenever $P \vdash F$, then $P \models F$. That is, whatever can be derived from P is also a logical consequence of P. An important question related to the use of inference rules is the problem of whether all logical consequences of an arbitrary set of premises P can be also derived from P. In this case the set of inference rules is said to be *complete*.

A set of premises is said to be *inconsistent* if any formula can be derived from the set. Inconsistency is the proof-theoretic counterpart of unsatisfiability, and when the inference system is both sound and complete the two are frequently used synonymously.

## 1.5 Substitutions

The chapter is concluded with some concepts needed in forthcoming chapters.

**Definition 1.16 (Substitutions)** A substitution is a finite set of pairs of the form $\{X_1/t_1, \ldots, X_n/t_n\}$ where each $t_i$ is a term and each $X_i$ a variable such that $X_i \neq t_i$ and $X_i \neq X_j$ if $i \neq j$. The empty substitution is denoted $\epsilon$. ∎

A substitution may be viewed as a finite representation of a mapping from variables to terms. In what follows $Dom(\{X_1/t_1, \ldots, X_n/t_n\})$ denotes the set $\{X_1, \ldots, X_n\}$ and $Range(\{X_1/t_1, \ldots, X_n/t_n\})$ designates the set of all variables in $t_1, \ldots, t_n$. For variables not included in $Dom(\theta)$, $\theta$ behaves as the identity mapping. It is natural to extend the domain of substitutions to include also terms and formulas. In other words, it is possible to *apply* a substitution to an arbitrary term or formula in the following way:

**Definition 1.17 (Application)** Let $\theta := \{X_1/t_1, \ldots, X_n/t_n\}$ be a substitution and $E$ a term or a formula. The application $E\theta$ of $\theta$ to $E$ is the term/formula obtained by simultaneously replacing $t_i$ for every occurrence of $X_i$ in $E$ ($1 \leq i \leq n$). $E\theta$ is called an *instance* of $E$. ∎

**Example 1.18**

$$p(f(X, Z), f(Y, a))\{X/a, Y/Z, W/b\} = p(f(a, Z), f(Z, a))$$
$$p(X, Y)\{X/f(Y), Y/b\} = p(f(Y), b)$$

**Definition 1.19 (Composition)** Let $\theta$ and $\sigma$ be two substitutions:

$$\theta := \{X_1/s_1, \ldots, X_m/s_m\}$$
$$\sigma := \{Y_1/t_1, \ldots, Y_n/t_n\}$$

The composition $\theta\sigma$ of $\theta$ and $\sigma$ is obtained from the set:

$$\{X_1/s_1\sigma, \ldots, X_m/s_m\sigma, Y_1/t_1, \ldots, Y_n/t_n\}$$

by removing all $X_i/s_i\sigma$ for which $X_i = s_i\sigma$ ($1 \leq i \leq m$) and by removing those $Y_j/t_j$ for which $Y_j \in \{X_1, \ldots, X_m\}$ ($1 \leq j \leq n$). ∎

**Example 1.20**

$$\{X/f(Z), Y/W\}\{X/a, Z/a, W/Y\} = \{X/f(a), Z/a, W/Y\}$$

**Proposition 1.21 (Properties of substitutions)** Let $\theta$, $\sigma$ and $\gamma$ be substitutions and let $E$ be a term or a formula. Then:

- $E(\theta\sigma) = (E\theta)\sigma$

- $(\theta\sigma)\gamma = \theta(\sigma\gamma)$

- $\epsilon\theta = \theta\epsilon = \theta$

∎

Proofs are left as exercises.

Notice that in general composition of substitutions is not commutative as illustrated by the following example:

$$\{X/f(Y)\}\{Y/a\} = \{X/f(a), Y/a\} \neq \{Y/a\}\{X/f(Y)\} = \{Y/a, X/f(Y)\}$$

# Exercises

1. Formalize the following sentences of natural language as formulas of predicate logic:

   a) Every natural number has a successor.
   b) Nothing is better than taking a nap.
   c) There is no such thing as negative integers.
   d) The names have been changed to protect the innocent.
   e) Logic plays an important role in all areas of computer science.
   f) People who cannot solve any of these problems should read some introductory book on logic.

2. Formalize the following sentences of natural language into predicate logic:

   a) A bronze medal is better than nothing.
   b) Nothing is better than a gold medal.
   c) A bronze medal is better than a gold medal.

3. Prove Proposition 1.13.

4. Prove the equivalences in connection with Definition 1.15.

5. Show that $F$ and $Q$ are logically equivalent iff $\models_{\mathfrak{I}}^{\sigma} (F \leftrightarrow G)$ for all interpretations $\mathfrak{I}$ and valuations $\sigma$.

6. Let $F := \forall X \, \exists Y p(X,Y)$ and $G := \exists Y \, \forall X p(X,Y)$. State for each of the following four formulas whether it is satisfiable or not. If it is, give a model with the natural numbers as domain, if it is not, explain why.

$$(F \wedge G) \quad (F \wedge \neg G) \quad (\neg F \wedge \neg G) \quad (\neg F \wedge G)$$

7. Let $F$ and $G$ be closed formulas. Show that $F \equiv G$ iff $\{F\} \models G$ and $\{G\} \models F$.

8. Show that P is unsatisfiable iff there is some closed formula $F$ such that $P \models F$ and $P \models \neg F$.

9. Show that the following set of formulas is satisfiable only if the interpretation has an infinite domain

$$\forall X \, \neg p(X, X)$$
$$\forall X \, \forall Y \, \forall Z \, (p(X,Y) \wedge p(Y,Z) \rightarrow p(X,Z))$$
$$\forall X \, \exists Y \, p(X,Y)$$

10. Let $F$ be a formula and $\theta$ a substitution. Show that $\forall F \models \forall(F\theta)$.

11. Let $P_1$, $P_2$ and $P_3$ be sets of closed formulas. Define $\models$ in such a way that $P_1 \models P_2$ iff every formula in $P_2$ is a logical consequence of $P_1$. Then show that $\models$ is transitive — that is, if $P_1 \models P_2$ and $P_2 \models P_3$ then $P_1 \models P_3$.

12. Let $P_1$ and $P_2$ be sets of closed formulas. Show that if $P_1 \subseteq P_2$ and $P_1 \models F$ then $P_2 \models F$.

13. Prove Proposition 1.21.

14. A substitution $\theta$ is *idempotent* iff $\theta\theta = \theta$. Show that $\theta$ is idempotent iff $Dom(\theta) \cap Range(\theta) = \emptyset$.

15. Which of the following statements are true?

- $\sigma\theta = \delta\theta$ implies $\sigma = \delta$
- $\theta\sigma = \theta\delta$ implies $\sigma = \delta$
- $\sigma = \delta$ implies $\sigma\theta = \delta\theta$

# Chapter 2

# Definite Logic Programs

## 2.1 Definite Clauses

The idea of logic programming is to use a computer for drawing conclusions from declarative descriptions. Such descriptions — called logic programs — consist of finite sets of logic formulas. This formulation shows that the idea has its roots in the research on automatic theorem proving. However, the transition from experimental theorem proving to applied logic programming requires improved efficiency of the system. This is achieved by introducing restrictions on the language of formulas. These restrictions make it possible to use the relatively simple and powerful inference rule called the *SLD-resolution principle.* This chapter first introduces a restricted language of *definite logic programs* and their computational principles. In subsequent chapters a more general language of so-called *normal* programs is introduced. In this way the foundations of the programming language Prolog are presented.

To start with, attention will be restricted to a special type of *declarative* sentences of natural language that describe positive *facts* and *rules.* A sentence of this type either states that a relation holds between individuals (in case of a fact), or that a relation holds between individuals provided that some other relations hold (in case of a rule). For example consider the sentences:

$F_1$: "Tom is John's child"
$F_2$: "Ann is Tom's child"
$F_3$: "John is Mark's child"
$F_4$: "Alice is John's child"

$R_1$: "The grandchild of a person is a child of a child of this person"

These sentences may be formalized in two steps. First atomic formulas describing facts are introduced:

$F_1'$ :  $child(tom, john)$
$F_2'$ :  $child(ann, tom)$
$F_3'$ :  $child(john, mark)$
$F_4'$ :  $child(alice, john)$

Applying this notation to $R_1$ yields:

$R_1'$:  "For all $X$ and $Y$, $grandchild(X, Y)$ if there exists a $Z$ such that $child(X, Z)$ and $child(Z, Y)$"

This can be further formalized using quantifiers and the logical connectives "$\rightarrow$" and "$\wedge$". To preserve the natural order of expression the implication arrow is written in the reverse order:

$R_1'$ :  $\forall X \, \forall Y \, (grandchild(X, Y) \leftarrow \exists Z \, (child(X, Z) \wedge child(Z, Y)))$

This formula can easily be transformed into equivalent forms using the equivalences given in connection with Definition 1.15:

$$\forall X \, \forall Y \, (grandchild(X, Y) \vee \neg \exists Z \, (child(X, Z) \wedge child(Z, Y)))$$
$$\forall X \, \forall Y \, (grandchild(X, Y) \vee \forall Z \, \neg (child(X, Z) \wedge child(Z, Y)))$$
$$\forall X \, \forall Y \, \forall Z \, (grandchild(X, Y) \vee \neg (child(X, Z) \wedge child(Z, Y)))$$
$$\forall X \, \forall Y \, \forall Z \, (grandchild(X, Y) \leftarrow (child(X, Z) \wedge child(Z, Y)))$$

We now focus our attention on the language of formulas exemplified by the example above. It consists of formulas of the form:

$H \leftarrow B_1 \wedge \cdots \wedge B_n$   (where $n \geq 0$)

or equivalently in one of the forms:

$H \vee \neg (B_1 \wedge \cdots \wedge B_n)$

or:

$H \vee \neg B_1 \vee \cdots \vee \neg B_n$

where $H$ and all $B_i$'s are atomic formulas and all variables occurring in a formula are (implicitly) universally quantified over the whole formula. The formulas of this form are called *definite clauses*. Facts are definite clauses where $n = 0$. The atomic formula $H$ is called the *head* of the clause whereas $B_1 \wedge \cdots \wedge B_n$ is called its *body*.

The initial example shows that definite clauses allow a restricted use of existential quantifiers — the variables which occur only in some body literals are, as a matter of fact, existentially quantified over the body, though formally this is equivalent to universal quantification on the level of clauses.

The notational convention used in what follows is to represent clauses of the form $H \leftarrow B_1 \wedge \cdots \wedge B_n$ as:

$$H \leftarrow B_1, \ldots, B_n$$

If the body is empty (i.e. if $n = 0$) the implication arrow is omitted. Alternatively the empty body can be seen as a 0-ary predicate symbol ∎ which is true in every interpretation. We will also refer to a 0-ary predicate symbol □ which is false in every interpretation.

## 2.2 Definite Programs and Goals

The first kind of logic program to be discussed is defined as follows:

**Definition 2.1 (Definite programs)** A *definite program* is a finite set of definite clauses. ∎

To explain the use of logic formulas as programs, a general view of logic programming is presented in Figure 2.1. The programmer attempts to describe the *intended model* by means of declarative sentences (i.e. when writing a program he has in mind an algebraic structure, usually infinite, whose relations are to interpret the predicate symbols of the program). So far these sentences are definite clauses — facts and rules. The program is a set of logic formulas and it may have many models, including the intended model (Figure 2.1(a)). The concept of intended model makes it possible to discuss correctness of logic programs — a program P is incorrect iff the intended model is not a model of P. (Notice that in order to prove programs to be correct or to test programs it is necessary to have an alternative description of the intended model, independent of P).

The program will be used by the computer to draw conclusions about the intended model (Figure 2.1(b)). However, the only information available to the computer about the intended model is the program itself. So the conclusions drawn must be true in *any* model of the program to guarantee that they are true in the intended model (Figure 2.1(c)). In other words — the soundness of the system is a necessary condition. This will be discussed in Chapter 3. Before that, attention will be focused on the practical question of how a logic program is to be used.

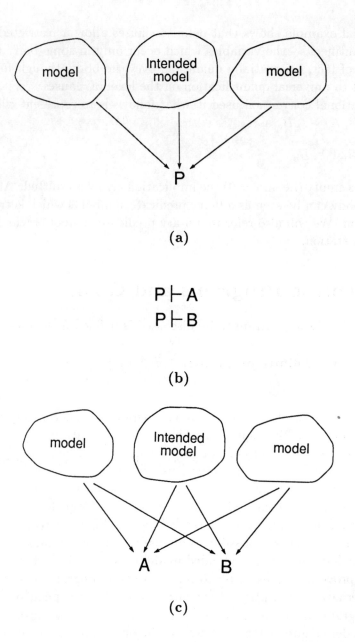

(a)

$$P \vdash A$$
$$P \vdash B$$

(b)

(c)

Figure 2.1:  General view of logic programming

The set of logical consequences of a program is infinite. Therefore the user is expected to *query* the program selectively for various aspects of the intended model. There is an analogy with relational databases — facts explicitly describe elements of the relations while rules give intensional characterization of some other elements. Since the rules may be recursive, the relation described may be infinite in contrast to the traditional relational databases. Another difference is the use of variables and compound terms. This chapter considers only "queries" of the form:

$$\forall(\neg(B_1 \wedge \cdots \wedge B_m))$$

Such formulas are called *definite goals* and are usually written as:

$$\leftarrow B_1, \ldots, B_m$$

where $B_i$'s are atomic formulas called *subgoals*. The goal where $m = 0$ is denoted $\Box$[1] and called the *empty* goal/clause. The logical meaning of a goal can be explained by referring to the equivalent universally quantified formula:

$$\forall X_1 \cdots \forall X_n \, \neg(B_1 \wedge \cdots \wedge B_m)$$

where $X_1, \ldots, X_n$ are all variables that occur in the goal. This is equivalent to:

$$\neg \, \exists X_1 \cdots \exists X_n \, (B_1 \wedge \cdots \wedge B_m)$$

This, in turn, can be seen as an existential question and the system attempts to deny it by constructing a counter-example. That is, it attempts to find terms $t_1, \ldots, t_n$ such that the formula obtained from $B_1 \wedge \ldots \wedge B_m$ when replacing the variable $X_i$ by $t_i$ ($1 \leq i \leq n$), is true in any model of the program, i.e. to construct a logical consequence of the program which is an instance of a conjunction of all subgoals in the goal.

By giving a definite goal the user selects the set of conclusions to be constructed. This set may be finite or infinite. The problem of how the machine constructs it will be discussed in Chapter 3.

The section is concluded with some examples of queries and the answers obtained to the corresponding goals in a typical Prolog system.

---

[1]Of course, formally it is not correct to write $\leftarrow B_1, \ldots, B_m$ since "$\leftarrow$" should have a formula also on the left-hand side. The problem becomes even more evident when $m = 0$ because then the right-hand side disappears as well. However, formally the problem can be viewed as follows — a definite goal has the form $\forall(\neg(B_1 \wedge \cdots \wedge B_m))$ which is equivalent to $\forall(\Box \vee \neg(B_1 \wedge \cdots \wedge B_m \wedge \blacksquare))$. A nonempty goal can thus be viewed as the formula $\forall(\Box \leftarrow (B_1 \wedge \cdots \wedge B_m))$. The empty goal can be viewed as the formula $\Box \leftarrow \blacksquare$ which is equivalent to $\Box$.

**Example 2.2** Referring to the family-example in Section 2.1 the user may ask questions like:

| Question | Goal |
|---|---|
| "Is Ann a child of Tom?" | $\leftarrow child(ann, tom)$ |
| "Who is a grandchild of Ann?" | $\leftarrow grandchild(X, ann)$ |
| "Whose grandchild is Tom?" | $\leftarrow grandchild(tom, X)$ |
| "Who is a grandchild of whom?" | $\leftarrow grandchild(X, Y)$ |

with expected answers:

- "yes".

- "none" (most Prolog implementations would answer "no").

- $X = mark$.

- This goal yields three answers:

$$
\begin{array}{llll}
X & = & tom & \qquad Y & = & mark \\
X & = & alice & \qquad Y & = & mark \\
X & = & ann & \qquad Y & = & john
\end{array}
$$

It is also possible to ask more complicated queries, for example "Is there a person whose grandchildren are Tom and Alice?", expressed formally as:

$$\leftarrow grandchild(tom, X), grandchild(alice, X)$$

whose (expected) answer is $X = mark$.        ∎

## 2.3   The Least Herbrand Model

Definite programs can only express positive knowledge — both facts and rules say which elements of a structure are in a relation, but they do not say when the relations do not hold. Therefore, using this language, it is not possible to construct contradictory descriptions, i.e. unsatisfiable sets of formulas. In other words, every definite program has a model. This section discusses this matter in more detail. It shows also that every definite program has a well defined *least* model. Intuitively this model reflects all information expressed by the program and nothing more.

We first focus attention on models of a special kind, called *Herbrand models*. The idea is to abstract from the actual meanings of the functors (here, constants are treated as 0-ary functors) of the language. More precisely, attention is restricted to the interpretations where the domain is the set of variable-free terms and the meaning of every ground term is this term. After all, it is a common practice in databases — the constants *tom* and *ann* may represent persons but the database describes relations between the persons by handling relations between the terms (symbols) no matter whom they represent.

The formal definition of such domains follows and is illustrated by two simple examples.

**Definition 2.3 (Herbrand universe, Herbrand base)** Let A be an alphabet containing at least one constant symbol. The set $U_A$ of all ground terms constructed from functors and constants in A is called the *Herbrand universe* of A. The set $B_A$ of all ground, atomic formulas over A is called the *Herbrand base* of A. ∎

The Herbrand universe and Herbrand base are often defined for a given *program*. In this case it is assumed that the alphabet of the program consists of exactly those symbols which appear in the program. It is also assumed that the program contains at least one constant (since otherwise, the domain would be empty).

**Example 2.4** Consider the following definite program P:

> $odd(s(0))$.
> $odd(s(s(X))) \leftarrow odd(X)$.

The program contains one constant $(0)$ and one unary functor $(s)$. Consequently the Herbrand universe looks as follows:

$$U_P = \{0, s(0), s(s(0)), s(s(s(0))), \ldots\}$$

Since the program contains only one (unary) predicate symbol $(odd)$ it has the following Herbrand base:

$$B_P = \{odd(0), odd(s(0)), odd(s(s(0))), \ldots\}$$

∎

**Example 2.5** Consider the following definite program P:

> $owns(owner(rabbit), rabbit)$.
> $happy(X) \leftarrow owns(X, rabbit)$.

In this case the Herbrand universe $U_P$ consists of the set:

$$\{rabbit, owner(rabbit), owner(owner(rabbit)), \ldots\}$$

and the Herbrand base $B_P$ of the set:

$$\{owns(x, y) \mid x, y \in U_P\} \cup \{happy(x) \mid x \in U_P\}$$

■

**Definition 2.6 (Herbrand interpretations)** A Herbrand interpretation of P is an interpretation $\Im$ such that:

- the domain of $\Im$ is $U_P$;

- for every constant $c$, $c_\Im$ is defined to be $c$ itself;

- for every $n$-ary functor $f$ the function $f_\Im$ is defined as follows

$$f_\Im(x_1, \ldots, x_n) := f(x_1, \ldots, x_n)$$

  That is, the function $f_\Im$ applied to $n$ ground terms composes them into the ground term with the principal functor $f$;

- for every $n$-ary predicate symbol $p$ the relation $p_\Im$ is a subset of $U_P^n$ (the set of all $n$-tuples of ground terms).

■

Thus Herbrand interpretations have predefined meanings of functors and to define a Herbrand interpretation it suffices to specify the relations associated with the predicate symbol. Hence, for an $n$-ary predicate symbol $p$ and a Herbrand interpretation $\Im$ the meaning $p_\Im$ of $p$ consists of the following set of $n$-tuples: $\{\langle t_1, \ldots, t_n \rangle \in U_P^n \mid \models_\Im p(t_1, \ldots, t_n)\}$.

**Example 2.7** One possible interpretation of the program P in Example 2.4 is $odd_\Im := \{\langle s(0) \rangle, \langle s(s(s(0))) \rangle\}$. A Herbrand interpretation can be specified by giving a family of such relations (one for every predicate symbol). ■

Since the domain of a Herbrand interpretation is the Herbrand universe the relations are sets of tuples of ground terms. One can define all of them at once by specifying a set of *labelled* tuples, where labels are predicate symbols. In other words a Herbrand interpretation $\Im$ can be seen as a subset of the Herbrand base (or a possibly infinite relational database), namely $\{A \in B_P \mid \models_\Im A\}$.

**Example 2.8** Consider some alternative Herbrand interpretations for P of Example 2.4.

$$\begin{aligned}
\Im_1 &:= \varnothing \\
\Im_2 &:= \{odd(s(0))\} \\
\Im_3 &:= \{odd(s(0)), odd(s(s(0)))\} \\
\Im_4 &:= \{odd(s^n(0)) \mid n \in \{1, 3, 5, 7, \ldots\}\} \\
&= \{odd(s(0)), odd(s(s(s(0)))), \ldots\} \\
\Im_5 &:= B_P
\end{aligned}$$

∎

**Definition 2.9 (Herbrand model)** A Herbrand model of a (closed) set of formulas is a Herbrand interpretation which is a model of every formula in the set. ∎

**Example 2.10** Clearly $\Im_2, \Im_3, \Im_4, \Im_5$ are models of $odd(s(0))$ since $odd(s(0)) \in \Im_i, (2 \leq i \leq 5)$.

However, $\Im_2$ is not a model of $odd(s(s(X))) \leftarrow odd(X)$ since there is an instance of the clause — namely $odd(s(s(s(0)))) \leftarrow odd(s(0))$ — such that all premises are true: $odd(s(0)) \in \Im_2$, but the conclusion is false: $odd(s(s(s(0)))) \notin \Im_2$. A similar reasoning proves that $\Im_3$ is not a model of the rule.

However, $\Im_4$ is a model also of the rule; let $odd(s(s(t))) \leftarrow odd(t)$ be any ground instance of the rule where $t \in U_P$. Clearly, $odd(s(s(t))) \leftarrow odd(t)$ is true if $odd(t) \notin \Im_4$ (check with Definition 1.6). Furthermore, if $odd(t) \in \Im_4$ then it must also hold that $odd(s(s(t))) \in \Im_4$ (check with the definition of $\Im_4$ above) and hence $odd(s(s(t))) \leftarrow odd(t)$ is true in $\Im_4$. Similar reasoning proves that $\Im_5$ is also a model of both clauses. ∎

Generally nonexistence of a Herbrand model of a set of formulas P does not mean that P is unsatisfiable. That is, there are sets of formulas P which lack a Herbrand model but which have other models.

**Example 2.11** Consider the formulas $\{\neg p(a), \exists X\, p(X)\}$ where $U_P := \{a\}$ and $B_P := \{p(a)\}$. Clearly, there are only two Herbrand interpretations — the empty set and $B_P$ itself. The former is not a model of the second formula. The latter is a model of the second formula but not of the first.

However, it is not very hard to find a model of the formulas — let the domain be the natural numbers, assign 0 to the constant $a$ and the relation $\{\langle 1 \rangle, \langle 3 \rangle, \langle 5 \rangle, \ldots\}$ to the predicate symbol $p$ (i.e. let $p$ denote the "odd"-relation). Clearly this is a model since "0 is not odd" and "there exists a natural number which is odd, e.g. 1". ∎

So what is the point in bringing up Herbrand interpretations? There are two reasons for this. Firstly, every non-Herbrand model of a definite program gives rise to a Herbrand model as shown below, so that the situation of Example 2.11 cannot happen. Secondly, the machine communicates with the user in the language of logic. The results of computations are some facts (or conjunctions of facts) which logically follow from the program. As seen later the concept of a Herbrand model makes it possible to characterize the set of all such facts.

The following theorem relates non-Herbrand models and Herbrand models of a definite program.

**Theorem 2.12** Let $\Im'$ be a model of a definite program P. The set $\Im := \{A \in B_P \mid \models_{\Im'} A\}$ is a Herbrand model of P. ∎

*Proof*:   Clearly, $\Im$ is a Herbrand interpretation. Now assume that $\Im'$ is a model and that $\Im$ is not a model of P. In other words, there exists a ground instance of a clause in P:

$$H \leftarrow B_1, \ldots, B_m \quad (m \geq 0)$$

which is not true in $\Im$.

Since this clause is false in $\Im$ then $B_1, \ldots, B_m$ are all true and $H$ is false in $\Im$. Hence, by the definition of $\Im$ we conclude that $B_1, \ldots, B_m$ are true and $H$ is false in $\Im'$. This contradicts the assumption that $\Im'$ is a model. Hence $\Im$ is a model of P. ∎

Notice that the Herbrand base of a definite program P *is* a Herbrand model of the program. To check that this is so, simply take an arbitrary ground instance of any clause $H \leftarrow B_1, \ldots, B_m$ in P. Clearly, all $B_i$'s and $H$ are in the Herbrand base. Hence the formula is true. However, this model is rather uninteresting — every $n$-ary predicate of the program is interpreted as the full $n$-ary relation over the domain of ground terms. More important is of course the question — what are the *interesting* models of the program? Intuitively there is no reason to expect that the model includes more ground atoms than those which follow from the program. By the analogy to databases — if John is not in the telephone directory he probably has no telephone. However, the directory gives only positive facts and if John has a telephone it is not a contradiction to what is said in the directory.

The rest of this section is organized as follows. First it is shown that there exists a *unique* minimal model called the least Herbrand model of a definite program. Then it is shown that this model really contains all positive information present in the program.

The Herbrand models of a definite program are subsets of its Herbrand base. Thus the set-inclusion is a natural ordering of such models. In order to show the existence of least models with respect to set-inclusion it suffices to show that the intersection of all Herbrand models is also a (Herbrand) model.

**Theorem 2.13 (Model intersection property)** Let $Mod_P := \{\mathfrak{I}_1, \mathfrak{I}_2, \ldots\}$ be a non-empty family of Herbrand models of a definite program P. Then the intersection $\mathfrak{I} := \mathfrak{I}_1 \cap \mathfrak{I}_2 \cap \ldots$ is a Herbrand model of P. ∎

*Proof*:  Assume that $\mathfrak{I}$ is not a model of P. Then there exists a ground instance of a clause of P:

$$H \leftarrow B_1, \ldots, B_m \quad (m \geq 0)$$

which is not true in $\mathfrak{I}$. This implies that $\mathfrak{I}$ includes $B_1, \ldots, B_m$ but not $H$. Then $B_1, \ldots, B_m$ are elements of every set of the family $Mod_P$. Moreover there must be at least one model $\mathfrak{I}_i$ in the family $Mod_P$ which does not include $H$. Thus $H \leftarrow B_1, \ldots, B_m$ is not true in this $\mathfrak{I}_i$. Hence $\mathfrak{I}_i$ is not a model of the program, which contradicts the assumption. This concludes the proof that the intersection of any set of Herbrand models of a program is also a Herbrand model. ∎

Thus by taking the intersection of all Herbrand models (it is known that every definite program P has at least one Herbrand models—namely $B_P$) the least Herbrand model of the definite program is obtained.

**Example 2.14** Let P be the definite program $\{male(adam), female(eve)\}$ with obvious intended interpretation. P has the following four Herbrand models:

$$\{male(adam), female(eve)\}$$
$$\{male(adam), male(eve), female(eve)\}$$
$$\{male(adam), female(eve), female(adam)\}$$
$$\{male(adam), male(eve), female(eve), female(adam)\}$$

It is not very hard to see that any intersection of these yields a Herbrand model. However, all but the first model contain atoms incompatible with the intended one. Notice also that the intersection of all four models yields a model which corresponds to the intended model. ∎

This example shows that there is a connection between the least Herbrand model and the intended model of a definite program. The intended model is an abstraction of the world to be described by the program. The world may be richer than the least Herbrand model. For instance, there may be more female individuals than just Eve. However, the information not included explicitly (via facts) or implicitly (via rules) in the program cannot be obtained as an answer to a goal. Answers correspond to logical consequences of the program and it therefore seems reasonable to expect that a tuple $\langle x_1, \ldots, x_n \rangle$ of individuals is in the relation $p_{\mathfrak{S}}$ of the intended model $\mathfrak{S}$ iff there is a tuple of ground terms $\langle t_1, \ldots, t_n \rangle$ such that, for $1 \leq i \leq n$, the meaning of $t_i$ is $x_i$ and the ground, atomic formula $p(t_1, \ldots, t_n)$ is a logical consequence of the program. The set of all such ground atoms can be seen as a "coded" version of the intended model. The following theorem relates it to the least Herbrand model.

**Theorem 2.15** The least Herbrand model $M_P$ of a definite program P is the set of all ground atomic logical consequences of the program. That is, $M_P = \{A \in B_P \mid P \models A\}$. ∎

*Proof*: Show first $M_P \supseteq \{A \in B_P \mid P \models A\}$: It is easy to see that every ground atom $A$ which is a logical consequence of P is an element of $M_P$. Indeed, by the definition of logical consequence $A$ must be true in $M_P$. On the other hand, the definition of Herbrand interpretation says that $A$ is true in $M_P$ iff $A$ is an element of $M_P$.

Then show that $M_P \subseteq \{A \in B_P \mid P \models A\}$: Assume that $A$ is in $M_P$. Hence it is true in every Herbrand model of P. Assume that it is not true in some non-Herbrand model $\mathfrak{S}'$ of P. But we know (see Theorem 2.12) that the set $\mathfrak{S}$ of all ground atomic formulas which are true in $\mathfrak{S}'$ is a Herbrand model of P. Hence $A$ cannot be an element of $\mathfrak{S}$ which contradicts the assumption that there exists a model of P where $A$ is false. Hence $A$ is true in every model of P, that is $P \models A$, which concludes the proof. ∎

The model intersection property expressed by Theorem 2.13 does not hold for arbitrary formulas as illustrated by the following example.

**Example 2.16** Consider the formula $p(a) \vee q(b)$. Clearly, both $\{p(a)\}$ and $\{q(b)\}$ are Herbrand models of the formula. However, the intersection $\{p(a)\} \cap \{q(b)\} = \emptyset$ is not a model. The two models are examples of *minimal* models — that is, you cannot remove any element from the model and still have a model. However, there is no *least* model — that is, a unique minimal model. ∎

## 2.4   Construction of Least Herbrand Models

The question arises how the least Herbrand model can be constructed, or approximated by successive enumeration of its elements. The answer to this question is given by a *fixpoint* approach to the semantics of definite programs. (A fixpoint of a function $f : D \rightarrow D$ is an element $x \in D$ such that $f(x) = x$.) Below follows an outline of this construction since the discussion of the relevant theory is outside of the scope of this book. However, the intuition behind the construction is the following:

A definite program consists of facts (unit clauses) and rules (nonunit clauses). Clearly, all ground instances of the facts must be included in every Herbrand model (if a Herbrand interpretation $\Im$ does not include a ground instance of a fact $A$ of the program then $A$ is not true in $\Im$ and $\Im$ is not a model).

Next, consider a rule $H \leftarrow B_1, \ldots, B_m$ where $(m > 0)$. This rule states that whenever $B_1, \ldots, B_m$ are true then so is $H$. In other words, take any ground instance $H' \leftarrow B_1', \ldots, B_m'$ of the rule. If $\Im$ includes $B_1', \ldots, B_m'$ it must also include $H'$ to be a model.

Consider the set $\Im_1$ of all ground instances of facts in the program. It is now possible to use every instance of each rule to augment $\Im_1$ with new elements which necessarily must belong to every model. In that way a new set $\Im_2$ is obtained which can be used again to generate more elements which must belong to the model. This process is repeated as long as new elements are generated. The new elements added to $\Im_{i+1}$ are those which *must immediately follow* from $\Im_i$.

The construction outlined above can be formally defined as an iteration of the transformation $T_P$ on Herbrand interpretations of the program P. The operation is called the *immediate consequence operator* and is defined as follows:

**Definition 2.17 (Immediate consequence operator)** Let $ground(\text{P})$ be the set of all ground instances of clauses in P. $T_P : \wp(B_P) \rightarrow \wp(B_P)$ is then defined as follows ($\wp(x)$ designates the set of all subsets of $x$):

$$T_P(x) := \{H \mid H \leftarrow B_1, \ldots, B_m \in ground(\text{P}) \wedge \{B_1, \ldots, B_m\} \subseteq x\}$$

∎

It can be shown that, for definite programs, there exists a least interpretation $\Im$ such that $T_P(\Im) = \Im$ and that $\Im$ is identical with the least Herbrand model $M_P$ (wrt set-inclusion). Moreover, $M_P$ is the limit of the increasing, possibly infinite sequence of iterations:

$$T_P(\varnothing), T_P(T_P(\varnothing)), T_P(T_P(T_P(\varnothing))), \ldots$$

There is a standard notation used to denote elements of the sequence of interpretations constructed for P. Namely:

$$T_P \uparrow 0 \; := \; \varnothing$$

$$T_P \uparrow (i+1) \; := \; T_P(T_P \uparrow i)$$

$$T_P \uparrow \omega \; := \; \bigcup_{i=0}^{\infty} T_P \uparrow i$$

The following illustrates the construction by means of an example:

**Example 2.18** Consider again the program of Example 2.4.

$$T_P \uparrow 0 \; = \; \varnothing$$
$$T_P \uparrow 1 \; = \; \{odd(s(0))\}$$
$$T_P \uparrow 2 \; = \; \{odd(s(s(s(0)))), odd(s(0))\}$$
$$\vdots$$
$$T_P \uparrow \omega \; = \; \{odd(s^n(0)) \mid n \in \{1,3,5,\ldots\}\}$$

∎

As already mentioned above it has been established that the set constructed in this way is identical to the least Herbrand model.

**Theorem 2.19** Let P be a definite program and $M_P$ its least Herbrand model. Then:

- $M_P$ is the least Herbrand interpretation such that $T_P(M_P) = M_P$ (i.e. it is the least fixpoint of $T_P$).

- $M_P = T_P \uparrow \omega$.

∎

For additional details and proofs see for example [5,105,172].

# Exercises

16. Rewrite the following formulas in the form $H \leftarrow B_1, \ldots, B_m$:

    1) $\forall X \, (p(X) \vee \neg q(X))$
    2) $\forall X \, (p(X) \vee \neg \exists Y \, (q(X,Y) \wedge r(X)))$
    3) $\forall X \, (\neg p(X) \vee (q(X) \rightarrow r(X)))$
    4) $\forall X \, (r(X) \rightarrow (q(X) \rightarrow p(X)))$

17. Give the Herbrand universe and Herbrand base for the following definite program:

$$p(f(X)) \leftarrow q(X, g(X)).$$
$$q(a, g(b)).$$
$$q(b, g(b)).$$

18. Give the Herbrand universe and Herbrand base for the following definite program:

$$p(s(X), Y, s(Z)) \leftarrow p(X, Y, Z).$$
$$p(0, X, X).$$

19. Consider the Herbrand universe consisting of the constants $a, b, c$ and $d$. Let $\Im$ be the Herbrand interpretation:

$$\{p(a), p(b), q(a), q(b), q(c), q(d)\}$$

Which of the following formulas are true in $\Im$?

1) $\forall X p(X)$
2) $\forall X q(X)$
3) $\exists X (q(X) \wedge p(X))$
4) $\forall X (q(X) \rightarrow p(X))$
5) $\forall X (p(X) \rightarrow q(X))$

20. Give the least Herbrand model of the program in exercise 17.

21. Give the least Herbrand model of the program in exercise 18. *Hint:* the model is infinite, but a certain pattern can be spotted when using the $T_P$-operator.

22. Let P be a definite program and $\Im$ a Herbrand interpretation. Show that $\Im$ is a model of P iff $T_P(\Im) \subseteq \Im$.

# Chapter 3

# SLD-Resolution

## 3.1 Informal Introduction

This chapter discusses the inference technique which is the basis for logic programming. Its cornerstone is the inference rule called the *resolution principle*. It was introduced by J. A. Robinson for a more general language than the language of definite programs. This chapter presents only a specialization of this rule which is applied to definite programs. For reasons explained later, it will be called the *SLD-resolution principle*. In the previous chapter a model-theoretic semantics of definite programs was discussed. The SLD-resolution principle makes it possible to draw correct conclusions from the program, thus giving a foundation for logically sound *operational semantics* of programs.

Every inference rule formalizes some natural way of reasoning. The presentation of the SLD-resolution principle will be preceded by an informal discussion about the underlying reasoning techniques. These will be illustrated by an example of such reasoning.

The sentences of logic programs have a general structure of implication:

$$H \leftarrow B_1, \ldots, B_m$$

or equivalently:

$$H \vee \neg (B_1 \wedge \cdots \wedge B_m)$$

where $H$ may be absent (a goal clause) and $m \geq 0$.

Now consider the following sentences:

- "Every good student taught by a logician knows logic"

37

- "Tom is a good student"

- "Peter is a logician"

- "Tom is Peter's student"

These give rise to the following definite program P:

$$knows\_logic(X) \leftarrow good\_student(X), teacher(Y, X), logician(Y).$$
$$good\_student(tom).$$
$$logician(peter).$$
$$teacher(peter, tom).$$

Notice that this program gives only positive knowledge — it does not say that the good students taught by logicians are the *only* persons knowing logic. This problem will be raised again in Chapter 4 when discussing the issue of negation.

Say now that we want to ask the question "Who knows logic?". The question concerns the world described by the program P, that is, the intended model of P. We would of course like to see the answer "Tom" to this question. However, predicate logic does not provide means for expressing this type of *interrogative* sentence — only *declarative* ones. Therefore the question is formalized as the goal clause:

$$\leftarrow knows\_logic(Z) \qquad\qquad\qquad (1)$$

which is an abbreviation for:

$$\forall Z \ \neg knows\_logic(Z)$$

equivalent to:

$$\neg \exists Z \ knows\_logic(Z)$$

whose reading is "Nobody knows logic" — i.e. a negative answer to the question asked above. The objective now is to show that this answer is a false statement in every model of P (and in particular in the intended model). By Proposition 1.13 it suffices to show unsatisfiability of the set of formulas $P \cup \{\neg \exists Z \ knows\_logic(Z)\}$. But this is equivalent to showing that:

$$P \cup \{\neg \exists Z \ knows\_logic(Z)\} \models \Box$$

Alas this would result only in a "yes"-answer to the original question, while the expected answer is "Tom". Thus, the objective is rather to find a substitution $\theta$ such that the set:

$$P \cup \{\neg\, knows\_logic(Z)\theta\}$$

is unsatisfiable or equivalently such that:

$$P \models knows\_logic(Z)\theta$$

The starting point of reasoning is the assumption (1) — "For any Z, Z does not know logic". By inspection of the program one discovers a rule concerning X's who know logic. Its equivalent reading is:

$$\neg knows\_logic(X) \rightarrow \neg(good\_student(X) \wedge teacher(Y,X) \wedge logician(Y))$$

Elimination of universal quantification and the use of *modus ponens* yields:

$$\neg\,(good\_student(Z) \wedge teacher(Y,Z) \wedge logician(Y))$$

or equivalently:

$$\leftarrow good\_student(Z), teacher(Y,Z), logician(Y) \tag{2}$$

Thus, one step of reasoning amounts to replacing a goal $G$ (in this case (1)) by another goal $G'$ (in this case (2)) which is true in any model of $P \cup \{G\}$. It now remains to be shown that $P \cup \{G'\}$ is unsatisfiable. Since (2) is equivalent to:

$$\forall Z\, \forall Y\, (\neg good\_student(Z) \vee \neg teacher(Y,Z) \vee \neg logician(Y))$$

the new goal says that every individual:

- is not a good student, or

- has no teacher, or

- none of his teachers is a logician.

Now, (2) can be shown to be unsatisfiable with P if in every model of P there is:

- a good student taught by a logician.

Thus, check first whether there are good students. Assume that there are no good students, i.e:

$$\forall Z\, \neg good\_student(Z)$$

or equivalently:

$$\leftarrow good\_student(Z)$$

But P contains the fact:

   $good\_student(tom)$

which is equivalent to:

   $\neg good\_student(tom) \rightarrow \square$

Hence, in every model of P there is a good student denoted by the constant *tom*. Consequently, if nobody knows logic, "none of Tom's teachers is a logician":

   $\leftarrow teacher(Y, tom), logician(Y)$                                    (3)

Next, check whether Tom has teachers. The program contains the fact:

   $teacher(peter, tom)$

or equivalently:

   $\neg teacher(peter, tom) \rightarrow \square$

Hence, if nobody knows logic "Peter must not be a logician":

   $\leftarrow logician(peter)$                                               (4)

But he is — there is a fact of P:

   $logician(peter)$

or:

   $\neg logician(peter) \rightarrow \square$

This leads to the final conclusion that:

   $P \cup \{\neg knows\_logic(tom)\} \models \square$

Hence, the reasoning process produced the answer $Z = tom$ for the goal:

   $\leftarrow knows\_logic(Z)$

   The way of reasoning used in this example is as follows: to show existence of something, assume the contrary and use *modus ponens* and elimination of the universal quantifier to find a counter-example for the assumption. This is a general idea to be used in computations of logic programs. As illustrated above, a single computation (reasoning) step transforms a set of atomic formulas — that is, a *definite goal* — into a new set of atoms. It uses a selected atomic formula $p(t_1, \ldots, t_n)$ of the goal and a selected program clause of the form $p(t'_1, \ldots, t'_n) \leftarrow$

$B_1, \ldots, B_m$ (where $m \geq 0$ and $B_1, \ldots, B_m$ are atoms) to find a common instance of $p(t_1, \ldots, t_n)$ and $p(t'_1, \ldots, t'_n)$. In other words a substitution $\theta$ is constructed such that $p(t_1, \ldots, t_n)\theta$ and $p(t'_1, \ldots, t'_n)\theta$ are identical (such a substitution is called a *unifier*. The problem of finding unifiers will be discussed in the next section). The new goal is constructed from the old one by replacing the selected atom by the set of body atoms of the clause and applying $\theta$ to all atoms obtained in that way. This basic computation step can be seen as an inference rule since it transforms logic formulas. It will be called the resolution principle for definite programs or *SLD-resolution* principle. As illustrated above it combines in a special way *modus ponens* with the elimination rule for the universal quantifier.

At the last step of reasoning the empty goal is obtained, which logically corresponds to falsity. The final conclusion then is the negation of the initial goal. Since this goal is of the form $\forall \neg (B_1 \wedge \cdots \wedge B_m)$, the conclusion is equivalent (by DeMorgan's laws) to the formula $\exists (B_1 \wedge \cdots \wedge B_m)$. This can be obtained by the inference rule known as *reductio ad absurdum*. Every step of reasoning produces a substitution. Unsatisfiability of the original goal $\leftarrow B_1, \ldots, B_m$ with P is demonstrated in $k$ steps by showing that its instance:

$$\leftarrow (B_1, \ldots, B_m)\theta_1 \cdots \theta_k$$

is unsatisfiable, or equivalently that:

$$P \models (B_1 \wedge \cdots \wedge B_m)\theta_1 \cdots \theta_k$$

In the example discussed, the goal "Nobody knows logic" is unsatisfiable with P since its instance "Tom does not know logic" is unsatisfiable with P. In other words — in every model of P the sentence "Tom knows logic" is true.

It is worth noticing that the unifiers may leave some variables unbound. In this case the universal closure of $(B_1 \wedge \cdots \wedge B_m)\theta_1 \cdots \theta_k$ is a logical consequence of P. Examples of such answers will appear below.

Notice also that generally the computation steps are not *deterministic* — any atom of a goal may be selected and there may be several clauses matching the selected atom. Another potential source of nondeterminism concerns the existence of alternative unifiers for two atoms. These remarks suggest that it may be possible to construct (sometimes infinitely) many solutions, i.e. counter-examples for the initial goal. On the other hand it may also happen that the selected atom has no matching clause. If so, it means that, using this method, it is not possible to construct any counter-example for the initial goal. The computation may also loop without producing any solution.

## 3.2   Most General Unifiers

Reasoning applied in the example of Section 3.1 is based on "matching" of atoms and terms. This section discusses the problem in more detail. It gives its abstract formulation and presents an algorithmic solution.

Syntactically atoms and terms are similar structures. Since we are dealing here with syntactical matching no distinction will be made between terms and atoms. They will simply be referred to as *structures*. The functors and the predicate symbols will, in this context, be called *constructors*.

For structures of the form $c(s_1, \ldots, s_n)$ the symbol $c$ will be called its *principal symbol* and $s_i$ its i-th *direct substructure*. The principal symbol of a constant or a variable is the term itself (obviously, constants and variables have no direct substructures).

**Definition 3.1 (Length of structure)** The *length* $|s|$ of a structure $s$ is defined as follows:

- if $s$ is a variable or a constant then $|s| := 1$;

- if $s$ has the form $c(s_1, \ldots, s_n)$, $n \geq 0$ then $|s| := |s_1| + \cdots + |s_n| + 1$.

∎

**Definition 3.2 (Unifier)** Let $s_1$ and $s_2$ be structures and let $\theta$ be a substitution. Then $\theta$ is called a *unifier* of $s_1$ and $s_2$ iff $s_1\theta$ and $s_2\theta$ are identical.  ∎

**Example 3.3** The substitution $\theta := \{X/f(a), Z/f(f(a))\}$ is a unifier of the two structures $p(X, f(X))$ and $p(f(a), Z)$ since:

$$p(X, f(X))\theta = p(f(a), Z)\theta = p(f(a), f(f(a)))$$

The substitution $\theta := \{X/a, Z/b\}$ is not a unifier of $p(X, Z)$ and $p(X, X)$ since:

$$p(X, Z)\theta = p(a, b) \neq p(X, X)\theta = p(a, a)$$

∎

Some structures have no unifier. Clearly, application of a substitution changes only the variables of a structure. Thus if two structures unify, either one of them is a variable, or both have the same principal symbol. The same must hold for their corresponding direct substructures.

**Example 3.4** The structures $p(X)$ and $q(Y)$ are not unifiable.   Neither are $p(a, X)$ and $p(b, b)$.   ∎

It is also easy to see that a variable $X$ and a nonvariable structure $s$ which includes $X$ as a substructure have no unifier — clearly the length of $s$ is greater than the length of $X$ ($= 1$). Hence for every substitution $\theta$ it holds that $|s\theta| > |X\theta|$ since $X$ occurs in $s$. Thus none of them can be a unifier.

Notice that a unifier $\theta$ of structures $s_1$ and $s_2$ may be such that $Range(\theta) \neq \varnothing$ as shown by the following example.

**Example 3.5** The substitution $\{X/f(Y), Z/Y\}$ is a unifier of the structures $p(X, Y)$ and $p(f(Z), Z)$. ∎

In this case composition of $\theta$ with an arbitrary substitution $\sigma$ such that $Dom(\sigma) \cap Range(\theta) \neq \varnothing$ is different from $\theta$ but still a unifier of $s_1$ and $s_2$. Clearly there are infinitely many such unifiers. Each of them is "more specific" than $\theta$ since it binds the variables of $s_1$ and $s_2$ to some particular instances of the terms to which they are bound by $\theta$. This observation gives rise to the following definition.

**Definition 3.6 (More general substitutions)** A substitution $\theta$ is *more general* than $\sigma$ iff there is a substitution $\omega$ such that $\sigma = \theta\omega$. ∎

**Example 3.7** This relation is not antisymmetric — take for example the substitutions $\theta := \{Y/X, Z/X\}$ and $\sigma := \{Y/Z, X/Z\}$. $\sigma$ is more general than $\theta$ since e.g. $\theta = \sigma\{Z/X\}$. Similarly $\theta$ is more general than $\sigma$ since $\sigma = \theta\{X/Z\}$. However, for any structure $t$ the structures $t\theta$ and $t\sigma$ are *identical up to renaming of the variables*. ∎

Let us briefly discuss the concept of *renaming*.

**Definition 3.8 (Renaming substitution)** Let $\theta := \{X_1/Y_1, \ldots, X_n/Y_n\}$. $\theta$ is called a *renaming substitution* iff $Y_1, \ldots, Y_n$ are distinct variables and $Dom(\theta) = Range(\theta)$. ∎

A renaming substitution represents a total, bijective mapping between variables. If $\theta$ is a renaming substitution, then $t\theta$ ($\sigma\theta$) will be called *renamings* of $t$ ($\sigma$). Since a renaming substitution represents a bijection there is also an "inverse".

**Definition 3.9 (Inverse)** Let $\theta := \{X_1/Y_1, \ldots, X_n/Y_n\}$ be a renaming substitution. Then $\{Y_1/X_1, \ldots, Y_n/X_n\}$ is called the *inverse* of $\theta$ and is denoted by $\theta^{-1}$. ∎

In fact, renaming substitutions are sometimes called *invertible* substitutions.

**Proposition 3.10** If $\theta$ is a renaming substitution then $\theta^{-1}$ is a renaming substitution and $\theta^{-1}\theta = \theta\theta^{-1} = \epsilon$. ∎

When searching for unifiers, our interest will be limited to the most general ones — a unifier $\theta$ of the structures $s_1$ and $s_2$ is called a *most general unifier* (mgu) iff it is more general than any other unifier of $s_1$ and $s_2$. That is, for any unifier $\sigma$ of $s_1$ and $s_2$ there exists a substitution $\omega$ such that $\sigma = \theta\omega$. The question arises whether most general unifiers are unique? The answer is given by the following theorem.

**Theorem 3.11 (Uniqueness of mgu's)** Let $\theta$ and $\sigma$ be mgu's of structures $s_1$ and $s_2$. Then $\theta$ and $\sigma$ are identical up to renaming (i.e. there are renaming substitutions $\delta$ and $\omega$ such that $\theta = \sigma\omega$ and $\sigma = \theta\delta$). ∎

*Proof:*  In what follows we will say that $\alpha$ and $\delta$ *agree* on $\theta$ iff $\theta\alpha = \theta\delta$. This will be denoted by $\alpha \simeq_\theta \delta$. Clearly, $\simeq_\theta$ is an equivalence relation.

Since $\theta$ and $\sigma$ are mgu's there must be substitutions $\alpha$ and $\beta$ such that:

$$\sigma = \theta\alpha \qquad (1)$$
$$\theta = \sigma\beta \qquad (2)$$

The general idea of the proof is to find a renaming substitution $\delta$ such that $\delta$ and $\alpha$ agree on $\theta$.

For this purpose we notice that any pair of the form $X/t$ where $X \in Dom(\theta)\setminus Range(\theta)$ can be added to, or deleted from $\alpha$ without invalidating equation (1).[1] Hence, let:

$$\alpha' := \{X/t \in \alpha \mid X \notin Dom(\theta) \setminus Range(\theta)\} \qquad (3)$$
$$\beta' := \{X/t \in \beta \mid X \notin Dom(\alpha')\} \qquad (4)$$

(i.e. $Dom(\beta \setminus \beta') \subseteq Dom(\alpha')$). Now since $\alpha \simeq_\theta \alpha'$ it holds that $\sigma = \theta\alpha'$ and:

$$\theta = \theta\alpha'\beta \qquad (5)$$

But in order for (5) to hold it is necessary that:

$$Dom(\alpha'\beta) \subseteq Dom(\theta) \setminus Range(\theta) \qquad (6)$$

Now assume $\alpha'$ is of the form $\{X_1/t_1, \ldots, X_m/t_m\}$. Then $\alpha'\beta$ is obtained from:

$$\{X_1/t_1\beta, \ldots, X_m/t_m\beta\} \cup \beta'$$

---

[1] Here $x \setminus y$ denotes the set-difference between $x$ and $y$.

by striking out those $X_i/t_i\beta$ where $X_i = t_i\beta$.

From (3) and (6) it follows that $X_1 = t_1\beta, \ldots, X_m = t_m\beta$. Consequently, $\{t_1/X_1, \ldots, t_m/X_m\} \subseteq \beta$ which implies that $t_1, \ldots, t_m$ must be distinct variables. Moreover:

$$\alpha'\beta = \beta' \tag{7}$$

Notice also that:

$$
\begin{aligned}
Range(\alpha') &\subseteq Dom(\beta) \\
&= Dom(\beta \setminus \beta') \cup Dom(\beta') \\
&\subseteq Dom(\alpha') \cup Dom(\theta) \setminus Range(\theta) \tag{8}
\end{aligned}
$$

using the fact that $Dom(\beta \setminus \beta') \subseteq Dom(\alpha')$ together with (6) and (7). We now know that $\alpha'$ is of the form $\{X_1/t_1, \ldots, X_m/t_m\}$ where:

- $t_1, \ldots, t_m$ are distinct variables;

- each of $t_1, \ldots, t_m$ appears either in $Dom(\alpha')$ or in $Dom(\theta) \setminus Range(\theta)$.

Now the general idea is to "extend" $\alpha'$ into a renaming substitution $\delta$ satisfying $\delta \simeq_\theta \alpha' \simeq_\theta \alpha$ by adding some extra pairs to it. Hence, let $\{Y_1, \ldots, Y_i\}$ be those variables which appear in the range but not in the domain of $\alpha'$. Since $t_1, \ldots, t_m$ are distinct there must be a corresponding set $\{Z_1, \ldots, Z_i\}$ of variables which appear in the domain but not in the range of $\alpha'$. Notice that:

- $\{Y_1, \ldots, Y_i\} \subseteq Dom(\theta) \setminus Range(\theta)$ (from (8));

- $\{Y_1, \ldots, Y_i\}$ and $\{Z_1, \ldots, Z_i\}$ are disjoint.

As a consequence $\delta := \alpha' \cup \{Y_1/Z_1, \ldots, Y_i/Z_i\}$ is a renaming substitution. Moreover, since $\alpha \simeq_\theta \delta$ it holds that $\sigma = \theta\delta$. Finally $\theta = \sigma\delta^{-1}$ by Proposition 3.10. ∎

Thus most general unifiers are unique up to renaming. In addition, if $\theta$ is an mgu of structures $s_1$ and $s_2$, then for any renaming substitution $\sigma$, $\theta\sigma$ is also an mgu of $s_1$ and $s_2$ (cf. exercise 27).

**Example 3.12** Consider the two structures $p(X, f(Y))$ and $p(Z, f(Z))$. Clearly $\sigma := \{X/a, Y/a, Z/a\}$ is a unifier but so is $\theta := \{X/Z, Y/Z\}$. The latter is more general than the former since $\sigma = \theta\{Z/a\}$. As a matter of fact $\theta$ is an mgu of the structures.

But $\theta$ is not their only mgu. For instance, $\delta := \{Z/X, Y/X\}$ is also an mgu since $\theta = \delta\omega$ and $\delta = \theta\omega^{-1}$ for $\omega := \{X/Z, Z/X\}$. ∎

The remaining problem is how to find a most general unifier of given distinct structures $s_1$ and $s_2$. First an auxiliary notion is introduced.

**Definition 3.13 (Disagreement pair)** A *disagreement pair* of the structures $s_1$ and $s_2$ is a pair of structures defined as follows:

- if $s_1$ and $s_2$ have distinct principal symbols then $\langle s_1; s_2 \rangle$ is the only disagreement pair of $s_1$ and $s_2$;

- if $s_1$ and $s_2$ have identical principal symbols and if the i-th direct substructures of $s_1$ and $s_2$ are distinct, then any disagreement pair of these substructures is also a disagreement pair of $s_1$ and $s_2$.

Notice that identical structures have no disagreement pairs.                  ∎

**Example 3.14** For the structures $p(f(X), Y)$ and $p(f(g(Y)), a)$ there are two disagreement pairs — $\langle X; g(Y) \rangle$ and $\langle Y; a \rangle$. For the structures $p(X, a)$ and $q(X, b)$ the only disagreement pair is $\langle p(X, a); q(X, b) \rangle$.                  ∎

If $\theta$ is an mgu of $s_1$ and $s_2$ and $\langle t_1; t_2 \rangle$ is one of their disagreement pairs, then $\theta$ must also be a unifier of $t_1$ and $t_2$. An mgu of $s_1$ and $s_2$ is thus the composition of an mgu $\sigma$ of $t_1$ and $t_2$ with an mgu of $s_1\sigma$ and $s_2\sigma$.

Notice that it is rather easy to find an mgu of the disagreement pair $\langle t_1; t_2 \rangle$ or to show that no unifier exists. The following cases are to be considered:

- Fail: Neither $t_1$ nor $t_2$ is a variable — by the definition of the disagreement pair this means that the principal symbols of $t_1$ and $t_2$ are distinct. Thus no unifier exists.

Otherwise at least one of the structures $t_1$ and $t_2$ is a variable. Thus $\langle t_1; t_2 \rangle$ is of the form $\langle X; t \rangle$ or $\langle t; X \rangle$. (Notice that there may be nondeterminism here in the case where $t$ is also a variable. This shows why there may be different mgu's.) Now there are two more cases:

- Occur-check: $X$ occurs as a proper substructure in $t$. In this case $t_1$ and $t_2$ have no unifier (as explained above).

- Success: otherwise the substitution $\{X/t\}$ is an mgu of $t_1$ and $t_2$.

The idea for construction of an mgu of structures $s_1$ and $s_2$ presented above has been used by Robinson to present a unification algorithm. A version of it is depicted in Figure 3.1 as a functional procedure on structures that returns either their mgu or the value *fail* in the case when the arguments have no unifier.

$mgu(s_1, s_2) :=$
    if $s_1 = s_2$ then $\epsilon$
    else let $\theta = mgu\text{-}of\text{-}disagreement\text{-}pair(s_1, s_2)$ in
        if $\theta = fail$ then $fail$ else $\theta\, mgu(s_1\theta, s_2\theta)$

$mgu\text{-}of\text{-}disagreement\text{-}pair(s_1, s_2) :=$
        let $\langle t_1; t_2 \rangle$ be a disagreement pair of $s_1$ and $s_2$ in
            cases of $\langle t_1; t_2 \rangle$
            Fail $\rightarrow$ $fail$
            Occur-check $\rightarrow$ $fail$
            Success $\rightarrow$ if $variable(t_1)$ then $\{t_1/t_2\}$ else $\{t_2/t_1\}$

**Figure 3.1: Unification algorithm**

As presented in Chapter 1 composition is defined only for substitutions. Since a call to $mgu(s_1, s_2)$ may also return the value $fail$ it is necessary to extend this definition by saying that $\theta\, fail := fail$ for any substitution $\theta$.

The algorithm presented in Figure 3.1 terminates for every input. Consider the number of variables in both arguments. If the mgu of their selected disagreement pair does not exist, the execution returns $fail$ and terminates. Otherwise the variable $X$ which is in the domain of the mgu does not appear in the arguments of the recursive call. Since no new variables are introduced by the mgu of the disagreement pair the number of variables decreases at every level of recursion.

It is also possible to give a formal proof that the algorithm indeed produces an mgu of the arguments if they are unifiable.

**Theorem 3.15 (Correctness of the unification algorithm)** If the structures $s_1$ and $s_2$ are unifiable the substitution computed by the algorithm in Figure 3.1 is an mgu of $s_1$ and $s_2$. ∎

*Proof*: The idea is to use induction on the number of recursive calls. For $n = 0$ the structures are identical and the result trivially holds.

Assume that for all unifiable structures for which the algorithm makes $n$ recursive calls, the result is an mgu of the structures. Let $s_1$ and $s_2$ be structures such that a unifier is computed in $n + 1$ calls and let $\langle t_1; t_2 \rangle$ be the selected disagreement-pair of $s_1$ and $s_2$, resulting in the substitution $\theta := \{X/t\}$. By the induction hypothesis $\sigma := mgu(s_1\theta, s_2\theta)$ will be an mgu of $s_1\theta$ and $s_2\theta$ obtained in $n$ recursive calls. The rest of the proof consists in proving that $\theta\sigma$ is an mgu of $s_1$ and $s_2$ — i.e. for any unifier $\gamma$ of $s_1$ and $s_2$ there exists a substitution $\omega'$ such that $\gamma = \theta \sigma \omega'$.

Let $\gamma$ be any unifier of $s_1$ and $s_2$. Then it is also a unifier of $s_1 \theta$ and $s_2 \theta$. Moreover:

$$\gamma = \sigma \omega \quad \text{for some substitution } \omega \tag{1}$$

Since $X$ appears neither in $s_1 \theta$ nor in $s_2 \theta$ it can appear neither in $Dom(\sigma)$ nor in $Range(\sigma)$. On the other hand since $X$ must be in $Dom(\gamma)$ it must hold that $X \in Dom(\omega)$. But since $X\gamma = t\gamma$ it follows that $X\sigma\omega = X\omega = t\omega$ implying that $\omega$ is a unifier of $X$ and $t\sigma$. It is straightforward to see that $\lambda := \{X/t\sigma\}$ is an mgu of $X$ and $t\sigma$. Hence:

$$\omega = \lambda \omega' \quad \text{for some substitution } \omega' \tag{2}$$

Additionally note that:

$$\sigma \lambda = \theta \sigma \tag{3}$$

since $\sigma\lambda = \sigma\{X/t\sigma\}$ is identical to $\theta\sigma = \{X/t\}\sigma$. Now by (1), (2) and (3):

$$\begin{aligned}
\gamma &= \sigma\omega \\
&= \sigma\lambda\omega' \\
&= \theta\sigma\omega'
\end{aligned}$$

Thus for any unifier $\gamma$ of $s_1$ and $s_2$ there exists a substitution $\omega'$ such that $\gamma = \theta\sigma\omega'$. Consequently $\theta\sigma$ is an mgu of $s_1$ and $s_2$.  ∎

**Example 3.16** Consider unification of $p(f(X,Y),a)$ and $p(f(Z,Z),Z)$:

$$mgu(p(f(X,Y),a), p(f(Z,Z),Z))$$

The structures are not identical so, for instance, the disagreement pair $\langle X; Z\rangle$ whose mgu is $\{X/Z\}$ is selected yielding:

$$\{X/Z\}\; mgu(p(f(Z,Y),a), p(f(Z,Z),Z))$$

However, the arguments are still not identical. The next recursive call selects $\langle Y; Z\rangle$ with mgu $\{Y/Z\}$ and:

$$\{X/Z\}\{Y/Z\}\; mgu(p(f(Z,Z),a), p(f(Z,Z),Z))$$

is obtained. Since composition of substitutions is associative (cf. Proposition 1.21) this is equivalent to:

$$\{X/Z, Y/Z\}\; mgu(p(f(Z,Z),a), p(f(Z,Z),Z))$$

> *mgu-of-disagreement-pair*$(s_1, s_2)$ :=
> > **let** $\langle t_1; t_2 \rangle$ be a disagreement pair of $s_1$ and $s_2$ **in**
> > > **cases of** $\langle t_1; t_2 \rangle$
> > > > Fail $\rightarrow$ *fail*
> > > > Success $\rightarrow$ **if** *variable*$(t_1)$ **then** $\{t_1/t_2\}$ **else** $\{t_2/t_1\}$

**Figure 3.2: Unification without occur-check**

In the next recursive call there is only one disagreement pair — namely $\langle a; Z \rangle$ whose mgu is $\{Z/a\}$ yielding:

$$\{X/Z, Y/Z\}\{Z/a\}\ mgu(p(f(a, a), a), p(f(a, a), a))$$

equivalent to:

$$\{X/a, Y/a, Z/a\}\ mgu(p(f(a, a), a), p(f(a, a), a))$$

Since the arguments are identical the empty substitution is returned and the final result is the substitution $\{X/a, Y/a, Z/a\}$ which is the mgu of the original structures $p(f(X, Y), a)$ and $p(f(Z, Z), Z)$. ∎

The algorithm presented in Figure 3.1 may be very inefficient. One of the reasons is the occur-check. Assume the time of occur-check is linear with respect to the length of the argument. Consider application of the algorithm to the structures of the form:

$$c(X_1, \ldots, X_n) \text{ and } c(f(X_0, X_0), f(X_1, X_1), \ldots, f(X_{n-1}, X_{n-1}))$$

where $X_i \neq X_j$ for $i \neq j$. Assume that the disagreement pair selected at each step is the "leftmost" one. Then the disagreement pair at the $k$-th recursive call, $(k > 0)$, will be of the form $\langle X_k; t_k \rangle$ where $t_k := f(t_{k-1}, t_{k-1})$ and $t_0 := X_0$. Hence, $|t_k| = 2 * |t_{k-1}| + 1$. That is, $|t_n| > 2^n$. This shows the exponential dependency of the unification time on the length of the structures. In this example the growth of the argument lengths is caused by duplication of subterms. As a matter of fact the same check is repeated many times which could be avoided by sharing various instances of the same structure. In the literature one can find linear algorithms but they are sometimes quite elaborate. On the other hand, Prolog systems usually "solve" the problem simply by omitting the occur-check during unification. Roughly speaking such an approach corresponds to the algorithm of Figure 3.2.

However this modification causes looping of the unification algorithm on structures which are not unifiable only because of the occur-check. For example, an attempt to unify $X$ and $f(X)$ by the modified algorithm will produce first the substitution $\theta := \{X/f(X)\}$. But $\theta$ is not a unifier since $X\theta = f(X) \neq f(X)\theta = f(f(X))$. Thus the second recursive call produces the same disagreement pair and the process never terminates. However, instead of the binding $X/f(X)$ Prolog systems usually bind $X$ to the infinite structure $f(f(f(\ldots)))$. (The notation $X/f(\infty)$ will be used to denote this binding.) Clearly, $\{X/f(\infty)\}$ is an infinite "unifier" of $X$ and $f(X)$. It can easily be represented in the computer by a finite cyclic data structure. But this amounts to generalization of the concepts of structure, substitution and unifier for the infinite case not treated in classical logic. Implementation of unification without occur-check may cause some strange behaviour of the system as illustrated in Example 3.26.

## 3.3   SLD-Resolution

The method of reasoning discussed informally in Section 3.1 can be summarized as the following inference rule:

$$\frac{\forall \neg (A_1 \wedge \cdots \wedge A_{i-1} \wedge A_i \wedge A_{i+1} \wedge \cdots \wedge A_m) \qquad \forall (H \leftarrow B_1 \wedge \cdots \wedge B_n)}{\forall \neg (A_1 \wedge \cdots \wedge A_{i-1} \wedge B_1 \wedge \cdots \wedge B_n \wedge A_{i+1} \wedge \cdots \wedge A_m)\theta}$$

where

- $A_1, \ldots, A_m$ and $H, B_1, \ldots, B_n$ are atomic formulas.

- $1 \leq i \leq m$ and $n \geq 0$.

- $\theta$ is a most general unifier of $A_i$ and $H$.

The rule has two premises — a goal clause and a definite clause. Notice that each of them is separately universally quantified. Thus the scopes of the quantifiers are disjoint. On the other hand, there is only one universal quantifier in the conclusion of the rule. Therefore it is required that the sets of variables in the premises are disjoint. Since all variables of the premises are bound it is always possible to *rename* the variables of the definite clause to satisfy this requirement (that is, to apply some renaming substitution to it).

The goal clause may include several atomic formulas which unify with the head of some clause in the program. In this case it may be desirable to introduce some deterministic choice of the selected atom $A_i$ for unification. In what follows it is assumed that this is given by some function which for a given goal selects the subgoal for unification. The function is called the *selection function* or the *computation rule.* It is sometimes desirable to generalize this concept so that, in one situation, the computation rule selects one subgoal from a goal $G$ but, in another situation, selects another subgoal from $G$. In that case the computation rule is not a function on goals but something more complicated. However, for the purpose of this book this extra generality is not needed.

The inference rule presented above is the only one needed for definite programs. It is a version of the inference rule called the *resolution principle*, which was introduced by J. A. Robinson in 1965. The resolution principle applies to clauses — that is, logic formulas of the form:

$$A_1 \vee \ldots \vee A_m \vee \neg B_1 \vee \ldots \vee \neg B_n$$

Since definite clauses are restricted clauses (where $m = 1$) the corresponding restricted form of resolution presented below is called *SLD-resolution* (Linear resolution for Definite clauses with Selection function).

Next the use of the SLD-resolution principle is discussed for a given definite program P. The starting point, as exemplified in Section 3.1, is a definite goal clause $G_0$ of the form:

$$\leftarrow A_1, \ldots, A_m \qquad (m \geq 0)$$

From this goal a subgoal $A_i$ is selected (if possible) by the computation rule. A new goal clause $G_1$ is constructed by selecting (if possible) some renamed program clause $H \leftarrow B_1, \ldots, B_n$ $(n \geq 0)$ whose head unifies with $A_i$ (resulting in an mgu $\theta_1$). If so $G_1$ will be of the form:

$$\leftarrow (A_1, \ldots, A_{i-1}, B_1, \ldots, B_n, A_{i+1}, \ldots, A_m)\theta_1$$

(According to the requirement above, the variables of the program clause are being renamed so that they are different from those of $G_0$.) Now it is possible to apply the resolution principle to $G_1$ thus obtaining $G_2$. This process may or may not terminate. There are two different cases where it is not possible to obtain $G_{i+1}$ from $G_i$:

- the first is when the selected subgoal cannot be resolved (i.e. is not unifiable) with the head of any program clause;

- the other case appears when $G_i = \square$ (i.e. the empty goal).

The process described above results in a finite or infinite sequence of goals starting with the initial goal. At every step a program clause (with renamed variables) is used to resolve the subgoal selected by the computation rule $\Re$ and an mgu is created. Thus, the full record of a reasoning step would be a pair $\langle G_i; C_i \rangle$, $i \geq 0$, where $G_i$ is a goal and $C_i$ a program clause with renamed variables. Clearly, the computation rule $\Re$ together with $G_i$ and $C_i$ determines (up to renaming of variables) the mgu (to be denoted $\theta_{i+1}$) produced at the $(i+1)$-th step of the process. Consequently the record of the whole process would be either a finite sequence:

$$\langle G_0; C_0 \rangle, \dots, \langle G_{n-1}; C_{n-1} \rangle, G_n$$

where $n \geq 0$, or an infinite sequence:

$$\langle G_0; C_0 \rangle, \langle G_1; C_1 \rangle, \langle G_2; C_2 \rangle, \dots$$

Such a sequence is called an *SLD-derivation* of $G_0$ (and P) via $\Re$. When no confusion arises as to what the computation rule is, it is omitted altogether. A goal $G_{i+1}$ is said to be *derived* (*directly*) from $G_i$ and $C_i$ via $\Re$ (or alternatively, $G_i$ and $C_i$ *resolve* into $G_{i+1}$).

Note that since there are usually infinitely many ways of renaming a clause there are formally infinitely many derivations. However, some of these differ only in the names of the variables used. To avoid some technical problems and to make the renaming of variables in a derivation consistent, the variables in the clause $C_i$ of a derivation are renamed by adding the index $i$ to *every* variable in the clause. In what follows we consider only derivations where this renaming strategy is used.

The composition

$$\theta := \begin{cases} \theta_1 \theta_2 \cdots \theta_n & \text{if } n > 0 \\ \epsilon & \text{if } n = 0 \end{cases}$$

of mgu's in a finite derivation:

$$\langle G_0; C_0 \rangle, \dots, \langle G_{n-1}; C_{n-1} \rangle, G_n$$

is called the *computed substitution* of the derivation.

**Example 3.17** A derivation of the goal $\leftarrow knows\_logic(Z)$ given the program discussed in Section 3.1 may thus look as follows:

$$
\begin{aligned}
G_0 &: \quad \leftarrow knows\_logic(Z) \\
C_0 &: \quad knows\_logic(X_0) \leftarrow good\_student(X_0), teacher(Y_0, X_0), \dots
\end{aligned}
$$

Unification of $knows\_logic(Z)$ and $knows\_logic(X_0)$ yields e.g. the mgu $\theta_1 = \{Z/X_0\}$. Assume that a computation rule which always selects the leftmost subgoal is used (if nothing else is said, this computation rule is used also in what follows). Such a computation rule will occasionally be referred to as *Prolog's* computation rule since this is the computation rule used in most Prolog systems. The first derivation step yields:

$$
\begin{aligned}
G_1 &: \ \leftarrow good\_student(X_0), teacher(Y_0, X_0), logical(Y_0) \\
C_1 &: \ good\_student(tom)
\end{aligned}
$$

In the second resolution step the mgu $\theta_2 = \{X_0/tom\}$ is obtained. The derivation then proceeds as follows:

$$
\begin{aligned}
G_2 &: \ \leftarrow teacher(Y_0, tom), logician(Y_0) \\
C_2 &: \ teacher(peter, tom)
\end{aligned}
$$

$$
\begin{aligned}
G_3 &: \ \leftarrow logician(peter) \\
C_3 &: \ logician(peter)
\end{aligned}
$$

$$
G_4 \ : \ \square
$$

The computed substitution of this derivation is:

$$
\begin{aligned}
\theta_1\theta_2\theta_3\theta_4 &= \ \{Z/X_0\}\{X_0/tom\}\{Y_0/peter\}\epsilon \\
&= \ \{Z/tom, X_0/tom, Y_0/peter\}
\end{aligned}
$$

■

**Example 3.18** Consider the definite program:

1) $p(X, Y) \leftarrow q(X, Z), r(Z, Y)$
2) $p(X, Y) \leftarrow r(Y, X)$
3) $q(X, Y) \leftarrow r(Y, X)$
4) $r(a, b)$

One possible SLD-derivation of the goal $\leftarrow p(b, X)$ is the following one (again a computation rule which selects the leftmost subgoal is used):

$$
\begin{aligned}
G_0 &: \ \leftarrow p(b, X) \\
C_0 &: \ p(X_0, Y_0) \leftarrow q(X_0, Z_0), r(Z_0, Y_0) \\
\theta_1 &: \ \{X_0/b, X/Y_0\}
\end{aligned}
$$

$$
\begin{aligned}
G_1 &: \ \leftarrow q(b, Z_0), r(Z_0, Y_0) \\
C_1 &: \ q(X_1, Y_1) \leftarrow r(Y_1, X_1) \\
\theta_2 &: \ \{X_1/b, Z_0/Y_1\}
\end{aligned}
$$

$$
\begin{aligned}
G_2 &: \ \leftarrow r(Y_1, b), r(Y_1, Y_0) \\
C_2 &: \ r(a, b) \\
\theta_3 &: \ \{Y_1/a\}
\end{aligned}
$$

$$G_3 \ : \ \leftarrow r(a, Y_0)$$
$$C_3 \ : \ r(a, b)$$
$$\theta_4 \ : \ \{Y_0/b\}$$

$$G_4 \ : \ \Box$$

The composition of all mgu's equals:

$$\theta_1\theta_2\theta_3\theta_4 = \{X_0/b, X/b, X_1/b, Z_0/a, Y_1/a, Y_0/b\}$$

∎

SLD-derivations that end in the empty goal and the bindings of variables in the initial goal of such derivations are of special importance:

**Definition 3.19 (SLD-refutation)** An (finite) SLD-derivation:

$$\langle G_0; C_0\rangle, \ldots, \langle G_n; C_n\rangle, G_{n+1}$$

where $G_{n+1} = \Box$ is called an *SLD-refutation* of $G_0$.                    ∎

**Definition 3.20 (Computed answer substitution)** The computed substitution of an SLD-refutation of $G_0$ restricted to the variables in $G_0$ is called a *computed answer substitution* for $G_0$.                    ∎

In Examples 3.17 and 3.18 the computed answer substitutions are $\{Z/tom\}$ and $\{X/b\}$ respectively.

For a given initial goal $G_0$ and computation rule, the sequence $G_1, \ldots, G_k$ of goals in a derivation $d$ is determined (up to renaming of variables) by the sequence $C_0, \ldots, C_{k-1}$ of (renamed) program clauses used. In particular this concerns refutations. Let $d$ be a refutation. It turns out that if the computation rule is changed there still exists a refutation $d'$ for $G_0$ which has (up to renaming) the same computed answer substitution and where the sequence $C'_0, \ldots, C'_{k-1}$ of clauses used is a permutation of the sequence $C_0, \ldots, C_{k-1}$. This property will be called *independence of the computation rule*.

The notion of SLD-derivation resembles the notion of derivation for formal grammars (cf. Chapter 10). By analogy to grammars a derivation can be mapped into a graph called the *derivation tree* (or *proof tree*). Such a tree is constructed by combining together some elementary trees representing instances of the clauses under the computed substitution of the derivation as illustrated in Figure 3.3. Notice that many derivations may map into the same derivation tree. The concept of derivation tree is related to the intuition behind the independence of the computation rule — take "copies" of the clauses to be combined together into

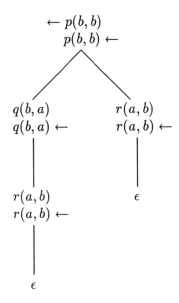

$$\leftarrow p(b, b)$$
$$p(b, b) \leftarrow$$

$$q(b, a) \qquad\qquad r(a, b)$$
$$q(b, a) \leftarrow \qquad\qquad r(a, b) \leftarrow$$

$$r(a, b) \qquad\qquad \epsilon$$
$$r(a, b) \leftarrow$$

$$\epsilon$$

**Figure 3.3: Derivation tree**

one derivation tree. Rename each copy so that it shares no variables with the
other copies. The problem of "combining" is to find unifiers for some pairs of
atoms. Each pair can be seen as an equation and the whole problem is to find
a solution to the set of equations. A computation rule determines the order in
which the equations are to be solved but the solution obtained does not depend
on this order. The existence of a solution is guaranteed by the existence of the
derivation for which the derivation tree was constructed.

**Definition 3.21 (Failed derivation)** A derivation of a goal clause $G_0$ whose
last element is not empty and cannot be resolved with any clause of the program
is called a *failed* derivation.                                              ∎

**Example 3.22** Consider the following derivation of the goal $\leftarrow p(a, X)$ together
with the program in Example 3.18:

$$G_0 \;:\; \leftarrow p(a, X)$$
$$C_0 \;:\; p(X_0, Y_0) \leftarrow q(X_0, Z_0), r(Z_0, Y_0)$$

$$G_1 \;:\; \leftarrow q(a, Z_0), r(Z_0, Y_0)$$
$$C_1 \;:\; q(X_1, Y_1) \leftarrow r(Y_1, X_1)$$

$$G_2 \;:\; \leftarrow r(Y_1, a), r(Y_1, Y_0)$$

Since the selected literal (the leftmost one) does not unify with any clause head, the derivation is failed. Hence, a derivation may be failed even though some other subgoal but the selected one unifies with a clause head.                              ∎

By a *complete derivation* we mean a *refutation*, a *failed derivation* or an *infinite derivation*. Generally, a given initial goal clause $G_0$ may have many complete derivations via a given computation rule $\Re$. This happens if the selected subgoal of some goal can be resolved with more than one program clause. All such derivations may be represented by a possibly infinite tree called the SLD-tree of $G_0$ (via $\Re$).

**Definition 3.23 (SLD-tree)** Let P be a definite program, $G_0$ a definite goal and $\Re$ a computation rule. The SLD-tree of $G_0$ wrt. P and $\Re$ is a (possibly infinite) labelled tree satisfying the following conditions:

- $G_0$ is the root of the tree;

- $G_{i+1}$ is a child of $G_i$ iff there is a renamed version of a clause $C_i$ in P such that $G_{i+1}$ is derived from $G_i$ and the renamed $C_i$ under $\Re$. The edge connecting $G_i$ and $G_{i+1}$ is labelled by $C_i$.

                                                                                        ∎

The nodes of an SLD-tree are thus goals of a derivation. The edges are labelled by the clauses of the program. There is in fact a one-to-one correspondence between the paths of the SLD-tree and the complete derivations of $G_0$ via $\Re$. The sequence:

$$\langle G_0; C_0 \rangle, \langle G_1; C_1 \rangle, \ldots, \langle G_k; C_k \rangle, \ldots$$

is a complete derivation of $G_0$ via $\Re$ iff there exists a path of the SLD-tree of the form $G_0, G_1, \ldots, G_k, \ldots$ such that for every $i$, the edge $\langle G_i; G_{i+1} \rangle$ is labelled by $C_i$ (usually this label is abbreviated when drawing the tree e.g. by numbering the clauses of the program). Additional labelling with the mgu $\theta_{i+1}$ (or some part of it) may also be included.

**Example 3.24** Consider again the program of Example 3.18. The SLD-tree of the goal $\leftarrow p(b, X)$ is depicted in Figure 3.4.                              ∎

The SLD-trees of a goal clause $G_0$ are often distinct for different computation rules. However, the independence of computation rules means that for every refutation path in one SLD-tree there exists a refutation path in the other SLD-tree with the same length and with the same computed answer substitution (up to renaming). The sequences of labelling clauses of both paths are permutations of each other.

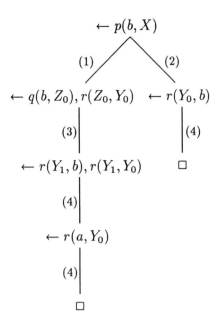

**Figure 3.4: SLD-tree**

## 3.4 Soundness of SLD-resolution

The method of reasoning presented informally in Section 3.1 has been formalized as the SLD-resolution principle. As a matter of fact one more inference rule is used after construction of a refutation. It applies the computed substitution of the refutation to the body of the initial goal to get the final conclusion. This is the most interesting part of the process since if the initial goal is seen as a query, the computed substitution of the refutation restricted to its variables is an answer to this query. It is therefore called a computed answer substitution. In this context it is also worth noticing the case when no answer substitution exists for a given query. Prolog systems may sometimes discover this and deliver a "no" answer. The logical meaning of "no" will be discussed in the next chapter.

As discussed in Chapter 1, the introduction of formal inference rules raises the questions of *soundness* and *completeness*. Soundness is an essential property which guarantees that the conclusions produced by the system are correct. Correctness in this context means that they are logical consequences of the program. That is, that they are true in every model of the program. Recall the discussion of Chapter 2 — a definite program describes many "worlds" (i.e. models), including the one which is meant by the user, the intended model. Soundness is necessary to be sure that the conclusions produced by any refutation are true in every world described by the program, in particular in the intended one.

One may ask the question about the soundness of the SLD-resolution principle. The discussion in Section 3.1 gives some arguments which may by used in a formal proof. However, the intermediate conclusions produced at every step of refutation are of little interest for the user of a definite program. Therefore the soundness of SLD-resolution is usually understood as correctness of computed answer substitutions. This can be stated as the following theorem (due to K. Clark [31]).

**Theorem 3.25 (Soundness of SLD-resolution)** Let P be a definite program and let $\theta$ be a computed answer substitution for a goal $\leftarrow A_1, \ldots, A_m$ via a computation rule $\mathfrak{R}$. Then $\forall((A_1 \wedge \cdots \wedge A_m)\theta)$ is a logical consequence of the program.                                                                                      ∎

*Proof:*   Any computed answer substitution is obtained by a refutation of the goal via $\mathfrak{R}$. The proof is based on induction over the number of resolution steps of the refutation.

First consider refutations of length one. This is possible only if $m = 1$ and $A_1$ resolves with some unit clause $A$ with the mgu $\theta_1$. Hence $A_1\theta_1$ is an instance of $A$. Now let $\theta$ be $\theta_1$ restricted to the variables in $A_1$. Then $A_1\theta = A_1\theta_1$.

It is a well-known fact that a universal closure of an instance of a formula $F$ is a logical consequence of the universal closure of $F$ (cf. exercise 10, Chapter 1). Hence the universal closure of $A_1\theta$ is a logical consequence of the clause $A$ and consequently of the program P.

Next, assume that the theorem holds for refutations with $n - 1$ steps. Take a refutation with $n$ steps of the form:

$$\langle G_0; C_0 \rangle, \langle G_1; C_1 \rangle, \ldots, \langle G_{n-1}; C_{n-1} \rangle, \square$$

where $G_0$ is the original goal clause $\leftarrow A_1, \ldots, A_m$.

Now, assume that in the first derivation step $A_j$ is the selected atom and that $C_0$ is a (renamed) clause $H \leftarrow B_1, \ldots, B_k$ $(k \geq 0)$ in P. Then $A_j\theta_1 = H\theta_1$ and $G_1$ is of the form:

$$\leftarrow (A_1, \ldots, A_{j-1}, B_1, \ldots, B_k, A_{j+1}, \ldots, A_m)\theta_1$$

By the induction hypothesis the formula:

$$\forall(A_1 \wedge \ldots \wedge A_{j-1} \wedge B_1 \wedge \ldots \wedge B_k \wedge A_{j+1} \wedge \ldots \wedge A_m)\theta_1 \cdots \theta_n \tag{1}$$

is a logical consequence of the program. It follows by definition of logical consequence that also the universal closure of:

$$(B_1 \wedge \ldots \wedge B_k)\theta_1 \cdots \theta_n \tag{2}$$

is a logical consequence of the program. By (1):

$$\forall (A_1 \wedge \ldots \wedge A_{j-1} \wedge A_{j+1} \wedge \ldots \wedge A_m)\theta_1 \cdots \theta_n \tag{3}$$

is a logical consequence of P. Now because of (2) and since:

$$\forall (H \leftarrow B_1 \wedge \ldots \wedge B_k)\theta_1 \cdots \theta_n$$

is a logical consequence of the program (being an instance of a clause in P) it follows that:

$$\forall H\theta_1 \cdots \theta_n \tag{4}$$

is a logical consequence of P. Hence by (3) and (4):

$$\forall (A_1 \wedge \ldots \wedge A_{j-1} \wedge H \wedge A_{j+1} \wedge \ldots \wedge A_m)\theta_1 \cdots \theta_n \tag{5}$$

is also a logical consequence of the program. But since $\theta_1$ is a most general unifier of $H$ and $A_j$, $H$ can be replaced by $A_j$ in (5). Now let $\theta$ be $\theta_1 \cdots \theta_n$ restricted to the variables in $A_1, \ldots, A_m$ then:

$$\forall (A_1 \wedge \ldots \wedge A_m)\theta$$

is a logical consequence of P, which concludes the proof. ∎

It should be noticed that the theorem does not hold if the unifier is computed by a "unification" algorithm without occur-check. For illustration consider the following example.

**Example 3.26** Consider the following "definitions": A term is said to be $f$-*constructed* with a term $T$ iff it is of the form $f(T, Y)$ for any term $Y$. A term $X$ is said to be *bizarre* iff it is $f$-constructed with itself. (As discussed in Section 3.2 there are no "bizarre" terms since no term can include itself as a proper subterm.) Finally a term $X$ is said to be *crazy* iff it is the second direct substructure of a bizarre term. These statements can be formalized as the following definite program:

1) $f\_constructed(f(T, Y), T)$.
2) $bizarre(X) \leftarrow f\_constructed(X, X)$.
3) $crazy(X) \leftarrow bizarre(f(Y, X))$.

Now consider the goal $\leftarrow crazy(X)$ — representing the query "Are there any crazy terms?". There is only one (up to renaming) complete SLD-derivation, namely:

$$G_0 \; : \; \leftarrow crazy(X)$$
$$C_0 \; : \; crazy(X_0) \leftarrow bizarre(f(Y_0, X_0))$$

$$G_1 \; : \; \leftarrow bizarre(f(Y_0, X))$$
$$C_1 \; : \; bizarre(X_1) \leftarrow f\text{-}constructed(X_1, X_1)$$

$$G_2 \; : \; \leftarrow f\text{-}constructed(f(Y_0, X), f(Y_0, X))$$

The only subgoal in $G_2$ does not unify with 1) because of the occur-check. This corresponds to our expectations: Since, in the intended model, there are no bizarre terms, there cannot be any crazy terms. Since SLD-resolution is sound, if there were any answers to $G_0$ they were correct also in the intended model.

Assume now that a "unification" algorithm without occur-check is used. Then the derivation can be extended as follows:

$$G_2 \; : \; \leftarrow f\text{-}constructed(f(Y_0, X), f(Y_0, X))$$
$$C_2 \; : \; f\text{-}constructed(f(T_2, Y_2), T_2)$$

$$G_3 \; : \; \square$$

The infinite "substitution" obtained by composing the mgu's $\theta_1$, $\theta_2$ and $\theta_3$ is $\{X/Y_2, Y_0/f(\infty, Y_2)\}$ (see Section 3.2). The corresponding answer substitution is a renaming of $X$ — namely $\{X/Y_2\}$. In other words the conclusion is that every term is crazy, which is not true in the intended model. Thus it is not a logical consequence of the program which shows that the inference is no longer sound.                                                                                    ∎

## 3.5   Completeness of SLD-resolution

Another important problem is whether all correct answers for a given goal (i.e. all logical consequences) can be obtained by SLD-resolution. The answer is given by the following theorem, called the completeness theorem for SLD-resolution (due to K. Clark [31]).

**Theorem 3.27 (Completeness of SLD-resolution)** Let P be a definite program, $\leftarrow B$ a definite goal and $\Re$ a computation rule. For every instance $B'$ of $B$ which is a logical consequence of P, there exists a refutation of $\leftarrow B$ via $\Re$ with the computed answer substitution $\theta$ such that $B'$ is an instance of $B\theta$.   ∎

The proof of the theorem is not very difficult but is rather long and requires some auxiliary notions and lemmas. It is therefore omitted. The interested reader is referred to e.g. [5,105].

Theorem 3.27 shows that even if all correct answers cannot be computed using SLD-resolution, every correct answer is an instance of some computed answer. This is due to the fact that only most general unifiers — not arbitrary unifiers — are computed in derivations. However every particular correct answer is a special instance of some computed answer since all unifiers can always be obtained by further instantiation of a most general unifier.

**Example 3.28** Consider the goal clause $\leftarrow p(X)$ together with the program:

$$p(f(Y)).$$
$$q(a).$$

Clearly, $\{X/f(a)\}$ is a correct answer to the goal — that is:

$$\{p(f(Y)), q(a)\} \models p(f(a))$$

However, the only (up to renaming) computed answer substitution is $\{X/f(Y_0)\}$. Clearly, this is a more general answer than $\{X/f(a)\}$. ∎

The completeness theorem confirms *existence* of a refutation which produces a more general answer than any given correct answer. However the problem of how to *find* this refutation is still open. The refutation corresponds to a complete path in the SLD-tree of the given goal and computation rule. Thus the problem reduces to a systematic search of the SLD-tree. Existing interpreters often exploit some ordering on the program clauses, e.g. the textual ordering in the source program. This imposes the ordering on the edges descending from a node of the SLD-tree. The tree is then traversed in a *depth-first* manner following this ordering. For a finite SLD-tree this strategy is complete. Whenever a leaf node of the SLD-tree is reached the traversal continues by *backtracking* to the last preceding node of the path with unexplored branches (see Figure 3.5). If it is the empty goal the answer substitution of the completed refutation is reported before backtracking. However, as discussed in Section 3.3 the SLD-tree may be infinite. In this case the traversal of the tree will never terminate and some existing answers may never be computed. This can be avoided by a different strategy of tree traversal, like for example the *breadth-first* strategy illustrated in Figure 3.6. However this creates technical difficulties in implementation due to very complicated memory management being needed in the general case. Because of this, the majority of Prolog systems use the depth-first strategy for traversal of the SLD-tree.

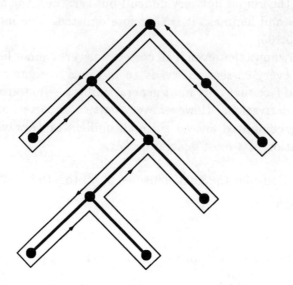

Figure 3.5: Depth-first search

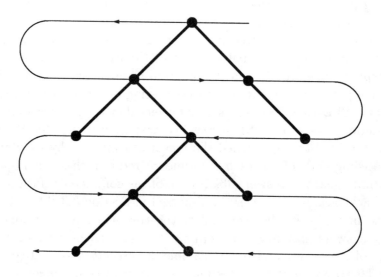

Figure 3.6: Breadth-first search

# Exercises

23. A substitution $\theta$ is idempotent iff $\theta\theta = \theta$. Show that the unification algorithm in Figure 3.1 produces only idempotent mgu's.

24. Find all disagreement pairs of the two structures $p(X, f(g(a), b), c)$ and $p(a, f(Y, b), Z)$.

25. What are the mgu's of the following pairs of structures:

$$\begin{array}{ll}
p(X, f(X)) & p(Y, f(a)) \\
p(f(X), Y, g(Y)) & p(Y, f(a), g(a)) \\
p(X, Y, X) & p(f(Y), a, f(Z)) \\
p(a, X) & p(X, f(X))
\end{array}$$

26. Give an example of two structures, $s$ and $t$, such that $s$ and $t$ have no common variables but unification fails because of occur-check.

27. Let $\theta$ be an mgu of $s$ and $t$ and $\omega$ a renaming substitution. Show that $\theta\omega$ is an mgu of $s$ and $t$.

28. Consider the following definite program:

$$\begin{array}{l}
p(Y) \leftarrow q(X, Y), r(Y). \\
p(X) \leftarrow q(X, X). \\
q(X, X) \leftarrow s(X). \\
r(b). \\
s(a). \\
s(b).
\end{array}$$

Draw the SLD-tree of the goal $\leftarrow p(X)$ if Prolog's computation rule is used. What are the computed answer substitutions?

29. Give an example of a definite program, a goal clause and two computation rules where one computation rule leads to a finite SLD-tree and where the other computation rule leads to an infinite tree.

30. Let $\theta$ be a renaming substitution. Show that there is only one substitution $\sigma$ such that $\sigma\theta = \theta\sigma = \epsilon$.

31. Show that if $A \in B_P$ and $\leftarrow A$ has a refutation of length $n$ then $A \in T_P \uparrow n$.

# Chapter 4

# Negation in Logic Programming

## 4.1 Definite Programs with Normal Goals

Definite programs deliver only positive knowledge. This statement can be explained in a technical way — the "knowledge" included in the program can be seen as the set of all atomic logical consequences of the program. This was discussed in Chapter 3 and compared with relational databases. The simplest piece of negative knowledge would be a negated atomic formula (in what follows such formulas will be called *negative literals* while atomic formulas are sometimes called *positive* literals). In the world described by Figure 1.1 John does not love Mary. However, because of the restricted syntax of definite programs this cannot be directly expressed in the corresponding definite program. Because of this no negative literal is a logical consequence of a definite program. The reason is that the Herbrand base of a definite program is always one of the program's models. This is a very uninteresting model — all predicates denote full relations. But every negative literal is false in this model so it cannot be a logical consequence of the program. (Recall that a logical consequence of the program is a formula true in every model of the program.)

By analogy to relational databases it seems natural to assume that the relations hold between individuals *only if* this can be concluded from the program. This is known as the *Closed World Assumption* (CWA), and may be understood as focusing attention to a specific class of models — not *all* models of the program.

The CWA-rule can be expressed as the "inference rule":

$$\frac{P \not\models A}{\neg A}$$

where $A$ is a (ground) atom.

Notice that the CWA-rule is not an inference rule in the traditional sense since P $\not\models$ A is not a formula of the object language (but of the meta-language).

**Example 4.1** Consider the following program:[1]

> $loves(X, Y) \leftarrow mother(X), child\_of(Y, X).$
> $loves(john, tom).$
> $loves(mary, john).$
> $mother(mary).$
> $child\_of(tom, mary).$

From this program $loves(john, mary)$ cannot be concluded — the SLD-tree for the definite goal $\leftarrow loves(john, mary)$ is finite and has no success branch. It then follows by the completeness theorem for SLD-resolution (Theorem 3.27) that $loves(john, mary)$ is *not* a logical consequence of the program. Thus, the atom is *not* in the least Herbrand model and, consequently, using the CWA-rule one can prove $\neg loves(john, mary)$.                                            ∎

Relational databases are finite. Hence, it is always possible to check in a finite time whether a given tuple is included in the database or not. In the case of definite programs the Herbrand base is usually infinite. It can be proved that the problem of whether a given atomic formula is a logical consequence of a program is undecidable. In other words there is no general algorithm which for an arbitrary given definite program and atom answers the question in a finite time. (It is not very difficult to relate this problem to the halting problem of Turing machines.)

Because of this, the CWA is inapplicable in the general case. A special case applies when, for some computation rule, the SLD-tree for a goal $\leftarrow A$ is *finitely failed*, as in Example 4.1 (a goal is said to be finitely failed if it has an SLD-tree containing only failed derivations).[2] By the completeness of SLD-resolution this means that no instance of $A$ is a logical consequence of P. In particular none of the *ground* instances of $A$ are included in the least Herbrand model of P. Thus CWA can be applied in this case to conclude $\forall(\neg A)$. This observation extends to the introduction of negative literals into the goals. Such goals are called *normal goals*. For instance, the normal goal $\leftarrow \neg A$ is refuted if the SLD-tree of $\leftarrow A$ is finitely failed for some computation rule. This was the case in

---

[1]Notice that Figure 1.1 describes only one of the program's models.

[2]The shape of the SLD-tree depends on the computation rule. It may happen that for some computation rule the SLD-tree of a goal is finitely failed while for another computation rule the SLD-tree of the same goal includes infinite branches.

the example with the goal $\leftarrow \neg loves(john, mary)$. Notice that the approach applies also to finitely failed nonground goals. The inferred formula in that case is the universal closure of $\neg A$. In Example 4.1 the goal $\leftarrow \neg loves(X, mary)$ would yield the answer "yes". In other words, "nobody loves Mary". Now obviously the SLD-tree of $\leftarrow A$ may also be infinite or contain success branches. If the computed answer substitution is empty then every instance of $A$ is a logical consequence of the program so that no negative conclusion is possible. This is reflected by the answer "no" to the normal goal. Notice that if the goal $\leftarrow \neg A$ is ground and $\leftarrow A$ succeeds, the computed answer substitution is always empty. However, consider the success of a nonground goal $\leftarrow A$ with a nonempty computed answer substitution $\theta$. This means that $A\theta$ is a logical consequence of the program. However, we are searching for those instances $A'$ of $A$ which are *not* logical consequences of the program in order to infer $\neg A'$. But the information obtained says nothing about the existence of such $A'$. Consider the goal $\leftarrow \neg loves(X, john)$ together with the program in Example 4.1. The definite goal $\leftarrow loves(X, john)$ succeeds with answer $X = mary$. But this is not sufficient to infer that there is no person who does not love John. For example, Tom does not love John.

The way of reasoning discussed above is called the *Negation as Failure* (NF) rule. It can be seen as a modification of CWA for the case of definite programs. Because of the difficulty in handling nonground negative subgoals it is often assumed that the NF-rule applies only when the selected negative subgoal is ground. The NF-rule can be summarized as the "inference rule":

$$\frac{\leftarrow A_1, \ldots, A_{i-1}, \neg A_i, A_{i+1}, \ldots, A_n \qquad \leftarrow A_i \text{ finitely fails with P}}{\leftarrow A_1, \ldots, A_{i-1}, A_{i+1}, \ldots, A_n}$$

As with the CWA-rule this is rather a meta-inference rule.

For the special case when $n = 1$ its effect is to derive $\neg A$ from a program P even though no negative literal is a logical consequence of a definite program. This raises the problem about the logical meaning of the NF-rule.

## 4.2   Completion of a Definite Program

The objective of this section is to give a logical justification of the NF-rule. The clauses of a definite program are *if*-statements, but to give a logical meaning to the NF-rule the clauses will be seen as shorthand for *if-and-only-if*-statements. (The general idea is due to K. Clark.) Thus, a definite program P with a normal goal is to be understood as a set of formulas obtained from the clauses by a special transformation of the program. Alternatively it can be seen as extending P with some additional axioms. This new set is called the *completion* of P and is denoted comp(P). It turns out that the conclusions drawn by the NF-rule are logical consequences of comp(P).

Before giving the formal method to construct the completion of definite programs the ideas are illustrated for the program of Example 4.1.

The first task is to combine all distinct clauses whose heads refer to the same predicate symbol $p$ into a single if-sentence for $p$. The idea is to take two (or more) clauses of the form $A \leftarrow B$ and $A \leftarrow C$ and replace them by the formula $A \leftarrow (B \vee C)$. This transformation is correct since $\Im$ is a model of $A \leftarrow B$ and $A \leftarrow C$ iff it is a model of $A \leftarrow (B \vee C)$. (The proof of this is left as an exercise).

Consider the predicate symbol *loves* in Example 4.1. The problem is that the heads of the relevant clauses are distinct — $loves(X, Y)$, $loves(john, tom)$ and $loves(mary, john)$ — hence, it is not possible to directly combine them into a single if-formula as described above. The solution is to introduce new variables for the arguments in the heads of the three clauses plus some additional restrictions on the values of these variables in the bodies.

$$loves(A, B) \leftarrow A = X, B = Y, mother(X), child\_of(Y, X).$$
$$loves(A, B) \leftarrow A = john, B = tom.$$
$$loves(A, B) \leftarrow A = mary, B = john.$$

Here the intended interpretation of the new binary predicate symbol "=" is identity on terms. There are two basic ways to handle this — one solution is to consider only interpretations where the symbol "=" has this particular interpretation. However, this means that concepts like model and logical consequence have to be redefined. The other approach is to add some axioms to the program which enforce this particular interpretation of "=". A set of such axioms will be presented later.

After this simple transformation of the clauses, all "old" variables are local to the right-hand sides of the clauses. Hence, they can be viewed as existentially quantified in the bodies. It is thus possible to write them as:

$$loves(A, B) \leftarrow \exists X, Y\ (A = X, B = Y, mother(X), child\_of(Y, X)).$$
$$loves(A, B) \leftarrow A = john, B = tom.$$
$$loves(A, B) \leftarrow A = mary, B = john.$$

These can now be combined into a single formula:

$$loves(A, B) \leftarrow \left[ \begin{array}{c} \exists X, Y\ (A = X, B = Y, mother(X), child\_of(Y, X)) \\ \vee \\ A = john, B = tom \\ \vee \\ A = mary, B = john \end{array} \right]$$

This example shows a general construction which for a given n-ary predicate symbol $p$ of the program P produces a logic formula denoted $IF(p, P)$.

**Definition 4.2 (Definition)** Let P be a definite program and $p/n$ a predicate symbol. The *definition* $def(p/n)$ of $p/n$ is the set of all clauses in P of the form $p(t_1, \ldots, t_n) \leftarrow B$ for arbitrary $t_1, \ldots, t_n$ and $B$. ∎

**Definition 4.3** Let $p/n$ be a predicate symbol in the program P and assume that $X_1, \ldots, X_n$ are "new" variables which do not appear in P.

- Let $C$ be a clause of the form:

$$p(t_1, \ldots, t_n) \leftarrow L_1, \ldots, L_m$$

  where $m \geq 0$, $t_1, \ldots, t_n$ are terms and $L_1, \ldots, L_m$ are literals. Then denote by $E(C)$ the formula:

$$\exists Y_1, \ldots, Y_k \ (X_1 = t_1, \cdots, X_n = t_n, L_1, \cdots, L_m)$$

  where $Y_1, \ldots, Y_k$ are all variables in $C$.

- Let $def(p/n) = \{C_1, \ldots, C_j\}$. The formula $IF(p, P)$ is obtained as follows:

$$\begin{aligned} p(X_1, \ldots, X_n) &\leftarrow E(C_1) \vee E(C_2) \vee \cdots \vee E(C_j) \quad \text{if } j > 0 \text{ and} \\ p(X_1, \ldots, X_n) &\leftarrow \square \qquad\qquad\qquad\qquad\qquad\qquad\quad \text{if } j = 0 \end{aligned}$$

Thus, if a predicate symbol $p/n$ does not appear in any head, then $IF(p, P)$ is the formula $p(X_1, \ldots, X_n) \leftarrow \square$. ∎

Now $IF(P)$ will be the set of all formulas $IF(q, P)$ for every predicate symbol $q$ occurring in P. The construction uses well-known logical equivalences, except for introduction of the equality in the bodies. Thus $IF(P)$ would be an equivalent formulation of P if appropriate axioms for equality were given (and they will be provided soon!). The next step of the construction is to transform the if-formulas of P into iff-formulas. More precisely, the occurrence of the connective "$\leftarrow$" in each formula of $IF(P)$ is replaced by "$\leftrightarrow$". The set of formulas obtained in this way is denoted $IFF(P)$. In doing this the meaning of our program is changed dramatically.

**Example 4.4** For the definite program P of Example 4.1 the set $IFF(P)$ is the following set of formulas:

$$loves(A,B) \leftrightarrow \left[ \begin{array}{c} \exists X, Y \ (A = X, B = Y, mother(X), child\_of(Y,X)) \\ \vee \\ A = john, B = tom \\ \vee \\ A = mary, B = john \end{array} \right]$$

$$mother(A) \leftrightarrow A = mary$$
$$child\_of(A,B) \leftrightarrow A = mary \wedge B = tom$$

                                                                     ■

It is not possible to deduce from the original program that John is Tom's father (nor the contrary). On the other hand, using IFF(P) the negative literal $\neg child\_of(john, tom)$ is equivalent to $\neg(john = mary \wedge tom = tom)$ which is evidently true in every Herbrand interpretation where the meaning of "=" is identity on ground terms. Hence, by adding to IFF(P) axioms for equality which enforce this condition it will be possible to deduce that "John is not a child of Tom". On the other hand it should be possible to deduce from IFF(P) all positive information deducible from P. Also for this some proper axiomatic characterization of the equality is needed.

    Next the formulation of the proposed equality theory is considered.

    The predicate symbol for equality ("=") introduced in the construction of IF(P) has been characterized by referring to its intended models. It was required that for any pair of ground terms $t_1$ and $t_2$, a Herbrand interpretation $\Im$ should be a model of $t_1 = t_2$ iff $t_1$ and $t_2$ are identical terms. In his construction Clark uses axioms, called Clark's Equality Theory (CET) in what follows, which enforce this condition. In other words, any model of CET has the required property. The axioms are the following:

**Definition 4.5 (CET)** In the following let $X \neq Y$ be a shorthand for $\neg X = Y$ and assume that all formulas are universally quantified:

1. $X = X$

2. $X = Y \rightarrow Y = X$

3. $X = Y \wedge Y = Z \rightarrow X = Z$

4. For any functor $f/m$:

$$X_1 = Y_1 \wedge \cdots \wedge X_m = Y_m \rightarrow f(X_1, \ldots, X_m) = f(Y_1, \ldots, Y_m)$$

5. For any predicate symbol $p/m$:

$$X_1 = Y_1 \wedge \cdots \wedge X_m = Y_m \rightarrow (p(X_1, \ldots, X_m) \rightarrow p(Y_1, \ldots, Y_m))$$

6. For all distinct functors $f/m$ and $g/n$, $(m, n \geq 0)$:

$$f(X_1, \ldots, X_m) \neq g(Y_1, \ldots, Y_n)$$

7. For all functors $f$:

$$f(X_1, \ldots, X_m) = f(Y_1, \ldots, Y_m) \rightarrow X_1 = Y_1 \wedge \cdots \wedge X_m = Y_m$$

8. For any term $t[X]$ containing $X$ as a proper subterm:

$$t[X] \neq X$$

∎

Now the notion of completion of P is defined as follows:

$$\mathrm{comp}(P) := \mathrm{IFF}(P) \cup \mathrm{CET}$$

Thus the definite program P has been transformed to a new set of axioms comp(P) with different semantics (different class of models). The justification for this construction is a psychological argument that the programmer really means "if and only if" when using "if" in the program. Even if it is not so, nothing really changes as long as the goals do not include negative literals (as discussed below).

Indeed, it can be proved that the terms $t_1$ and $t_2$ are unifiable iff the formula $\exists (t_1 = t_2)$ is a logical consequence of CET [30]. A most general unifier $\theta$ of $t_1$ and $t_2$ can thus be used as the answer substitution for the goal $\leftarrow t_1 = t_2$. This is exploited in Prolog where the binary predicate symbol "=" is a so called built-in predicate. (Notice, however, that Prolog systems usually do not employ the occur-check, thus violating axiom number 8 of the equality theory.)

The completion of a definite program P preserves the "positive knowledge" represented by P. By construction of IFF(P) and CET it follows that comp(P) $\models$ P (the proof of this is left as an exercise). Thus, if $A$ is a logical consequence of P it is also a logical consequence of comp(P). By soundness of SLD-resolution the computed answer $\theta$ for a definite goal $\leftarrow B$ gives also a logical consequence $B\theta$ of comp(P). In other words the computed answers remain correct also for the if-and-only-if reading of a definite program.

The remaining problem is to determine the logical meaning of answers obtained by the NF-rule for goals including negative literals.

# 4.3   Soundness of the NF-Rule

Completion of a definite program P introduces by its only-if-part some negative information not present in P. The example of the previous section shows
that the sentence "Tom is not John's child" is not a logical consequence of the
original program. But it is a logical consequence of the completion. This can
also be derived by the NF-rule from the original program — since the atom
*child_of*(*tom, john*) unifies with no head of the program clauses, then the goal
← ¬*child_of*(*tom, john*) yields the answer "yes" by the NF-rule. The following
result shows that this is a general law.

**Theorem 4.6 (Soundness of NF-rule)** Let P be a definite program and $G$ be
a definite goal of the form ← $A_1, \ldots, A_m$. If there exists a computation rule $\Re$
such that the SLD-tree for $G$ and P via $\Re$ is finitely failed then $\forall\neg(A_1 \wedge \cdots \wedge A_m)$
is a logical consequence of comp(P).                                      ∎

The theorem can be proved by induction on the depth of the SLD-tree (i.e. the
maximal length of a path in the tree) using some properties of the equality theory.
    This theorem has a particular importance for the case $m = 1$ since it makes it
possible to combine SLD-resolution with the NF-rule. The subgoal $L_k$ selected by
the computation rule from the normal goal ← $L_1, \ldots, L_k, \ldots, L_n$ is then treated
as follows:[3]

- if $L_k$ is a positive literal then ordinary SLD-resolution is used;

- if $L_k$ is a negative literal of the form ¬$A$ and if ← $A$ has a finitely failed
  SLD-tree then ¬$A$ has been solved and the next goal in the sequence is
  ← $L_1, \ldots, L_{k-1}, L_{k+1}, \ldots, L_n$.

This way of constructing derivations is called *SLDNF-resolution* for definite programs with normal goals.
    Consider the program of Example 4.1 and the goal:

    ← *loves*(*X, Y*), ¬*mother*(*X*)

SLDNF-resolution (using Prolog's computation rule) produces the answer $X =$
*john*, $Y = tom$, and by the soundness theorem this answer is correct. That is,
comp(P) ⊨ *loves*(*john, tom*) ∧ ¬*mother*(*john*).

---

[3]Some authors impose the additional requirement that if the selected literal is negative, it
must be ground. Such computation rules are said to be *safe*. A computation which at some
state under a given computation rule selects a nonground negative subgoal is said to *flounder*.

Notice however that so far no method to check whether there exists a finitely failed SLD-tree for a given goal and program has been suggested. In the example above the selection of leftmost subgoals is sufficient for that purpose but this may not work in other cases where the SLD-tree of the goal is finitely failed for some computation rule and infinite for another rule. Theoretically the problem can be solved by a so called *fairness* requirement on the computation rule. Fairness means that every literal of the goal (or its instance obtained by intermediate steps of derivation) is selected within a finite number of derivation steps. If there is a finitely failed SLD-tree of $G$ for some computation rule, every fair rule will also have a finitely failed SLD-tree. Clearly, Prolog's computation rule is unfair — the selected atom is explored in a depth-first manner and the other subgoals are not selected until this subderivation is completed. But if it is infinite they are never selected. In practice implementation of fair computation rules creates severe efficiency problems. On the other hand, use of unfair rules creates no danger of incorrect answers — computation with unfair rules may loop in some cases when a fair rule would be sufficient for termination. But looping computations do not produce any answers. A looping program can often be transformed into an equivalent one which terminates under Prolog's computation rule.

The second question concerns the completeness of SLDNF-resolution. That is, whether every correct answer can be found. Let P be a definite program, $\leftarrow A$ a normal goal and $\theta$ a substitution such that $A\theta$ is a logical consequence of comp(P). The problem is whether $\theta$ can always be constructed by SLDNF-resolution. The answer is no, as illustrated by the following simple example.

**Example 4.7**

>     $teacher(john).$
>     $student(tom).$
>     $takes\_courses(X) \leftarrow student(X).$

The completion of this program describes the situation when only the students take courses. But the question whether there are individuals who do not take courses cannot be answered by SLDNF-resolution. Consider the goal $\leftarrow \neg takes\_courses(Y)$. Since it contains only a negative literal, the goal $\leftarrow takes\_courses(X)$ is considered. But it succeeds with $X = tom$. Thus the SLDNF-resolution provides no answer. On the other hand the answer $X = john$ is correct, that is, the goal $\leftarrow \neg takes\_courses(john)$ succeeds which implies that $\neg takes\_courses(john)$ is a logical consequence of comp(P). ∎

The reason for this is that the NF-rule is only a test. It can check whether a negated literal is a logical consequence of the completion of a program, but since it is based on the concept of failure it cannot find an instance of the literal which has this property.

## 4.4   Normal and Stratified Programs

Formalization of some "worlds" requires the use of negative literals as conditions of the rules, not just in the goals. Take for instance:

**Example 4.8** Every professor gives courses if he is not on sabbatical leave. Professors are the only persons who give courses. This can be reflected by the following rule with the iff-reading.

$$gives\_courses(X) \leftarrow professor(X), \neg on\_sabbatical(X).$$

∎

Programs with such rules are called *normal* (or general) logic programs. More precisely — a normal clause is a clause of the form $A \leftarrow L_1, \ldots, L_n$ where $n \geq 0$, $A$ is an atomic formula and $L_1, \ldots, L_n$ are positive or negative literals. A normal program is a finite set of such normal clauses.

The notion of completion carries over from definite programs to normal programs — negative literals are simply treated as if they were positive ones. Unfortunately, the completion of a normal program may be inconsistent, that is, it may happen that the completion has no models. For example consider the program P:

$$p \leftarrow \neg p$$

By the definition of completion, IFF(P) is the formula:

$$p \leftrightarrow \neg p$$

which is false in every interpretation.

To avoid this problem a sufficient syntactic condition can be given which characterizes a subset of all normal programs whose completion is consistent. The condition seems to be reasonable from the pragmatic point of view and reflects a certain methodology for constructing normal programs. The intuition is to provide a certain discipline in defining predicates of the program. First a number of predicates are defined by a definite program. Then new predicates may be defined by normal clauses using negations of predicates defined only at previous levels. All predicates are defined in a finite number of such steps. The program constructed in this way is said to be *stratified*. A precise definition may be given using the auxiliary notion of *dependency graph*. It is a directed graph with edges labelled by '+' or '−' and nodes labelled by the predicate symbols of the program. The nodes are connected as follows:

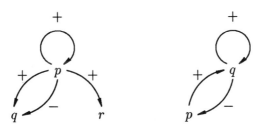

**Figure 4.1: Dependency graphs**

- there is an edge labelled '+' from $p/m$ to $q/n$ iff P contains a clause of the form $p(s_1, \ldots, s_m) \leftarrow \ldots, q(t_1, \ldots, t_n), \ldots$;

- there is an edge labelled '−' from $p/m$ to $q/n$ iff P contains a clause of the form $p(s_1, \ldots, s_m) \leftarrow \ldots, \neg q(t_1, \ldots, t_n), \ldots$

A program is stratified iff in its dependency graph there are no cycles containing a negative edge. Intuitively this means that no predicate is defined in terms of its own negation (directly or indirectly) which was the source of the problems in the example above.

**Example 4.9** The dependency graphs of the two programs:

$$p(X) \leftarrow \neg q(X). \qquad\qquad p(X) \leftarrow q(X).$$
$$p(X) \leftarrow q(X), r(X), p(X). \qquad q(X) \leftarrow \neg p(X).$$
$$r(X). \qquad\qquad\qquad q(X) \leftarrow q(X).$$

are depicted in Figure 4.1. Clearly, the first program is stratified but the second one is not. ∎

Most typical programs are stratified but the question arises whether there are useful normal programs which are not stratified? Clearly there are nonstratified programs whose completion is consistent. For instance, consider the following one:

$$odd(X) \leftarrow \neg even(X).$$
$$even(X) \leftarrow \neg odd(X).$$

However, even if the program makes perfect sense it is difficult to make any useful deductions from it. Very few people would be happy with the following circular explanation:

Q: What are the odd numbers?

A: The odd numbers are those which are not even.

Q: OK, in that case, what are the even numbers?

A: The even numbers are anything but the odd numbers.

etc.

However, there *are* useful and constructive programs which are not stratified. One such program appears in Chapter 9 (on page 169).

**Definition 4.10 (Stratified programs)** A normal program P is *stratified* iff the set of P's predicate symbols can be partitioned into disjoint sets $S_0, \ldots, S_m$ such that if:

$$p(\ldots) \leftarrow L_1, \ldots, L_j \in P$$

and $p \in S_k$, $(0 \le k \le m)$ then for each $L_i \in \{L_1, \ldots, L_j\}$:

- if $L_i$ is of the form $q(\ldots)$ then $q$ is contained in $S_0 \cup \cdots \cup S_k$;

- if $L_i$ is of the form $\neg q(\ldots)$ then $q$ is contained in $S_0 \cup \cdots \cup S_{k-1}$.

Each $S_i$, $(0 \le i \le m)$, is called a *stratum* of P.  ∎

Partitioning of a stratified program can be done as follows — first let $S_0$ be the set of all predicate symbols which do not occur in any clause head of P. That is $S_0 := \{p \mid def(p) = \varnothing\}$. For each predicate symbol $p$, denote by $Min(p)$ the set of predicate symbols $q$ such that there exists a path with at least one negative edge from $p$ to $q$ in the dependency graph of P. Then for $i \ge 0$:

$$S_{i+1} := \{p \mid Min(p) \subseteq S_0 \cup \cdots \cup S_i \text{ and } p \notin S_0 \cup \cdots \cup S_i\}$$

A program P is said to be *m-stratified* iff $m$ is the least index such that $S_0 \cup \cdots \cup S_m$ is the set of all predicate symbols of P.

**Example 4.11** For some department the following information is available — names of students, names of graduate students, names of employees. For example:

*student(tom).*
*student(mary).*
*student(liz).*
*graduate(mary).*
*employee(liz).*
*employee(mary).*
*employee(john).*

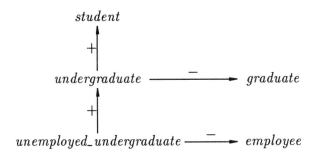

**Figure 4.2: Dependency Graph**

Assume also that the program contains information about the undergraduate students who are not employed at the department. For this the following stratified program can be given:

$unemployed\_undergraduate(X) \leftarrow$
$\quad\quad undergraduate(X), \neg employee(X).$

$undergraduate(X) \leftarrow$
$\quad\quad student(X), \neg graduate(X).$

The dependency graph of the program is depicted in Figure 4.2.
   It follows that:

$$Min(student) = Min(graduate) = Min(employee) = \varnothing;$$
$$Min(undergraduate) = \{graduate\};$$
$$Min(unemployed\_undergraduate) = \{employee, graduate\}$$

The program is 2-stratified with the following strata:

$$S_0 = \varnothing$$
$$S_1 = \{student, graduate, employee\}$$
$$S_2 = \{undergraduate, unemployed\_undergraduate\}$$

∎

The following result has been proved concerning the consistency of stratified programs.

**Theorem 4.12** For every stratified program P its completion has a Herbrand model. ∎

The intuition behind this result is clear. Denote by $P_i$ the set of clauses defining the predicates of the set $S_i$ for $1 \leq i \leq m$ obtained by the construction discussed above. Thus $P_0$ is the empty program and its completion has a Herbrand model $M_0$ which is the empty subset of the Herbrand base. The clauses of $P_1$ have no predicates of $P_0$ in their heads. Thus, when $M_0$ is fixed, $P_1$ can be seen as a definite program using some (in this case negative) facts of $M_0$. Therefore its completion has a Herbrand model $M_1$, including $M_0$ as a subset. Repeating this procedure the model $M_m$ can be finally constructed as the model of comp(P).

**Example 4.13** Consider the program consisting of the clause $p(a) \leftarrow \neg q(b)$. Clearly, $S_0 = \{q\}$ and $S_1 = \{p\}$. Then $M_0 = \emptyset$ and $M_1 = \{p(a)\}$ (since $M_0$ makes the right-hand side true). To the final model one must add all possible atoms of the form $t = t$ where $t$ is a ground term.                    ∎

As opposed to definite programs, stratified programs do not in general have one unique minimal Herbrand model. The model in Example 4.13 is a minimal Herbrand model but $\{q(b), a = a, b = b\}$ is another minimal model of the same program.

## 4.5    SLDNF-resolution for Normal Programs

The next problem to be discussed is how to handle normal programs with normal goals. The idea is to extend the approach discussed for definite programs and normal goals. The difference is that the resolution of normal clauses may introduce new negative subgoals.

However, presentation of SLDNF-resolution for normal programs leads to certain technical problems. The definition consists of two new notions — the concept of SLDNF-derivation (for normal programs) and the concept of failed SLDNF-derivation. However, there is one little hitch to it — the two are mutually dependent and it is not possible to define one of them without making use of the other. In order to handle this problem a concept of *level* is introduced. Informally the level of a goal can be explained as follows: when having normal programs, nested use of negation is possible — i.e. while trying to solve a negative literal it may happen that another negative literal is encountered — the intuition behind the level is to control the number of nested uses of negation.

Before presenting SLDNF-resolution the auxiliary notion of SLD$^+$-derivation is introduced:

**Definition 4.14 (SLD$^+$-derivation)** Let P be a normal program, $G_0$ a normal goal and $\mathfrak{R}$ a computation rule. An SLD$^+$-derivation of $G_0$ is either a finite sequence:

$$\langle G_0; C_0 \rangle, \ldots, \langle G_{i-1}; C_{i-1} \rangle, G_i$$

or an infinite sequence:

$$\langle G_0; C_0 \rangle, \langle G_1; C_1 \rangle, \langle G_2; C_2 \rangle, \ldots$$

where in each step $m+1$ ($m \geq 0$), $\mathfrak{R}$ selects a positive literal in $G_m$ and obtains $G_{m+1}$ in the usual way. ∎

In other words, an SLD$^+$-derivation basically is an SLD-derivation where, in addition, clauses and goals are allowed to contain negative literals. The notion of computed substitution of an SLD$^+$-derivation is defined in the same way as for SLD-derivations.

Apart from infinite SLD$^+$-derivations there are three more cases when a derivation $\langle G_0; C_0 \rangle, \ldots, \langle G_{i-1}; C_{i-1} \rangle, G_i$ cannot be extended (i.e. is complete):

- when the selected subgoal in $G_i$ is negative (say $\neg A$). Such derivations are said to be *blocked* (on $\neg A$);

- when $G_i = \square$ (refutation);

- when the selected subgoal in $G_i$ is positive but fails to unify with any clause head (failed SLD$^+$-derivation).

To cope with infinite nesting of negation the notion of *level* is introduced.

**Definition 4.15 (Level of goals)** Let P be a normal program, $G_0$ a normal goal and $\mathfrak{R}$ a computation rule. The level of $G_0$ is said to be:

- 0 iff no SLD$^+$-derivation of $G_0$ under $\mathfrak{R}$ is blocked;

- $k+1$ iff the maximum level of all goals $\leftarrow A$ such that $\neg A$ blocks an SLD$^+$-derivation of $G_0$ is $k$.

∎

In other words, the level of a goal $G_0$ is the maximum number of blocked SLD$^+$-derivations which may be constructed starting from $G_0$ and initiating a new SLD$^+$-derivation for $\leftarrow A$ whenever $\neg A$ blocks for the old one.

Thus, goals which only have failed, infinite or successful derivations are of level 0. Notice also that there are goals which do not have any (finite) level depending on what P looks like. For instance, the goal $\leftarrow p$ does not have a level together with the program:

$$p \leftarrow \neg p$$

It follows that if the program is stratified every goal has a level but not necessarily the other way around.

Having defined the auxiliary concept of $\text{SLD}^+$-derivation it is possible to give the definition of SLDNF-derivation:

**Definition 4.16 (SLDNF-derivation)** Let P be a normal program, $G_0$ a normal goal and $\Re$ a computation rule. The set of SLDNF-derivations and the subset of failed SLDNF-derivations of $G_0$ are the least sets such that:

- any $\text{SLD}^+$-derivation of $G_0$ is an SLDNF-derivation of $G_0$. In particular, any failed $\text{SLD}^+$-derivation of $G_0$ is a failed SLDNF-derivation of $G_0$;

- if $\langle G_0; C_0 \rangle, \ldots, G_i$ is an $\text{SLD}^+$ derivation which is blocked on $\neg A$ (that is, $G_i$ is of the form $\leftarrow L_1, \ldots, L_{m-1}, \neg A, L_{m+1} \ldots, L_n$) and $\leftarrow A$ is a goal of level $k$, then:

  - if every complete SLDNF-derivation of $\leftarrow A$ is failed under $\Re$, then $\langle G_0; C_0 \rangle, \ldots, \langle G_i; @ \rangle, (\leftarrow L_1, \ldots, L_{m-1}, L_{m+1}, \ldots, L_n)$ is an SLDNF-derivation of $G_0$ (the symbol "@" is used to indicate that the derivation step is negative and the substitution computed in the step is $\epsilon$);

  - if there is an SLDNF-refutation of $\leftarrow A$ under $\Re$ with the empty computed answer substitution then $\langle G_0; C_0 \rangle, \ldots, G_i$ is a failed SLDNF-derivation.

- if $\langle G_0; C_0 \rangle, \ldots, G_i$ is an SLDNF-derivation of $G_0$ and $\langle G_i; C_i \rangle, \ldots$ is an SLDNF-derivation of $G_i$, then the "composition" $\langle G_0; C_0 \rangle, \ldots, \langle G_i; C_i \rangle, \ldots$ is a (possibly infinite) SLDNF-derivation of $G_0$;

- if, for any $i \geq 0$, $\langle G_0; C_0 \rangle, \ldots, \langle G_{i-1}; C_{i-1} \rangle, G_i$ is an SLDNF-derivation of $G_0$, then $\langle G_0; C_0 \rangle, \langle G_1; C_1 \rangle, \ldots$ is an infinite SLDNF-derivation of $G_0$.

■

The notion of computed answer substitution carries over from Chapter 3 with the exception that resolution steps involving negative literals produce the empty substitution.

Apart from infinite SLDNF-derivations we distinguish four cases when an SLDNF-derivation $\langle G_0; C_0 \rangle, \ldots, \langle G_{i-1}; C_{i-1} \rangle, G_i$ cannot be extended:

- when $G_i = \square$ (refutations);

- when the derivation is *failed* (as defined above). That is, if the selected subgoal in $G_i$ is positive and fails to unify with any clause head, or if it is negative ($\neg A$) and $\leftarrow A$ has a refutation with the empty computed answer substitution;

- when the selected subgoal in $G_i$ is negative (say $\neg A$) and $\leftarrow A$ has at least one refutation, but none with the empty computed answer substitution. In this case $G_i$ (and $G_0$) are said to *flounder*;

- finally it may happen that the selected subgoal in $G_i$ is negative ($\neg A$) and $\leftarrow A$ has no finite level. Such SLDNF-derivations are called *blocked*.

The notion of level is of little practical interest since, in general, it is undecidable whether a goal has a (finite) level or not. A practical way of constructing SLDNF-derivations (for instance, in Prolog), is to initiate a new SLD$^+$-derivation for any blocked one without checking the level of the blocking goal. As shown in Example 4.20 this may lead to a new kind of looping computation. It is worth noticing that Prolog systems usually do not even check floundering but treats it as failure, so that the computed answers are not logically sound.

It should also be noted that if it is known that $\Re$ never selects nonground negative subgoals for a given program and goal, then there is no risk of floundering since ground goals always result in the empty computed answer substitution (if any). Moreover, if the program is stratified one can see that blocked derivations are impossible. In other words, if these restrictions are imposed SLDNF-derivations are either successful, failed or infinite.

In order to prove a goal $G_0$ it may be necessary to traverse all possible SLDNF-derivations of $G_0$. By analogy to SLD-trees we can define a notion of SLDNF-tree to facilitate a systematic traversal of all possible derivations.

**Definition 4.17 (SLDNF-tree)** Let P be a normal program, $G_0$ a normal goal and $\Re$ a computation rule. The SLDNF-tree of $G_0$ is a tree such that:

- $G_0$ is the root of the tree;

- $G_{i+1}$ is a child of $G_i$ (through an edge labelled by $C_i$) iff there is an SLDNF-derivation $\langle G_0; C_0 \rangle, \ldots, \langle G_i; C_i \rangle, G_{i+1}$.

∎

The root of an SLDNF-tree all of whose branches correspond to failed derivations is said to be *finitely failed*.

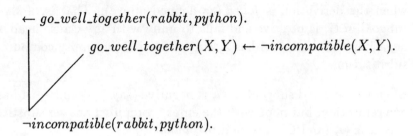

$\leftarrow go\_well\_together(rabbit, python).$

$go\_well\_together(X, Y) \leftarrow \neg incompatible(X, Y).$

$\neg incompatible(rabbit, python).$

**Figure 4.3: Failed SLDNF-derivation**

A procedure for constructing (or traversing) such a tree would proceed analogously to construction of SLD-trees as long as only positive subgoals are selected. However, when a negative literal ($\neg A$) is encountered the construction is suspended while trying to establish whether $\leftarrow A$ is finitely failed or if it has a refutation with the empty computed answer substitution.

**Example 4.18** Consider the normal program:

$C_1 : \quad go\_well\_together(X, Y) \leftarrow \neg incompatible(X, Y).$
$C_2 : \quad incompatible(X, Y) \leftarrow \neg likes(X, Y).$
$C_3 : \quad incompatible(X, Y) \leftarrow \neg likes(Y, X).$
$C_4 : \quad likes(X, Y) \leftarrow harmless(Y).$
$C_5 : \quad likes(X, Y) \leftarrow eats(X, Y).$
$C_6 : \quad harmless(rabbit).$
$C_7 : \quad eats(python, rabbit).$

The (only) complete SLDNF-derivation of the goal:

$\leftarrow go\_well\_together(rabbit, python).$

is depicted in Figure 4.3.The derivation is failed since the goal:

$\leftarrow incompatible(rabbit, python).$

has an SLDNF-refutation (needless to say with the empty substitution). The SLDNF-tree of this goal is depicted in Figure 4.4. The leftmost branch in the tree is a refutation since the goal:

$\leftarrow likes(rabbit, python).$

is finitely failed. The rightmost branch is a failed derivation since the goal:

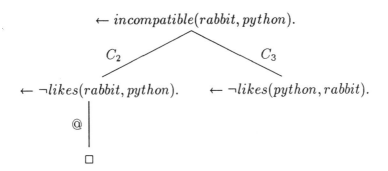

**Figure 4.4: SLDNF-tree**

$\leftarrow likes(python, rabbit).$

has a refutation (in fact, two). Similarly the SLDNF-tree of the goal:

$\leftarrow go\_well\_together(rabbit, rabbit).$

contains a refutation as demonstrated by Figures 4.5–4.7. ∎

To demonstrate floundering and blocked derivations consider the following two examples:

**Example 4.19** Let P be the program:

$C_1: \quad p(a) \leftarrow \neg q(X).$
$C_2: \quad q(b).$

Then surely $\langle \leftarrow p(a); C_1 \rangle, \leftarrow \neg q(X_0)$ is an $SLD^+$-derivation and, as a consequence, an SLDNF-derivation. Since $\leftarrow q(X_0)$ only has a single derivation and since this is a refutation with a nonempty computed answer substitution, it follows that the initial goal flounders. ∎

**Example 4.20** Let P be the program:

$C_1: \quad p \leftarrow \neg p.$

Then $\langle \leftarrow p; C_1 \rangle, \leftarrow \neg p$ is an SLDNF-derivation. But since $\leftarrow p$ has no (finite) level it follows that the derivation is blocked. Computationally this amounts to infinitely many attempts to construct an SLDNF-tree for the goal $\leftarrow p$. ∎

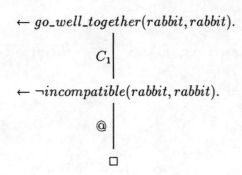

**Figure 4.5: SLDNF-tree**

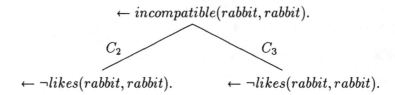

**Figure 4.6: Finitely failed SLDNF-tree**

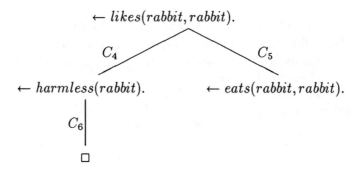

**Figure 4.7: SLDNF-tree of** $\leftarrow likes(rabbit, rabbit)$

Concerning soundness and completeness of SLDNF-resolution for normal programs at least the following can be proved:

**Theorem 4.21 (Soundness of SLDNF-resolution)** Let P be a normal program, $\leftarrow B$ a normal goal and $\Re$ a computation rule. If $\theta$ is a computed answer substitution of an SLDNF-refutation of $\leftarrow B$. Then $B\theta$ is a logical consequence of comp(P). ∎

The proof is similar to that of SLD-resolution but in addition one has to use induction on the level of goals using as a basis the soundness of the NF-rule for definite programs with normal goals.

Since SLDNF-resolution for normal programs includes definite programs with normal goals as a special case there is no hope for *completeness* in the general case. A possible solution seems to be introduction of certain restrictions on the class of programs and goals for which completeness can be achieved. Several results of this type can be found in the literature but none of them has gained broad acceptance. The research on this topic resulted, however, in better understanding of the problem. Among the questions raised the following seems to be particularly interesting:

Is it justified to take comp(P) as the intended meaning of a normal program? The answer is not so simple and the only possible answer appears to be "sometimes". Take for instance the clause:

P : $p(a) \vee q(b)$

From the logical point of view P is equivalent to each of the following two normal programs:

$P_1$ : $p(a) \leftarrow \neg q(b)$.

$P_2$ : $q(b) \leftarrow \neg p(a)$.

Now, the set of models of comp($P_1$) and comp($P_2$) are not the same! The Herbrand model $\{p(a), a = a, b = b\}$ is a model of comp($P_1$) but not a model of comp($P_2$) (verify this!). This seems to contradict the claim that the completion is what the programmer really means when he writes a normal program.

Another possible approach would be not to transform P (by adding new axioms to P) but to restrict the class of models under consideration — in the extreme, take just one model, for instance, the least model or a special minimal model if there is no least model. However, this introduces basically the same problems as above: namely to characterize the intended model since, as stated in Chapter 2, the only information available concerning the intended model is the program itself.

Another problem concerns the restriction to stratified programs. As stated above the set of all stratified programs is a proper subset of all normal programs whose completion is consistent. This subset can be extended to so called *locally stratified programs*. Roughly speaking, a normal program is locally stratified if it is possible to partition the Herbrand base into strata such that every ground instance of each clause satisfies the requirements in Definition 4.10. The class of locally stratified programs encompasses also stratified programs and this larger class of normal programs has been shown to be consistent.

Now what about the use of negation in Prolog? It turns out that most Prolog systems do not implement a sound version of SLDNF-resolution. When a Prolog system encounters a negative literal $\neg A$ in a derivation, it tries to prove the goal $\leftarrow A$. If this goal succeeds the original derivation is failed. As pointed out, this causes no problem as long as there is a refutation of $\leftarrow A$ with the *empty* computed answer substitution. However, most Prolog implementations do not perform this check since it may be rather costly. As a result, Prolog computations involving nested use of negation may produce erroneous answers (see exercise 48). The responsibility of making sure that such situations do not arise is the responsibility of the user. It is good practice, when using negation in Prolog, to make sure that negative literals are positioned only in such places where it is guaranteed that the literal is *ground* when selected by Prolog's computation rule. Obviously, if $\neg A$ is ground and $\leftarrow A$ succeeds, the computed answer substitution will be empty and the problem raised above does not appear. Usage of negation resulting in nonground negative literals being selected is commonly referred to as *unsafe use of negation*.

Unsafe use of negation can be exploited in a way which abuses the normal declarative understanding of logic programs. For instance, it is quite common that people write clauses like:

$$orphan(X) \leftarrow \neg parent(Y, X). \tag{*}$$

interpreting this as "$X$ is an orphan if there is no $Y$ such that $Y$ is the parent of $X$". However, the standard way of understanding the clause is by considering it as being universally quantified. That is:

$$\forall X \, \forall Y \, (orphan(X) \leftarrow \neg \, parent(Y, X))$$

which is equivalent to:

$$\forall X \, (orphan(X) \leftarrow \exists Y \, \neg \, parent(Y, X))$$

whose reading is "$X$ is an orphan if there is some $Y$ such that $Y$ is not the parent of $X$" which is something completely different than what was intended. The point is that the program works as intended as long as $orphan/1$ is called with a ground argument. For instance, assume that the goal $\leftarrow parent(Y, brian)$ finitely fails. Then according to Theorem 4.21, $\forall Y \neg parent(Y, brian)$ is a logical consequence of comp(P) and no matter how the clause (*) is understood the conclusion $orphan(brian)$ follows from comp(P). There is a very simple solution to avoid the ambiguity of (*). Namely to revert to safe use of negation; this can be achieved by rewriting (*) into two clauses removing any doubts as to what the meaning of the program is:

$$orphan(X) \leftarrow \neg has\_a\_parent(X).$$
$$has\_a\_parent(X) \leftarrow parent(Y, X).$$

Unsafe use of negation is often used to prevent the possibility of solving subgoals using two different clauses. Such programs are of the form:

$$p(X) \leftarrow q(X, Y), \ldots$$
$$p(X) \leftarrow \neg q(X, Y), \ldots$$

Also in this case the standard interpretation of clauses is abandoned. Intuitively the first clause says that "$p(X)$ is true if *there is* a $Y$ such that $q(X, Y)$ and ...". The second clause says that "$p(X)$ is true if *there is not* a $Y$ such that $q(X, Y)$ and ...". Again it is possible to avoid such ambiguities by adding an extra clause to the program but in practice this is seldom done.

# Exercises

32. Let P be a definite program. Show that P is a logical consequence of comp(P).

33. Consider the following definite program:

    $$p(Y) \leftarrow q(X, Y), r(X).$$
    $$p(X) \leftarrow r(X).$$
    $$q(f(X), Y) \leftarrow q(X, Y).$$
    $$r(b).$$

    Show that there are two computation rules, $\Re_1$ and $\Re_2$, such that $\leftarrow p(a)$ finitely fails under $\Re_1$ and has an infinite SLD-tree under $\Re_2$.

34. Show that $\{p \leftarrow q, p \leftarrow r\}$ has exactly the same set of models as $\{p \leftarrow (q \lor r)\}$ (where $p$, $q$ and $r$ are arbitrary formulas).

35. Construct the completion of the program in exercise 33. Show that $\neg p(a)$ is a logical consequence of comp(P).

36. Let $s$ and $t$ be terms. Show that CET $\models \exists(s = t)$ iff $s$ and $t$ are unifiable.

37. Show that in any model $\Im$ of CET, $=_\Im$ is an equivalence relation.

38. Let P be a definite program and $G$ a definite goal. Show that if $G$ has a finitely failed SLD-tree of depth $n$ (i.e. the longest branch in the tree has length $n$) then any instance $G\theta$ of $G$ also has a finitely failed SLD-tree of depth $m$ where $m \leq n$.

39. Construct the completion of the program:

$$p(a) \leftarrow q(X).$$
$$p(b) \leftarrow r(X).$$
$$r(a).$$
$$r(b).$$

40. Consider the normal program:

$$p(a) \leftarrow \neg q(X).$$
$$q(a).$$

Construct its completion and show that $\neg p(a)$ is not a logical consequence of comp(P).

41. Find a fair computation rule for the following program and goal clause:

$$\leftarrow p(X), q(X, Y).$$
$$p(f(X)) \leftarrow p(X).$$
$$q(X, Y) \leftarrow p(Y), s(X, a).$$
$$s(X, X).$$

42. Which of the following four programs are stratified?

$$P_1 \quad \begin{array}{l} p(X) \leftarrow q(X), r(X). \\ p(X) \leftarrow \neg r(X). \\ q(X) \leftarrow \neg r(X), s(X). \\ r(X) \leftarrow \neg s(X). \end{array} \qquad P_2 \quad \begin{array}{l} p(X) \leftarrow p(X), s(X). \\ s(X) \leftarrow r(X). \\ r(X) \leftarrow \neg p(X). \\ r(a). \end{array}$$

$$P_3 \quad \begin{array}{l} p(X) \leftarrow \neg q(X), r(X). \\ r(X) \leftarrow q(X). \\ q(X) \leftarrow \neg s(X). \end{array} \qquad P_4 \quad \begin{array}{l} p(X) \leftarrow r(X), p(X). \\ r(X) \leftarrow \neg p(X). \\ r(X) \leftarrow r(X). \end{array}$$

43. Construct the completion of the normal program:

$p(a) \leftarrow \neg q(b)$.

and show that $\{p(a), a = a, b = b\}$ is a Herbrand model of the completion. Show also that the model is minimal.

44. Consider the normal program:

$flies(X) \leftarrow bird(X), \neg abnormal(X)$.
$bird(tom)$.
$bird(sam)$.
$bird(donald)$.
$abnormal(donald)$.
$abnormal(X) \leftarrow isa(X, penguin)$.
$isa(sam, eagle)$.
$isa(tom, penguin)$.
$isa(donald, duck)$.

Construct an SLDNF-tree for the goal $\leftarrow flies(X)$.

45. Consider the program in Example 4.18. Show that

$\leftarrow go\_well\_together(python, rabbit)$

is a finitely failed goal.

# Chapter 5

# Towards Prolog: Cut and Arithmetic

Computations of logic programs require the construction and traversal of SLD-trees. This is not necessarily the most efficient way of computing. Two observations lead to two ideas for speeding-up computations. The ideas are incorporated in Prolog and will be presented separately in Sections 5.1 and 5.2. For the sake of simplicity the exposition covers only definite programs but all the concepts relating to SLD-derivations and SLD-trees trivially carry over to normal programs, SLDNF-derivations and SLDNF-trees.

## 5.1  Cut: Pruning the SLD-tree

An SLD-tree may have many failed branches and very few or just one success branch. Control information supplied by the user may prevent the interpreter from construction of failed branches. This idea relies on the operational semantics of logic programs. To give the required information, the user has to know how the SLD-tree is constructed and traversed. However, the user has to take this information into account anyway — for the depth-first search employed in Prolog-interpreters, existence of an infinite branch of the SLD tree may prevent the interpreter from finding an existing correct answer. To control the search the concept of *cut* is introduced in Prolog. Syntactically the cut is denoted by the symbol "!" and it may be placed in the body of a clause or a goal as one of its atoms. Its meaning can be best explained as a "shortcut" in the traversal of the SLD-tree. Thus, the presence of cut in a clause results in omitting some subtrees of the SLD-tree. For more precise explanation some auxiliary notions are needed.

Every node $N$ of an SLD-tree corresponds to a goal of an SLD-derivation and has a selected atom $A$. Assume that $A$ is not an instance of a subgoal in the initial goal. Then $A$ is an instance of a body atom $B_i$ of a clause $H \leftarrow B_1, \ldots, B_i, \ldots, B_n$ whose head unifies with the selected subgoal in some node $N'$ between the root and $N$. Denote by origin($A$) the node $N'$.

Prolog interpreters traverse the nodes of the SLD-tree in a depth-first manner as depicted in Figure 3.5. The ordering of branches corresponds to the textual ordering of the clauses in the program. When a leaf of the tree is reached, backtracking takes place. The process terminates when no more backtracking is possible (that is, when all subtrees of the root are traversed). The atom "!" is handled as an ordinary atom in the body of a clause. When a cut is selected for resolution it succeeds immediately (with the empty substitution). The node where "!" is selected will be called the *cut-node*. A cut-node may be reached again during backtracking. In this case the normal order of tree-traversal illustrated in Figure 3.5 is altered — by definition of cut the backtracking continues *above* the node origin(!) (if cut occurs in the initial goal the execution simply terminates). This is illustrated by the following simple example.

**Example 5.1** The father of a person is its male parent. Assume that the following world is given:

> (1)  $father(X,Y) \leftarrow parent(X,Y), male(X).$
> (2)  $parent(ben, tom).$
> (3)  $parent(mary, tom).$
> (4)  $parent(sam, ben).$
> (5)  $parent(alice, ben).$
> (6)  $male(ben).$
> (7)  $male(sam).$

The SLD-tree for the goal $\leftarrow father(X, tom)$ under Prolog's computation rule is shown in Figure 5.1.

After first finding the solution $X = ben$ another attempt will fail since Mary is not male. By the formulation of the problem it is clear that there may be at most one solution for this type of goal (that is, when the second argument is fully instantiated). When a solution is found the search can be stopped since no person has more than one father. To enforce this, cut may be inserted at the end of (1). The modified SLD-tree is shown in Figure 5.2 (The dashed line designates the branch cut off by "!"). The origin of the cut-node is the root of the tree so the search is completed after backtracking to the cut-node. Hence, the other branch of the tree is not traversed.

Notice that the modified version of (1) cannot be used for computing more than one element of the relation "... is the father of ...". The cut will stop the

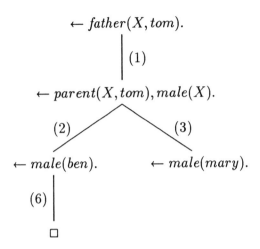

**Figure 5.1: SLD-tree**

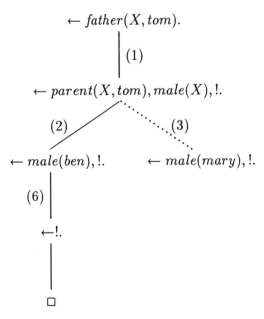

**Figure 5.2: Pruning failing branches**

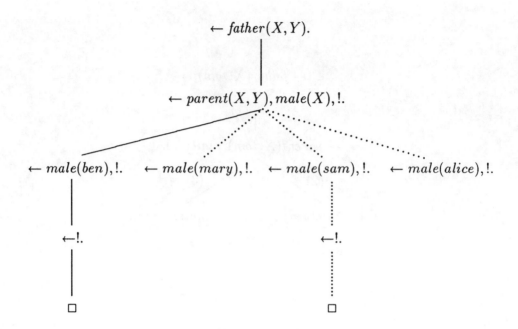

**Figure 5.3: Pruning success-branches**

search after finding the first answer to the goal ← *father*(*X*, *Y*) (consider the
SLD-tree in Figure 5.3). ■

It follows by the definition that the cut has the following effect:

- It divides the body into two parts where backtracking is done separately
  — after success of "!" no backtracking to the literals in the left-hand part
  is possible. However, in the right-hand part execution goes on as usual.

- It cuts off unexplored branches directly below origin(!). In other words
  there will be no more attempts to match the selected subgoal of origin(!)
  with the remaining clauses of the program.

Cut is, to put it mildly, a controversial construct. The intention of introducing
cut is to control the execution of a program without changing its logical meaning. Therefore the logical reading of cut is "true". Operationally, if it removes
only the failed branches of the SLD-tree it does not influence the meaning of
the program. However, it may also cut off some success branches, thus destroying completeness of definite programs and soundness of normal programs. To
illustrate this consider the following example.

**Example 5.2** It is a well known fact that fathers of newborn children are proud. This proposition is reflected by the following definite clause:

(1)  $proud(X) \leftarrow father(X, Y), newborn(Y)$.

Take additionally the clauses:

(2)  $father(X, Y) \leftarrow parent(X, Y), male(X)$.
(3)  $parent(john, mary)$.
(4)  $parent(john, chris)$.
(5)  $male(john)$.
(6)  $newborn(chris)$.

The answer to the initial goal $\leftarrow proud(john)$ is "yes" since, as described, John is the father of Chris who is newborn.

Now, replace (2) by the version with cut used in Example 5.1, that is:

(2')  $father(X, Y) \leftarrow parent(X, Y), male(X), !$.

This time the answer to the goal $\leftarrow proud(john)$ is "no". It is so because the first "listed" child of John is Mary — the sister of Chris. After having found this answer there will be no more attempts to find any more children of John because of the cut.

This makes the program incomplete — some correct answer substitutions cannot be found. More seriously, this incompleteness may result in incorrect answers if negation is involved. For example, the goal $\leftarrow \neg proud(john)$ will succeed — implying that John is not proud. ∎

So far two principal uses of cut have been distinguished — it may be used to cut off failing branches of the SLD-tree and it may also be used to prune succeeding branches. Cutting off failing branches is generally considered harmless since it does not alter the answers produced during the execution. However, this restricted use of cut is usually tied to some particular use of the program. Thus, as illustrated in Figures 5.2 and 5.3, for some goals only failing branches are cut off whereas for other goals succeeding branches are also pruned.

In general, cutting succeeding branches *is* considered harmful. However, there are some cases when it is motivated. This section is concluded with two examples — in the first the use of cut is sometimes (rightfully) advocated. The second example demonstrates a very harmful (albeit common) use of cut.

Consider the following (not fully specified) program:

$$proud(X) \leftarrow father(X, Y), newborn(Y).$$
$$\vdots$$

$$father(john, sue).$$
$$father(john, mary).$$
$$\vdots$$

$$newborn(sue).$$
$$newborn(mary).$$

The SLD-tree for the goal $\leftarrow proud(X)$ has two success-leaves since John has two children both of which are newborn. However, both answers give the same binding for $X$ — namely $X = john$. In general the user is not interested in getting the same answer twice or more. To avoid this, cut may be inserted at the very end of the first clause (or possibly as the rightmost subgoal in the goal).

$$proud(X) \leftarrow father(X, Y), newborn(Y), !.$$

Next consider the following example[1] which describes the relation between two integers and their minimum:

$$min(X, Y, X) \leftarrow X < Y, !.$$
$$min(X, Y, Y).$$

At first glance this program may look correct. People used to imperative programming languages often reason as follows — "If X is less than Y then the minimum of X and Y is X, else it is Y". Actually the program returns the expected answer both to the goal $\leftarrow min(2, 3, X)$ and $\leftarrow min(3, 2, X)$ — in both cases the answer $X = 2$ is obtained. However, the program is simply not correct. This is demonstrated by giving the goal $\leftarrow min(2, 3, 3)$. This goal succeeds implying that "3 is the minimum of 2 and 3"! The program above is an example of an incorrect program where (some of) the false answers are discarded by means of cut. The intended model is simply not a model of the program since the second clause says that "For any two integers X and Y, Y is their minimum". This use of cut is harmful. It may not only produce incorrect answers, but it

---

[1]Here $<$ is a binary predicate symbol written in infix notation designating the less-than relation over natural numbers. Intuitively it may be thought of as an infinite collection of facts:

$$0 < 1. \quad 1 < 2. \quad 2 < 3. \quad \cdots$$
$$0 < 2. \quad 1 < 3. \quad 2 < 4. \quad \cdots$$
$$\vdots \quad\quad \vdots \quad\quad \vdots \quad\quad \ddots$$

In Prolog $<$ is implemented as a so called built-in predicate but more about that in the next section.

also makes the program hard to read and understand. If cut is to be used it should be added to a program which is true in the intended model. Thus, the recommended version of the minimum program (with cut) would look as follows:

$$min(X, Y, X) \leftarrow X < Y, !.$$
$$min(X, Y, Y) \leftarrow X \geq Y.$$

This program is true in the intended model and the goal $\leftarrow min(2, 3, 3)$ does not succeed any longer.

As a final remark, cut may be used to implement negation in Prolog. Consider the following clauses (where *fail* is a Prolog predicate which lacks a definition and cannot be defined by the user):

$$not\ student(X) \leftarrow student(X), !, fail.$$
$$not\ student(X).$$

This definition relies entirely on the operational semantics of Prolog. That is, subgoals must be solved from left to right and clauses are searched in the textual order. If we want to know whether "John is not a student" the goal $\leftarrow not\ student(john)$ may be given. Then there are two cases to consider — if the subgoal $student(john)$ succeeds (i.e. if John is a student), "!" will cut off the second clause and the negated goal will fail. That is, Prolog produces the answer "no". However, if the subgoal $student(john)$ finitely fails, the second clause will be tried (on backtracking) and the negated goal immediately succeeds.

To avoid having to write a separate definition for every predicate that the user may want to negate it is possible to use a predefined meta-predicate named $call/1$ which is available in most Prolog implementations. The argument of $call$ must be a nonvariable when the subgoal is selected and a call to the predicate succeeds iff the argument succeeds. In other words — the goal $\leftarrow call(G)$ succeeds iff the goal $\leftarrow G$ succeeds. Using this predicate $not/1$ may be defined for arbitrary goals:

$$not\ X \leftarrow call(X), !, fail.$$
$$not\ X.$$

Notice that the success of $call(t)$ may produce bindings for variables in $t$. Hence the implementation is not logically correct, as discussed in Chapter 4. However, it works as intended when the argument of $not/1$ is a *ground* atom.

In general it is possible to avoid using cut in most cases by sticking to negation instead. This is in fact advocated since unrestricted use of cut often leads to incorrect programs. It is not unusual that people on their first contacts with Prolog and faced with a program that produces incorrect answers clutter the program with cuts at random places instead of writing a logically correct program in the first place. In the following chapters the use of cut is avoided to make this point quite clear. However, this does not mean that cut should be abandoned altogether — correctly used, it can improve the efficiency of programs considerably.

## 5.2   Arithmetic

It has been proved that definite programs can describe any computable relation. That is, any Turing machine can be coded as a logic program. This means that from a theoretical point of view logic programming is not less expressive than other programming paradigms. In other words, resolution and exhaustive search provide a universal tool for computation. But from a practical point of view it is not desirable to compute everything in that way. Take for example the arithmetic operations on natural numbers. They are efficiently implemented in the hardware of computers. Therefore, from a practical point of view, it is desirable to allow logic programs to access machine arithmetic. A similar argument concerns any other operation or procedure whose efficient implementation in hardware or software is available. The problem is whether it is possible to do that without destroying the declarative nature of logic programs using these *external* features. This section discusses the problem for the example of arithmetic operations and shows the solution adopted in Prolog.

Notice first that arithmetic operations like plus or times can be easily described by a definite logic program. The natural numbers can be represented by ground terms. A standard way for that is to use the constant 0 for representing zero and the unary functor $s$ for representing the successor of a number. Thus, the consecutive natural numbers are represented by the following terms:

$$0, s(0), s(s(0)), \ldots$$

The operations of addition and multiplication are binary functions on natural numbers. Logic programs provide only a formalism for expressing relations. However, a binary function can be seen as a ternary relation consisting of all triples $\langle x, y, z \rangle$ such that $z$ is the result of applying the function to the arguments $x$ and $y$. It is well known that the operations of addition and multiplication on natural numbers can be characterized by the following Peano axioms:

$$
\begin{aligned}
0 + X &= X \\
s(X) + Y &= s(X + Y) \\
0 * X &= 0 \\
s(X) * Y &= (X * Y) + Y
\end{aligned}
$$

These axioms relate arguments and results of the operations. In the relational notation of definite programs they can be reformulated as follows:

$$plus(0, X, X).$$
$$plus(s(X), Y, s(Z)) \leftarrow plus(X, Y, Z).$$

$$times(0, X, 0).$$
$$times(s(X), Y, Z) \leftarrow times(X, Y, W), plus(W, Y, Z).$$

This program can be used to add and multiply natural numbers represented by ground terms.

For example, to add 2 and 3 the goal $\leftarrow plus(s(s(0)), s(s(s(0))), X)$ can be given. The computed answer then becomes $X = s(s(s(s(s(0)))))$. To compute it an SLD-refutation is constructed.

On the other hand, the program can be used also for subtraction and (a limited form of) division. For example, in order to subtract 2 from 5 the goal $\leftarrow plus(X, s(s(0)), s(s(s(s(s(0))))))$ can be used. The program can also perform certain symbolic computations. For example, one can add 2 to an unspecified natural number using the goal $\leftarrow plus(s(s(0)), X, Y)$. The computed answer is $Y = s(s(X))$. Thus, for any ground term $t$ the result is obtained by adding two instances of the symbols $s$ in front of $t$ (and some parentheses).

When comparing this with the usual practice in programming languages, the following observations can be made:

- the representation of numbers by terms is not convenient for humans;

- the computations of the example program do not make use of arithmetic operations available in the hardware — therefore they are much slower. For instance, adding numbers $N$ and $M$ requires $N + 1$ procedure-calls;

- arithmetic expressions cannot be constructed, since the predicate symbols $plus/3$ and $times/3$ represent relations. For example, to compute $2 + (3 * 4)$ one has to introduce new temporary variables representing the values of subexpressions:

$$\leftarrow times(s(s(s(0))), s(s(s(s(0)))), X), plus(X, s(s(0)), Y).$$

The first problem can be easily solved by introducing some "syntactic sugar", like the convention that the decimal numeral for the natural number $n$ represents the term $s^n(0)$ — for instance, 3 represents the term $s(s(s(0)))$. Techniques for compiling arithmetic expressions into machine code are also well known. Thus the main problem is how to incorporate arithmetic expressions into logic programs without destroying the declarative meaning of the programs.

Syntactically arithmetic expressions are terms built from numerals, variables and specific arithmetic functors, like "+", "*", etc. usually written in infix notation. The intended meaning of a ground arithmetic expression is a number. It is thus essential that distinct expressions may denote the same number, take for example $2+2$, $2*1+4-2$ and $4$. There is thus a binary relation on ground arithmetic expressions which holds between arbitrary expressions $E_1$ and $E_2$ iff $E_1$ and $E_2$ denote the same number. Clearly this relation is an equivalence relation. Every equivalence class includes one numeral which is the simplest representation of all terms in the class. The machine operations give a possibility of efficient reduction of a given ground arithmetic expression to this numeral.

Assume that arithmetic expressions may appear as terms in definite logic programs. The answers of such programs should take into account equivalence between the arithmetic expressions. For example, consider the following rule for computing tax — "if the annual income is greater than $150,000$ then the tax is 50%, otherwise 25% of the income reduced by $30,000$":

$$tax(Income, 0.5 * Income) \leftarrow greater(Income, 150000).$$
$$tax(Income, 0.25 * (Income - 30000)) \leftarrow \neg greater(Income, 150000).$$

A tax-payer received a decision from the tax department to pay $25,000$ in tax from his income of $130,000$. To check whether the decision is correct (s)he may want to use the rules above by giving the goal $\leftarrow tax(130000, 25000)$. But the rules cannot be used to find a refutation of the goal since none of the heads of the clauses unify with the subgoal in the goal. The reason is that standard unification is not sufficient since it does not take into account the fact that the intended interpretations of the terms $25000$ and $0.25 * (130000 - 30000)$ are the same. The equivalence must be described by *equality* axioms for arithmetic but they are not included in the program.

This discussion shows the need for an extension of the concept of logic programs. For our example the program should consist of two parts — a set of definite clauses P and a set of equality axioms $E$ describing the equivalences of terms. This type of program has been studied in the literature. The most important result is a concept of generalized unification associated with a given equality theory $E$ and called $E$-unification. A brief introduction follows below. A more extensive account is provided in Chapter 13.

A *definite clause equality theory* is a possibly infinite set of definite clauses, where every atom is of the form $t_1 = t_2$ and $t_1$ and $t_2$ are terms. Sometimes the form of the clauses is restricted to facts.

A *definite program with equality* is a pair $\langle P; E \rangle$ where P is a definite program which contains no occurrences of the predicate symbol $=/2$ and $E$ is a definite clause equality theory.

Let $E$ be a definite clause equality theory. A substitution $\theta$ is an $E$-*unifier* of the terms $t_1$ and $t_2$ iff $t_1\theta = t_2\theta$ is a logical consequence of $E$.

**Example 5.3** Let $E$ be an equality theory describing the usual equivalence of arithmetic expressions. Consider the expressions:

$$t_1 := (2 * X) + 1 \quad \text{and} \quad t_2 := Y + 2$$

For instance, the substitution $\theta := \{Y/(2 * X - 1)\}$ is an $E$-unifier of $t_1$ and $t_2$. To check this, notice that $t_1\theta = t_1$ and that $t_2\theta = (2 * X - 1) + 2$ which is equivalent to $t_1$. ∎

Now, for a given program $\langle P; E \rangle$ and goal $\leftarrow A_1, \ldots, A_m$ the refutation of the goal can be constructed in the same way as for definite programs, with the only difference that $E$-unification is used in place of unification as presented in Chapter 3.

Finding $E$-unifiers can be seen as solving of equations in an algebra defined by the equality axioms. It is known that the problem of $E$-unification is in general undecidable. Even if it is decidable for some theory $E$ there may be many different solutions of a given equation. The situation when there exists one most general unifier is rather unusual. This means that even if it is possible to construct all $E$-unifiers, a new dimension of nondeterminism is introduced.

Assume now that an equality theory $E$ describes all external functions used in a logic program, including arithmetic operations. This means that for any ground terms $t_1$ and $t_2$ whose main functors denote external functions, the formula $t_1 = t_2$ is a logical consequence of $E$ iff the invocation of $t_1$ returns the same result as the invocation of $t_2$. In other words in the special case of ground terms their $E$-unifiability can be decided — they either $E$-unify with the identity substitution, if both reduce to the same result, or they are not $E$-unifiable, if their results are different. This can be exploited in the following way — whenever a call of an external function is encountered as a term to be $E$-unified, it is invoked and its reduced form is being unified instead by the usual unification algorithm. However, the external procedures can be invoked only with ground arguments. If some variables of the call are not instantiated, the computation cannot proceed and no $E$-unifier can be found. In this case a run time error may be reported.

This idea is incorporated in Prolog in a restricted form for arithmetic operations. Before explaining it, some syntactic issues should be mentioned.

The natural numbers are represented in Prolog as numerals, for example 0, 1, 1989, etc. Logically the numerals are constants. A number of predefined arithmetic functors for use in the infix notation is available. They denote standard arithmetic functions on integers and refer to the operations of the computer. The most important are:

| Functor | Operation |
|:---:|:---|
| + | Addition |
| − | Subtraction |
| * | Multiplication |
| / | (Integer) division |
| *mod* | Remainder after division |

Additionally unary minus is used to represent negative integers.

A ground term $t$ constructed from the arithmetic functors and numerals represents an integer, which can also be represented by a numeral $n$, possibly prefixed by "−". The machine operations of the computer make it possible to construct this term $t'$ in an efficient way. The arithmetic operations can be axiomatized as an equational theory $E$ such that $t = t'$ is its logical consequence. Two predefined predicates of Prolog handle two specific cases of $E$-unification. They are $is/2$ and $=:=/2$ both of which are used in the infix notation.

The binary predicate $=:=/2$ checks whether two ground terms are E-unifiable. For example the goal:

$$\leftarrow 2 + 3 =:= 1 + 4.$$

succeeds with the answer "yes" (corresponding to the empty substitution). If the arguments are not ground arithmetic expressions, the execution aborts with an error message in most Prolog implementations.

The binary predicate $is/2$ unifies a variable with the reduced form of a term constructed from the arithmetic functors and numerals. For example the goal:

$$\leftarrow X \; is \; 2 + 2.$$

succeeds with the substitution $\{X/4\}$.

The first argument of this predicate need not be variable. Operationally the reduced form of the second argument, which is either a numeral or a numeral preceded by "−", is being unified with the first argument. If the latter is an arithmetic expression in the reduced form then this is a special case of $E$-unification handled also by $=:=/2$. Otherwise the answer is "no". But an $E$-unifier may still exist. For example the goal:

$$\leftarrow X + 1 \; is \; 2 + 3.$$

will fail, while the terms $X + 1$ and $2 + 3$ have an $E$-unifier — namely $\{X/4\}$.

Another standard predicate $=\backslash=/2$ (also in infix notation) checks whether two ground terms are not $E$-unifiable.

Prolog also provides predefined predicates for comparing the integers represented by ground arithmetic expressions. These are the binary infix predicates $<, >, \geq$ and $\leq$.

The notion of $E$-unification seems to be a fundamental concept relating logic programming and functional programming. The on-going research on amalgamation of logic programming and functional programming will hopefully result in successors of Prolog with better efficiency and clean declarative semantics.

# Exercises

46. Consider the following definite program:

    $$top(X, Y) \leftarrow p(X, Y).$$
    $$top(X, X) \leftarrow s(X).$$
    $$p(X, Y) \leftarrow true(1), q(X), true(2), r(Y).$$
    $$p(X, Y) \leftarrow s(X), r(Y).$$
    $$q(a).$$
    $$q(b).$$
    $$r(c).$$
    $$r(d).$$
    $$s(e).$$
    $$true(X).$$

    Draw the SLD-tree for the goal $\leftarrow top(X, Y)$. Then show what branches are cut off:

    - when $true(1)$ is replaced by cut;

    - when $true(2)$ is replaced by cut.

47. Consider the following program:

    $$p(Y) \leftarrow q(X, Y), r(Y).$$
    $$p(X) \leftarrow q(X, X).$$
    $$q(a, a).$$
    $$q(a, b).$$
    $$r(b).$$

    Add cut at different places in the program above and say what answers you get in response to the goal $\leftarrow p(Z)$.

48. Consider the definition of $not/1$ given on page 97. From a logical point of view, $\leftarrow p(X)$ and $\leftarrow not\ not\ p(X)$ are equivalent formulas. However, they behave differently when given to the program that consists of a single clause $p(a)$ — in what way?

49. Prolog implementations often incorporate a built-in predicate $var/1$ which succeeds (with the empty substitution) if the argument is an uninstantiated variable when the call is made and fails otherwise. That is:

$$\leftarrow var(X), X = a.$$

succeeds whereas:

$$\leftarrow X = a, var(X).$$

fails under the assumption that Prolog's computation rule is used. Define $var/1$ given the definition of $not/1$ on page 97.

50. Write a program which defines the relation between integers and their factorial. First use Peano arithmetic and then the built-in arithmetic predicates of Prolog.

51. Write a predicate $between(X, Y, Z)$ which holds if $X \leq Y \leq Z$. That is, given a goal $\leftarrow between(1, X, 10)$ the program should generate all integers in the closed interval (via backtracking).

52. Write a program that describes the relation between integers and their square using Peano arithmetic.

53. Implement the Euclidean algorithm for computing the greatest common divisor of two integers. Do this using both Peano arithmetic and built-in arithmetic.

54. The polynomial $c_n * x^n + \cdots + c_1 * x + c_0$ where $c_0, \ldots, c_n$ are integers may be represented by the term

$$c_n * x\hat{\ }n + \cdots + c_1 * x + c_0$$

where $\hat{\ }/2$ is written with infix notation and binds stronger than $*/2$ which in turn binds stronger than $+/2$. Now write a program which evaluates such polynomials given the value of $x$. For instance:

$$\leftarrow eval(2 * x\hat{\ }2 + 5, 4, X).$$

should succeed with answer $X = 37$. To solve the problem you may presuppose the existence of a predicate $integer/1$ which succeeds if the argument is an integer.

# Part II

# Programming in Logic

# Chapter 6

# Logic and Databases

This chapter discusses the relationship between logic programs and relational databases. It is demonstrated how logic can be used to represent — on a conceptual level — not only *explicit* data, but also *implicit* data (corresponding to *views* in relational database theory) and how it can be used as a *query language* for retrieval of information in a database. We do not concern ourselves with implementation issues but only remark that SLD-resolution does not necessarily provides the best inference strategy for full-scale databases. On the other hand, logic not only provides a uniform language for representation of databases — its additional expressive power also enables description, in a concise and intuitive way, of more complicated relations — for instance, relations which exhibit certain common properties (like transitivity) and relations involving structured data objects.

## 6.1 Relational Databases

As the name implies, the foundation of relational databases originates from the concept of a mathematical relation. The section begins with a brief recapitulation of the basic mathematical theory.

Let $D_1, D_2, \ldots, D_n$ be collections of individuals called *domains*. In the context of database theory the domains are usually assumed to be finite although, for practical reasons, they normally include an infinite domain of integers or floating point numbers. Additionally, the individuals are assumed to be atomic or indivisible — that is, it is not possible to access any proper part of an individual.

The *cartesian product* of the domains $D_1, \ldots, D_n$ is denoted $D_1 \times \cdots \times D_n$ and is the set of all $n$-tuples $\langle x_1, \ldots, x_n \rangle$ such that $x_i \in D_i$ for $1 \leq i \leq n$. A *relation*

$R$ over the domains $\mathbf{D}_1, \ldots, \mathbf{D}_n$ is a subset of $\mathbf{D}_1 \times \cdots \times \mathbf{D}_n$. $R$ is in this case said to be $n$-ary. A *relational database* is a finite number of such (finite) relations. Database relations and domains will be denoted by identifiers in capital letters.

**Example 6.1** Let $MALE := \{adam, bill\}$, $FEMALE := \{anne, beth\}$ and let $PERSON := MALE \cup FEMALE$. Then:

$$
MALE \times PERSON = \left\{ \begin{array}{ll}
\langle adam; adam \rangle & \langle bill; adam \rangle \\
\langle adam; bill \rangle & \langle bill; bill \rangle \\
\langle adam; anne \rangle & \langle bill; anne \rangle \\
\langle adam; beth \rangle & \langle bill; beth \rangle
\end{array} \right\}
$$

Now, let *FATHER*, *MOTHER* and *PARENT* be relations over the domains $MALE \times PERSON$, $FEMALE \times PERSON$ and $PERSON \times PERSON$ defined as follows:

$$
\begin{array}{lll}
FATHER & := & \{\langle adam; bill \rangle, \langle adam; beth \rangle\} \\
MOTHER & := & \{\langle anne; bill \rangle, \langle anne; beth \rangle\} \\
PARENT & := & \{\langle adam; bill \rangle, \langle adam; beth \rangle, \langle anne; bill \rangle, \langle anne; beth \rangle\}
\end{array}
$$

∎

It is of course possible to imagine alternative syntactic representations of these relations. For instance in the form of tables:

*FATHER:*

| $C_1$ | $C_2$ |
|-------|-------|
| adam  | bill  |
| adam  | beth  |

*MOTHER:*

| $C_1$ | $C_2$ |
|-------|-------|
| anne  | bill  |
| anne  | beth  |

*PARENT:*

| $C_1$ | $C_2$ |
|-------|-------|
| adam  | bill  |
| adam  | beth  |
| anne  | bill  |
| anne  | beth  |

or as a collection of labelled tuples (that is, facts):

father(adam, bill).
father(adam, beth).
mother(anne, bill).
mother(anne, beth).
parent(adam, bill).
parent(adam, beth).
parent(anne, bill).
parent(anne, beth).

The table-like representation is the one found in most textbooks on relational databases whereas the latter is a logic program. The two representations are isomorphic if no notice is taken of the names of the columns in the tables. Such names are called *attributes* and are needed only to simplify the specification of some of the operations discussed in Section 6.3. It is assumed that the attributes of a table are distinct. In what follows the notation $R(A_1, A_2, \ldots, A_n)$ will be used to describe the name, $R$, and attributes, $\langle A_1, A_2, \ldots, A_n \rangle$, of a database table (i.e. relation). $R(A_1, A_2, \ldots, A_n)$ is sometimes called a *relation scheme*. When not needed, the attributes are omitted and a table will be named only by its relation-name.

A major difference between the two representations which is not evident above, is the set of values which may occur in each column/argument-position of the representations. In logic there is only a single domain of terms and the user may without problem write:

$father(anne, adam)$.

whereas in a relational database this is not possible since $anne \notin MALE$. To avoid such problems a notion of type is needed.

Despite this difference it should be clear that any relational database can be represented as a logic program (where each domain of the database is extended to the set of all terms) consisting solely of ground facts. Such a set of facts is commonly called the *extensional database* (EDB).

## 6.2 Deductive Databases

Now, after having established the relationship between relational databases and a (very simple) class of logic programs, different extensions to the relational database-model are studied. We first consider the usage of variables and a simple form of rules. By such extensions we are able to describe — in a more succinct and intuitive way — many database relations. For instance, using rules and variables the database above can be represented by the program:

$parent(X, Y) \leftarrow father(X, Y)$.
$parent(X, Y) \leftarrow mother(X, Y)$.
$father(adam, bill)$.
$father(adam, beth)$.
$mother(anne, bill)$.
$mother(anne, beth)$.

The part of a logic program which consists of rules and nonground facts is called the *intensional database* (IDB). Because logic programs facilitate definition of new facts which are ultimately *deduced* from explicit facts, logic programs are often referred to as *deductive databases*. The programs above are also examples of a class of logic programs called *datalog* programs. They are characterized by the absence of functors. In other words, the set of terms used in the program solely consists of constant symbols and variables. For the representation of relational databases this is sufficient since the domains of the relations are assumed to be finite and it is therefore always possible to represent the individuals with a finite set of constant terms. In the last section of this chapter logic programs which make also use of compound terms are considered, but until then our attention will be restricted to datalog programs.

**Example 6.2** Below is given a deductive family-database whose extensional part consists of definitions of *male/1*, *female/1*, *father/2* and *mother/2* and whose intensional part consists of *parent/2* and *grandparent/2*:

$$grandparent(X, Z) \leftarrow parent(X, Y), parent(Y, Z).$$

$$parent(X, Y) \leftarrow father(X, Y).$$
$$parent(X, Y) \leftarrow mother(X, Y).$$

$$father(adam, bill).$$
$$father(adam, beth).$$
$$father(bill, cathy).$$
$$father(donald, eric).$$

$$mother(anne, bill).$$
$$mother(anne, beth).$$
$$mother(cathy, donald).$$
$$mother(diana, eric).$$

$$female(anne).$$
$$female(beth).$$
$$female(cathy).$$
$$female(diana).$$

$$male(adam).$$
$$male(bill).$$
$$male(donald).$$
$$male(eric).$$

∎

In most cases it is possible to organize the database in alternative ways. Which organization to choose is of course highly dependent on what information one needs to retrieve. Moreover, it often determines the size of the database. Finally, in the case of updates to the database, the organization is very important to avoid inconsistencies in the database — how should, for instance, the removal of the labelled tuple $parent(adam, bill)$ from the database in Example 6.2 be handled? Although updates are very important, they will not be discussed in this book.

Another thing worth noticing about Example 6.2 is that the unary definitions $male/1$ and $female/1$ can be seen as *type declarations*. It is easy to add another such type declaration for the domain of persons:

$person(X) \leftarrow male(X).$
$person(X) \leftarrow female(X).$

It is now possible to "type" e.g. the database on page 111 by adding to the body of every clause the type of each argument in the head of the clause:

$parent(X, Y) \leftarrow person(X), person(Y), father(X, Y).$
$parent(X, Y) \leftarrow person(X), person(Y), mother(X, Y).$

$father(adam, bill) \leftarrow male(adam), person(bill).$
$father(adam, beth) \leftarrow male(adam), person(beth).$

$\vdots$

$person(X) \leftarrow male(X).$
$person(X) \leftarrow female(X).$

$\vdots$

In this manner, "type-errors" like $father(anne, adam)$ may be avoided.

## 6.3 Relational Algebra vs. Logic Programs

In database textbooks one often encounters the concept of *views*. A view can be thought of as a relation which is not explicitly stored in the database, but which is created by means of operations on existing database relations and other views. Such implicit relations are described by means of some *query-language* which is usually based on *relational algebra* for the purpose of computing the views. Below we shall see that all standard operations of relational algebra can be mimicked in logic programming (with negation) in a more natural way. The objective of this section is twofold — on the one hand it shows that logic programs have the computational power of relational algebra. On the other hand, it also provides an alternative to SLD-resolution as the operational semantics of a class of logic programs.

The most primitive operations in relational algebra are union, set difference, cartesian product, projection and selection.

Given two $n$-ary relations over the same domains, the *union* of the two relations, $R_1$ and $R_2$ (denoted $R_1 \cup R_2$), is the set:

$$\{\langle x_1, \ldots, x_n \rangle \mid \langle x_1, \ldots, x_n \rangle \in R_1 \vee \langle x_1, \ldots, x_n \rangle \in R_2\}$$

Using definite programs the union of two relations — represented by the predicate symbols $r_1/n$ and $r_2/n$ — can be specified by the two rules:

$$r(X_1, \ldots, X_n) \leftarrow r_1(X_1, \ldots, X_n).$$
$$r(X_1, \ldots, X_n) \leftarrow r_2(X_1, \ldots, X_n).$$

For instance, if the EDB includes the definitions *father*/2 and *mother*/2, then *parent*/2 can be defined as the union of the relations *father*/2 and *mother*/2:[1]

$$parent(X, Y) \leftarrow father(X, Y).$$
$$parent(X, Y) \leftarrow mother(X, Y).$$

The *difference* $R_1 \setminus R_2$ of two relations $R_1$ and $R_2$ over the same domains yields the new relation:

$$\{\langle x_1, \ldots, x_n \rangle \in R_1 \mid \langle x_1, \ldots, x_n \rangle \notin R_2\}$$

In logic programming it is not possible to define such relations without the use of negation; however, with negation it may be defined thus:

$$r(X_1, \ldots, X_n) \leftarrow r_1(X_1, \ldots, X_n), not\ r_2(X_1, \ldots, X_n).$$

For example, let *parent*/2 and *mother*/2 belong to the EDB. Now, *father*/2 can be defined as the difference of the relations *parent*/2 and *mother*/2:

$$father(X, Y) \leftarrow parent(X, Y), not\ mother(X, Y).$$

The *cartesian product* of two relations $R_1$ and $R_2$ (denoted $R_1 \times R_2$) yields the new relation:

$$\{\langle x_1, \ldots, x_m, y_1, \ldots, y_n \rangle \mid \langle x_1, \ldots, x_m \rangle \in R_1 \wedge \langle y_1, \ldots, y_n \rangle \in R_2\}$$

---

[1] In what follows we will sometimes, by abuse of language, write "the relation $p/n$". Needless to say, $p/n$ is not a relation but a predicate symbol which *denotes* a relation.

Notice that $R_1$ and $R_2$ do not need to have either the same domains or the same arity. Moreover, if $R_1$ and $R_2$ contain disjoint sets of attributes then they are simply carried over to the resulting relation. However, if the original relations contain some joint attribute the attribute of the two columns in the new relation must be renamed into distinct ones. This can be done e.g. by prefixing the joint attributes in the new relation by the relation where they came from. For instance, in the relation $R(A, B) \times S(B, C)$ the attributes are, from left to right, $A$, $R.B$, $S.B$ and $C$. Obviously, it is possible to achieve the same effect in other ways.

In logic programming the cartesian product is mimicked by the rule:

$$r(X_1, \ldots, X_m, Y_1, \ldots, Y_n) \leftarrow r_1(X_1, \ldots, X_m), r_2(Y_1, \ldots, Y_n).$$

For instance, let $male/1$ and $female/1$ belong to the EDB. Then the set of all male/female couples can be defined by the rule:

$$couple(X, Y) \leftarrow male(X), female(Y).$$

*Projection* can be seen as the deletion and/or rearrangement of one or more "columns" of a relation. For instance, by projecting the $F$- and $C$-attributes of the relation $FATHER(F, C)$ on the $F$-attribute (denoted $\pi_F(FATHER(F, C))$) the new relation:

$$\{\langle x_1 \rangle \mid \langle x_1; x_2 \rangle \in FATHER\}$$

is obtained. The same can be achieved in Prolog via the rule:

$$father(X) \leftarrow father(X, Y).$$

The *selection* of a relation $R$ is denoted $\sigma_F(R)$ (where $F$ is a formula) and is the set of all tuples $\langle x_1, \ldots, x_n \rangle \in R$ such that "$F$ is true for $\langle x_1, \ldots, x_n \rangle$". How to translate such an operation to a logic program depends on the appearance of the constraining formula $F$. In general $F$ is only allowed to contain atomic objects, attributes, $\wedge$, $\vee$, $\neg$ and some simple comparisons (e.g. "$=$" and "$<$"). For instance, the database relation defined by $\sigma_{Y \geq 1,000,000} INCOME(X, Y)$ may be defined as follows in Prolog:

$$millionaire(X, Y) \leftarrow income(X, Y), Y \geq 1000000.$$

Some other operations (like intersection and composition) are sometimes encountered in relational algebra but they are usually all defined in terms of the mentioned, primitive ones and are therefore not discussed here. However, one of them deserves special attention — namely the *natural join*.

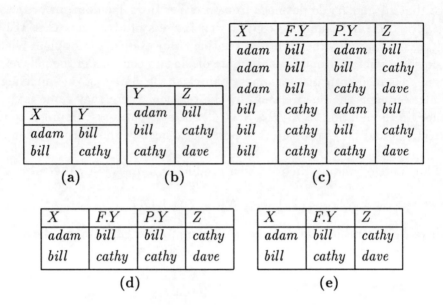

**Figure 6.1: Natural Join**

The natural join of two relations $R$ and $S$ can be computed only when the columns are named by attributes. Thus, assume that $T_1, \ldots, T_k$ are the attributes which appear both in $R$ and in $S$. Then the natural join of $R$ and $S$ is defined thus:

$$R \bowtie S := \pi_A \, \sigma_{R.T_1 = S.T_1 \, \wedge \, \cdots \, \wedge \, R.T_k = S.T_k} \, (R \times S)$$

where $A$ is the list of all attributes of $R \times S$ with exception of $S.T_1, \ldots, S.T_k$. Thus, the natural join is obtained by (1) taking the cartesian product of the two relations, (2) selecting those tuples which have identical values in the columns with the same attribute and (3) filtering out the superfluous columns. Notice that if $R$ and $S$ have disjoint sets of attributes, then the natural join reduces to an ordinary cartesian product.

To illustrate the operation, consider the relation defined by the expression $F(X, Y) \bowtie P(Y, Z)$ where $F(X, Y)$ and $P(Y, Z)$ are defined according to Figure 6.1(a) and 6.1(b) and denote the relation between fathers/parents and their children.

Now $F(X, Y) \bowtie P(Y, Z)$ is defined as $\pi_{X, F.Y, Z} \, \sigma_{F.Y = P.Y} \, (F(X, Y) \times P(Y, Z))$. Hence the first step consists in computing the cartesian product $F(X, Y) \times$

$P(Y,Z)$ (cf. Figure 6.1(c)). Next the tuples with equal values in the columns named by $F.Y$ and $P.Y$ are selected (Figure 6.1(d)). Finally this is projected on the $X$, $F.Y$ and $Z$ attributes yielding the relation in Figure 6.1(e).

If we assume that $father/2$ and $parent/2$ are used to represent the database relations $F$ and $P$ then the same relation may be defined with a single definite clause as follows:

$$grandfather(X,Y,Z) \leftarrow father(X,Y), parent(Y,Z).$$

Notice that the standard definition of $grandfather/2$:

$$grandfather(X,Z) \leftarrow father(X,Y), parent(Y,Z).$$

is obtained by projecting $X, F.Y, Z$ on $X$ and $Z$, that is, by performing the operation $\pi_{X,Z}(F(X,Y) \bowtie P(Y,Z))$.

It is interesting to notice a similarity between variables of Prolog and attributes of relational algebra.

## 6.4    Logic as a Query-Language

In previous sections it was observed that logic provides a uniform language for representing both explicit data and implicit data (so-called views). However, deductive databases are of little or no interest if it is not possible to retrieve information from the database. In traditional databases this is achieved by so-called *query-languages*. Examples of existing query-languages for relational databases are e.g. ISBL, SQL, QUEL and Query-by-Example.

By now it should come as no surprise to the reader that logic programming can be used as a query-language in the same way it was used to define views. For instance, to retrieve the children of Adam from the database in Example 6.2 one only has to give the goal:

$$\leftarrow parent(adam, X).$$

To this Prolog-systems would reply with the answers $X = bill$ and $X = beth$, or put alternatively — the unary relation $\{\langle bill \rangle, \langle beth \rangle\}$. Likewise, in response to the goal:

$$\leftarrow mother(X,Y).$$

Prolog produces four answers:

$$
\begin{array}{ll}
X = anne, & Y = bill \\
X = anne, & Y = beth \\
X = cathy, & Y = donald \\
X = diana, & Y = eric
\end{array}
$$

That is, the relation:

$$\{\langle anne; bill\rangle, \langle anne; beth\rangle, \langle cathy; donald\rangle, \langle diana; eric\rangle\}$$

Notice that a failing goal (for instance $\leftarrow parent(X, adam)$) computes the empty relation as opposed to a succeeding goal without variables (like the goal $\leftarrow parent(adam, bill)$) which computes a singleton relation containing a 0-ary tuple.

Now consider the following excerpt from a database:

$$likes(X, Y) \leftarrow baby(Y).$$
$$baby(mary).$$
$$\vdots$$

Informally the two clauses say that "Everybody likes babies" and "Mary is a baby". Consider the result of the query "Is anyone liked by someone?". In other words the goal clause:

$$\leftarrow likes(X, Y).$$

Clearly Prolog will reply with $Y = mary$ and $X$ being unbound. This is interpreted as "Everybody likes Mary" but what does it mean in terms of a database relation? One solution to the problem is to declare a type-predicate and to extend the goal with calls to this new predicate:

$$\leftarrow likes(X, Y), person(X), person(Y).$$

In response to this goal Prolog would enumerate all individuals of type $person/1$. It is also possible to add the extra literal $person(X)$ to the database rule. Another approach which is often employed when describing deductive databases is to adopt certain assumptions about the world which is modelled. One such assumption was mentioned already in connection with Chapter 4 — namely the closed world assumption (CWA). Another assumption which is usually adopted in deductive databases is the so-called *domain closure assumption* (DCA) which says that "the only existing individuals are those mentioned in the database". In terms of logic this can be expressed through the additional axiom:

$$\forall X(X = c_1 \vee X = c_2 \vee \cdots \vee X = c_n)$$

where $c_1, c_2, \ldots, c_n$ are all the constants occurring in the database. With this axiom the relation defined by the goal above becomes $\{\langle t; mary\rangle \mid t \in U_P\}$. However, this assumes that the database contains no functors and only a finite number of constants.

## 6.5   Relations with Common Properties

The main objective of this section is to briefly show how to define relations which exhibit certain properties that frequently occur both in real life and in mathematics. This includes properties like reflexivity, symmetry and transitivity.

Let $R$ be a binary relation over some domain $\mathbf{D}$. Then:

- $R$ is said to be *reflexive* iff for all $x \in \mathbf{D}$, it holds that $\langle x; x \rangle \in R$;

- $R$ is *symmetric* iff $\langle x; y \rangle \in R$ implies that $\langle y; x \rangle \in R$;

- $R$ is *anti-symmetric* iff $\langle x; y \rangle \in R$ and $\langle y; x \rangle \in R$ implies that $x = y$;

- $R$ is *transitive* iff $\langle x; y \rangle \in R$ and $\langle y; z \rangle \in R$ implies that $\langle x; z \rangle \in R$;

- $R$ is *asymmetric* iff $\langle x; y \rangle \in R$ implies that $\langle y; x \rangle \notin R$.

To define an EDB which possesses one of these properties is usually a rather cumbersome task if the domain is large. For instance, to define a reflexive relation over a domain with $N$ elements requires $N$ tuples, or $N$ facts in the case of a logic program. Fortunately, in logic programming, relations can be defined to be reflexive with a single clause of the form:

$$r(X, X).$$

However, in many cases one thinks of the Herbrand universe as the coded union of several domains. For instance, the Herbrand universe consisting of the constants *bill*, *kate* and *love* may be thought of as the coded union of persons and abstract notions. If — as in this example — the intended domain of $r/2$ (encoded as terms) ranges over proper subsets of the Herbrand universe and if the type predicate $t/1$ characterize this subset, a reflexive relation can be written as follows:

$$r(X, X) \leftarrow t(X).$$

For instance, in order to say that "persons look like themselves" we may write the following program:

$$looks\_like(X, X) \leftarrow person(X).$$
$$person(bill).$$
$$person(kate).$$
$$abstract(love).$$

In order to define a symmetric relation $R$ it suffices to specify only one of the pairs $\langle x; y \rangle$ and $\langle y; x \rangle$ if $\langle x; y \rangle \in R$. Finally the program is extended with the rule:

$$r(X, Y) \leftarrow r(Y, X).$$

However, as shown below such programs suffer from operational problems.

**Example 6.3** Consider the domain:

$$\{sarah, diana, elizabeth, philip, andrew, charles\}$$

The relation "... is married to ..." clearly is symmetric and it may be written either as an extensional database:

> $married(sarah, andrew)$.
> $married(diana, charles)$.
> $married(elizabeth, philip)$.
> $married(andrew, sarah)$.
> $married(charles, diana)$.
> $married(philip, elizabeth)$.

or more briefly as a deductive database:

> $married(X, Y) \leftarrow married(Y, X)$.
> $married(sarah, andrew)$.
> $married(diana, charles)$.
> $married(elizabeth, philip)$.

∎

Transitive relations can also be simplified by means of rules. Instead of a program P consisting solely of facts, P can be fully described by the clause:

$$r(X, Z) \leftarrow r(X, Y), r(Y, Z).$$

together with all $r(a, c) \in$ P for which either $a = c$ or there exists no $b$ ($b \neq a$ and $b \neq c$) such that $r(a, b) \in$ P and $r(b, c) \in$ P.

**Example 6.4** Consider the world consisting of the "objects" $a$, $b$, $c$ and $d$:

The relation "... is positioned over ..." clearly is transitive and may be defined either through a purely extensional database:

$over(a, b)$.
$over(a, c)$.
$over(a, d)$.
$over(b, c)$.
$over(b, d)$.
$over(c, d)$.

or alternatively as the deductive database:

$over(X, Z) \leftarrow over(X, Y), over(Y, Z)$.
$over(a, b)$.
$over(b, c)$.
$over(c, d)$.

∎

Although the definitions above are perfectly correct, they suffer from operational problems when executed by a Prolog interpreter. Consider the goal clause $\leftarrow married(diana, charles)$ together with the deductive database of Example 6.3. Clearly $married(diana, charles)$ is a logical consequence of the program but any Prolog interpreter would go into an infinite loop — first by trying to prove:

$\leftarrow married(diana, charles)$.

Via unification with the rule a new goal clause is obtained:

$\leftarrow married(charles, diana)$.

When trying to satisfy $married(charles, diana)$ the subgoal is once again unified with the rule yielding a new goal, identical to the initial one. This process will obviously go on forever. The misbehaviour can, to some extent, be avoided by moving the rule textually after the facts. By doing so it may be possible to find some (or all) refutations before going into an infinite loop. However, no matter how the clauses are ordered, goals like $\leftarrow married(diana, diana)$ always lead to loops.

A better way of avoiding such problems is to use instead an auxiliary anti-symmetric relation and to take the *symmetric closure* of this relation. This can be done by renaming the predicate symbol of the EDB with the auxiliary predicate symbol and then introducing two rules which define the symmetric relation in terms of the auxiliary one.

**Example 6.5** The approach is illustrated by defining $married/2$ in terms of the auxiliary definition $wife/2$ which is anti-symmetric:

$married(X,Y) \leftarrow wife(X,Y).$
$married(X,Y) \leftarrow wife(Y,X).$

$wife(sarah, andrew).$
$wife(diana, charles).$
$wife(elizabeth, philip).$

This program has the nice property that it never loops — simply because it is not recursive.                                                                                      ∎

A similar approach can be applied when defining transitive relations. A new auxiliary predicate symbol is introduced and used to rename the EDB. Then the *transitive closure* of this relation is defined by means of the following two rules (where $p/2$ denotes the transitive relation and $q/2$ the auxiliary one):

$p(X,Y) \leftarrow q(X,Y)$
$p(X,Y) \leftarrow q(X,Z), p(Z,Y).$

**Example 6.6** $over/2$ may be defined in terms of the predicate symbol $on/2$:

$over(X,Y) \leftarrow on(X,Y).$
$over(X,Z) \leftarrow on(X,Y), over(Y,Z).$

$on(a, b).$
$on(b, c).$
$on(c, d).$

Notice that recursion is not completely eliminated. It may therefore happen that the program loops. As shown below this depends on properties of the auxiliary relation.                                                                                  ∎

The transitive closure may be combined with the *reflexive closure* of a relation. Given an auxiliary relation denoted by $q/2$, its reflexive and transitive closure is obtained through the additional clauses:

$p(X,X).$
$p(X,Y) \leftarrow q(X,Y).$
$p(X,Z) \leftarrow q(X,Y), p(Y,Z).$

Actually, the second clause is superfluous since it follows logically from the first and third clause: any goal, $\leftarrow p(a,b)$, which is refuted through unification with the second clause can be refuted through unification with the third clause where the recursive subgoal is unified with the first clause.

Next we consider two frequently encountered types of relations — namely *partial orders* and *equivalence relations*.

A binary relation is called a *partial order* if it is reflexive, anti-symmetric and transitive whereas a relation which is reflexive, symmetric and transitive is called an *equivalence relation*.

**Example 6.7** Consider a directed, acyclic graph (e.g. the following one):

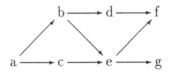

It is easy to see that the relation "there is a path from ... to ..." is a partial order given the graph above. To formally define this relation we start with an auxiliary, asymmetric relation (denoted by *edge*/2) which describes the edges of the graph:

$edge(a, b)$.
$edge(a, c)$.
$edge(b, d)$.
$edge(b, e)$.
$edge(c, e)$.
$edge(d, f)$.
$edge(e, f)$.
$edge(e, g)$.

Finally the reflexive and transitive closure of this relation is described through the two clauses:

$path(X, X)$.
$path(X, Z) \leftarrow edge(X, Y), path(Y, Z)$.

This program does not suffer from infinite loops. In fact, no partial order defined in this way will loop as long as the domain is finite. However, if the graph contains a loop it may happen that the program starts looping — consider the addition of a cycle in the graph above. For instance, an additional edge from $b$ to $a$:

$edge(b, a)$.

Part of the SLD-tree for the goal $\leftarrow path(a, f)$ is depicted in Figure 6.2. The SLD-tree clearly contains an infinite branch and hence it may happen that the program starts looping without returning any answers. In Chapter 11 this problem will be discussed and a solution will be suggested. ∎

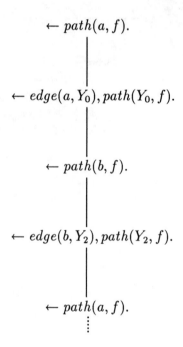

Figure 6.2: Infinite branch in the SLD-tree

**Example 6.8** Next consider some points on a map and bi-directed edges between the points, e.g:

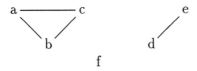

This time the relation "there is a path from … to …" is an equivalence relation. To define the relation we may start by describing one half of each edge in the graph:

> $edge(a, b).$
> $edge(a, c).$
> $edge(b, c).$
> $edge(d, e).$

Next the other half of each edge is described by means of the symmetric closure of the relation denoted by $edge/2$:

> $bi\_edge(X, Y) \leftarrow edge(X, Y).$
> $bi\_edge(X, Y) \leftarrow edge(Y, X).$

Finally, $path/2$ is defined by taking the reflexive and transitive closure of this relation:

> $path(X, X).$
> $path(X, Z) \leftarrow bi\_edge(X, Y), path(Y, Z).$

Prolog programs defining equivalence relations usually suffer from termination problems unless specific measures are taken (cf. Chapter 11).  ∎

## 6.6  Databases with Compound Terms

In relational databases it is usually required that the domains consist of atomic objects, something which simplifies the mathematical treatment of relational databases. Naturally, when using logic programming, nothing prevents us from using structured data when writing deductive databases. This allows for data abstraction and in most cases results in greater expressive power and improves readability of the program.

**Example 6.9** Consider a database which contains members of families and the addresses of the families. Imagine that a family is represented by a ternary term *family*/3 where the first argument is the name of the husband, the second the name of the wife and the last a structure which contains the names of the children. The absence of children is represented by the constant *none* whereas the presence of children is represented by the binary term of the form $c(x, y)$ whose first argument is the name of one child and whose second argument recursively contains the names of the remaining children (intuitively *none* can be thought of as the empty set and $c(x, y)$ can be thought of as a function which constructs a set by adding $x$ to the set represented by $y$). An excerpt from such a database might look as follows:

$address(family(john, mary, c(tom, c(jim, none))), main\_street(3)).$
$address(family(bill, sue, none), main\_street(4)).$

$parent(X, Y) \leftarrow$
$\qquad address(family(X, Z, Children), Street),$
$\qquad among(Y, Children).$
$parent(X, Y) \leftarrow$
$\qquad address(family(Z, X, Children), Street),$
$\qquad among(Y, Children).$

$husband(X) \leftarrow$
$\qquad address(family(X, Y, Children), Street).$

$wife(Y) \leftarrow$
$\qquad address(family(X, Y, Children), Street).$

$married(X, Y) \leftarrow$
$\qquad address(family(X, Y, Children), Street).$
$married(Y, X) \leftarrow$
$\qquad address(family(X, Y, Children), Street).$

$among(X, c(X, Y)).$
$among(X, c(Y, Z)) \leftarrow$
$\qquad among(X, Z).$

∎

The database above *can* be represented in the form of a traditional database by introducing a unique key for each family. For example as follows:

$husband(f1, john).$
$husband(f2, bill).$

$wife(f1, mary).$
$wife(f2, sue).$

$child(f1, tom).$
$child(f1, jim).$

$address(f1, main\_street, 3).$
$address(f2, main\_street, 4).$

$parent(X, Y) \leftarrow husband(Key, X), child(Key, Y).$
$\vdots$

However, the latter representation is less readable and it may also require some extra book-keeping to make sure that each family has a unique key.

To conclude — the issues discussed in this chapter were raised to demonstrate the advantages of using logic as a uniform language for representing databases. Facts, rules and queries can be written in a single language. Moreover, logic supports definition of relations via recursive rules, something which is not allowed in traditional databases. Finally, the use of structured data facilitates definition of relations which cannot be made in traditional relational databases. From this stand-point logic programming provides a very attractive conceptual framework for describing relational databases. On the other hand we have not raised important issues like how to implement such databases let alone how to handle updates to deductive databases.

# Exercises

55. Reorganize the database in Example 6.2 in such a way that *father*/2 and *mother*/2 become part of the intensional database.

56. Extend Example 6.2 with some more persons. Then define the following predicate symbols (with obvious intended interpretations):

   • *grandchild*/2
   • *sister*/2
   • *brother*/2
   • *cousins*/2

- *uncle*/2
- *aunt*/2

57. Consider an arbitrary planar map of countries. Write a program which colours the map using only four colours so that no two adjacent countries have the same colour. NOTE: Two countries which meet only pointwise are not considered to be adjacent.

58. Define the input-output behaviour of AND- and inverter-gates. Then describe the relation between input and output of the following nets:

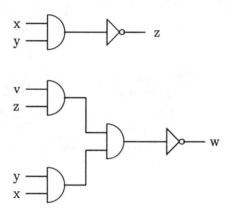

59. Translate the following relational algebra expressions into definite clauses.

- $\pi_{X,Y}(HUSBAND(Key, X) \bowtie WIFE(Key, Y))$
- $\pi_X(PARENT(X, Y) \cup \pi_X\ \sigma_{Y \leq 20,000}\ INCOME(X, Y))$

60. The following clauses define a binary relation denoted by $p/2$ in terms of the relations $q/2$ and $r/2$. How would you define the same relation using relational algebra?

$$p(X, Y) \leftarrow q(Y, X).$$
$$p(X, Y) \leftarrow q(X, Z), r(Z, Y).$$

61. Let $R_1$ and $R_2$ be subsets of $\mathbf{D} \times \mathbf{D}$. Define the composition of $R_1$ and $R_2$ using (1) definite programs; (2) relational algebra.

62. Let $R_1$ and $R_2$ be subsets of $\mathbf{D} \times \mathbf{D}$. Define the intersection of $R_1$ and $R_2$ using (1) definite programs; (2) relational algebra.

63. An ancestor is a parent, a grandparent, a great-grandparent etc. Define a relation *ancestor*/2 which is to hold if someone is an ancestor of somebody else.

64. Andrew, Ann, and Adam are siblings and so are Bill, Beth and Basil. Describe the relationships between these persons using as few clauses as possible.

65. Define a database which relates dishes and all of their ingredients. For instance, pancakes contain milk, flour and eggs. Then define a relation which describes the available ingredients. Finally define two relations:

    - *can_cook*($X$) which should hold for a dish $X$ if all its ingredients are available;

    - *needs_ingredient*($X, Y$) which holds for a dish $X$ and an ingredient $Y$ if $X$ contains $Y$.

66. Modify the previous exercise as follows — add to the database the quantity available of each ingredient and for each dish the quantity needed of each ingredient. Then modify the definition of *can_cook*/1 so that the dish can be cooked if each of its ingredients is available in sufficient quantity.

# Chapter 7

---

# Programming with Recursive
# Data Structures

## 7.1  Recursive Data Structures

In the previous chapter we studied a class of programs which operate on simple data objects — mostly constants. However, the last section of the chapter discussed the use of compound terms for representation of more complex worlds — like families and their members. Such data objects are typically used when there is a need to represent some collection of individuals where the size is not fixed or when the set of individuals is infinite. In the example a family may have anything between 0 and (in principle) infinitely many children. Such objects are usually represented by means of so called *recursive data structures*. A recursive data structure is so called because its data objects may contain, recursively as substructures, objects of the same "type". In the previous chapter the functor $c/2$ was used to represent the children of a family — the first argument contained the name of one child and the second, recursively, a representation of the remaining children.

This chapter discusses some recursive data structures used commonly in logic programs and programming techniques for dealing with such structures.

## 7.2  Lists

Some well-known programming languages — for instance Lisp — use lists as the primary representation of data (and programs). Although logic programming only allows terms as representations of individuals, it is not very hard to *represent* lists as terms. Most Prolog systems even support usage of lists by means of special syntax. We introduce first a precise concept of list.

Let **D** be some domain of objects. The set of all lists (over **D**) is defined inductively as the smallest set satisfying:

- the empty list (denoted $\epsilon$) is a list (over **D**);

- if $T$ is a list (over **D**) and $H \in$ **D** then the pair $\langle H;T \rangle$ is a list (over **D**).

For instance $\langle 1; \langle 2; \epsilon \rangle \rangle$ is a list over the domain of natural numbers.

In Prolog the empty list $\epsilon$ is usually represented by the constant $[\,]$ whereas a pair is represented using the binary functor ./2. The list above is thus represented by the term $.(1, .(2, [\,]))$ and is said to have 2 *elements* — "1" and "2". The possibility of having different types of lists (depending on what domain **D** one uses) introduces a technical problem since logic programs lack a type-system. In general we will only consider types over a universal domain which will be represented by the Herbrand universe.

To avoid having to refer to the "representation of lists" every time such a term is referred to, it will simply be called a *list* in what follows. However, when the word "list" is used it is important to keep in mind that the object is in fact only a term.

Every list (but the empty one) has a *head* and a *tail*. For a list of the form $.(H, T)$ the first argument is called the head and the second the tail of the list. For instance, $.(1, .(2, [\,]))$ has the head 1 and tail $.(2, [\,])$. To avoid this rather awkward notation, most Prolog systems employ special syntax for lists. The general idea is to write $[H|T]$ instead of $.(H, T)$. However, since $[1|[2|[\,]]]$ is about as difficult to write (and read) as the standard notation, certain simplifications are allowed. Thus, instead of writing:

- $[X_1, \ldots, X_m | [Y_1, \ldots, Y_n]]$ one usually writes $[X_1, \ldots, X_m, Y_1, \ldots, Y_n]$;

- $[X_1, \ldots, X_m | [Y_1, \ldots, Y_n | Z]]$ one usually writes $[X_1, \ldots, X_m, Y_1, \ldots, Y_n | Z]$.

Hence, instead of writing $[a|[b|[c|[\,]]]]$ (which is equivalent to $.(a, .(b, .(c, [\,]))))$ the notation $[a, b, c]$ will be used (to see why, we note that $[c|[\,]]$ is written as $[c]$, $[b|[c]]$ is written as $[b, c]$ and $[a|[b, c]]$ is written as $[a, b, c]$). Similarly $[a, b|[c|X]]$ is written as $[a, b, c|X]$. In standard notation this is written as $.(a, .(b, .(c, X)))$.

It is surprisingly easy to write procedures which correspond to the operations "CAR" and "CDR" of Lisp:

```
car(Head, [Head|Tail]).
cdr(Tail, [Head|Tail]).
```

By giving as goal $\leftarrow cdr(X, [a, b, c])$ Prolog replies with the expected answer $X = [b, c]$.

Now consider the definition of lists again. Looking more closely at the two statements defining what a list is, it is not very hard to see that they are both expressible as definite clauses — the first one as a fact and the second as a recursive rule.

**Example 7.1** Formally the definition of lists can be expressed as follows:

$list([])$.
$list([Head | Tail]) \leftarrow list(Tail)$.

This "type"-declaration has two different uses — it can (1) be used to *test* whether a term is a list or (2) to *enumerate/generate* all possible lists. By giving the definite goal $\leftarrow list(X)$ — "Is there some $X$ such that $X$ is a list?" — Prolog starts enumerating all possible lists starting with [] and followed by $[X_1], [X_1, X_2]$, etc. Remember that answers containing variables are understood to be universally quantified — that is, the second answer is interpreted as "For any $X_1$, $[X_1]$ is a list". (Of course the names of the variables may differ but are not important anyway.)

The next program considered is actually a version of the *among/2* program from the previous chapter. Here it is called *member/2* and it is used to describe membership in a list. The definition looks as follows:

- $X$ is a member of any list whose head is $X$;

- if $X$ is a member of *Tail* then $X$ is a member of any list whose tail is *Tail*.

Again observe that the definition is directly expressible as a definite program!

**Example 7.2**

$member(X, [X | Tail])$.
$member(X, [Y | Tail]) \leftarrow member(X, Tail)$.

As a matter of fact, the first clause is not quite correct since, for instance, the goal $\leftarrow member(a, [a | b])$ has a refutation despite the fact that $[a | b]$ is not a proper list. Thus, to make the program correct the first clause should be turned into a rule of the form:

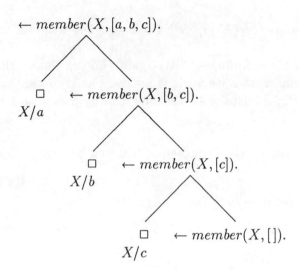

**Figure 7.1: SLD-tree of the goal** $\leftarrow member(X,[a,b,c])$

$$member(X,[X|\,Tail]) \leftarrow list(\,Tail).$$

However, for pragmatic reasons this is normally not done since a goal of the form:

$$\leftarrow member(x_m,[x_1,\ldots,x_m,\ldots,x_{m+n}]).$$

requires $n + 1$ extra procedure calls in order to be refuted.

Just as $list/1$ has more than one use depending on how the arguments are instantiated, $member/2$ can be used either to test or to generate answers. For instance, the goal $\leftarrow member(b,[a,b,c])$ has a refutation whereas the goal $\leftarrow member(d,[a,b,c])$ fails.

By leaving the first argument uninstantiated the $member/2$-program will enumerate the elements of the list in the second argument. For instance, the goal $\leftarrow member(X,[a,b,c])$ has three refutations with three different answers — under Prolog's depth-first search strategy the first answer is $X = a$, followed by $X = b$ and finally $X = c$. The SLD-tree of the goal is shown in Figure 7.1. (To avoid cluttering the SLD-trees with too much information the labels of the edges are usually omitted subsequently.)

Notice that the program produces exactly the expected answers. Consider instead the goal $\leftarrow member(a,X)$ which reads "Is there some list which contains $a$?". The SLD-tree of the goal is depicted in Figure 7.2.

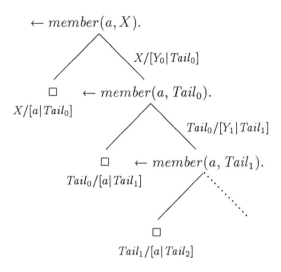

**Figure 7.2: SLD-tree of the goal** $\leftarrow member(a, X)$

The first answer produced is $X = [a \mid Tail_0]$ which is interpreted as — "For any $Tail_0$, $[a \mid Tail_0]$ has $a$ as a member" or less strictly "Any list starting with $a$ contains $a$". The second success branch first binds $X$ to $[Y_0 \mid Tail_0]$ and then binds $Tail_0$ to $[a \mid Tail_1]$. Hence the complete binding obtained for $X$ is $[Y_0 \mid [a \mid Tail_1]]$ which is equivalent to $[Y_0, a \mid Tail_1]$ and is interpreted as "Any list with $a$ as the second element contains $a$". Similarly the third answer is interpreted as "Any list with $a$ as the third element contains $a$". It is not hard to see that there are infinitely many answers of this kind and the SLD-tree obviously contains infinitely many success branches. This brings us to an important question discussed briefly in Chapter 3 — what impact has the textual ordering of clauses in Prolog?

What happens if the positions of the clauses in the $member/2$-program are swapped? Referring to Figure 7.1 one sees that instead of first traversing the leftmost branch in the SLD-tree the rightmost branch is traversed first. This branch will eventually fail, so the computation backtracks until the first answer (which is $X = c$) is found. Then the computation backtracks again and the answer $X = b$ is found followed by the final answer which is $X = a$. Thus, nothing much happens — the SLD-tree is simply traversed in an alternative fashion which means that the answers show up in a different order. This may, of course, have serious impacts if the tree contains some infinite branch — consider the rightmost branch of the tree in Figure 7.2. Clearly no clause ordering will affect the size of the tree and it is therefore not possible to traverse the whole tree (that is, find all answers). However if the rightmost branch in the tree is always selected before the leftmost one the computation will loop for ever without reporting *any* answers (although there are answers to the goal).

The halting problem is of course undecidable (i.e. it is in general not possible to determine whether a program will loop or not), but it is good practice to put facts before recursive clauses when writing a recursive program. In doing so it is often possible to find all, or at least some, of the answers to a goal before going into an infinite loop. There is also another good reason for doing this which has to do with the implementation of modern Prolog compilers. By letting the rightmost subgoal in the very last clause of a definition be a recursive call, the Prolog compiler can use what is commonly called *tail recursion optimization* which results in a more efficient machine code.

The next program considered is that of "putting two lists together". The name commonly used for the program is *append*/3 although a more appropriate name would be *concatenate*/3. As an example, appending a list $[c, d]$ to another list $[a, b]$ yields the new list $[a, b, c, d]$. More formally the relation is defined as follows:

- appending any list $X$ to the empty list gives as result the list $X$;

- if appending $Z$ to $Y$ yields $W$, then appending $Z$ to $[X|Y]$ yields $[X|W]$.

Again there is a direct translation of the definition into a definite program:

## Example 7.3

$$append([\,], X, X).$$
$$append([X|Y], Z, [X|W]) \leftarrow append(Y, Z, W).$$

∎

Just like the previous programs, the *append*/3-program can be used for some alternative tasks. Obviously, it can be used to test whether the concatenation of two lists equals a third list e.g. by giving the goal:

$$\leftarrow append([a, b], [c, d], [a, b, c, d])$$

It can also be used "as a function" to concatenate two lists into a third by giving the goal:

$$\leftarrow append([a, b], [c, d], X)$$

in which case the computation succeeds with the answer $X = [a, b, c, d]$. However, it is also possible to give the goal:

$$\leftarrow append(Y, Z, [a, b, c, d])$$

which reads — "Are there two lists, $Y$ and $Z$, such that $Z$ appended to $Y$ yields $[a, b, c, d]$?". Clearly there are two such lists — there are in fact five different possibilities:

$$
\begin{array}{ll}
Y = [] & Z = [a, b, c, d] \\
Y = [a] & Z = [b, c, d] \\
Y = [a, b] & Z = [c, d] \\
Y = [a, b, c] & Z = [d] \\
Y = [a, b, c, d] & Z = []
\end{array}
$$

By now it should come as no surprise that all of these answers are reported by Prolog. The SLD-tree of the goal is depicted in Figure 7.3.

The program can actually be used for even more sophisticated tasks. For instance, the rule:

$$unordered(List) \leftarrow append(Front, [X, Y|End], List), X > Y.$$

describes the property of being an unordered list of integers. The clause expresses the fact that a list is unordered if there are two consecutive elements where the first is greater than the second.

Another example of the use of $append/3$ is shown in the following clause, which defines the property of being a list with multiple occurrences of some element:

$$multiple(List) \leftarrow append(L1, [X|L2], List), append(L3, [X|L4], L2).$$

However, maybe the following is a more natural definition of the same property:

$$multiple([Head|Tail]) \leftarrow member(Head, Tail).$$
$$multiple([Head|Tail]) \leftarrow multiple(Tail).$$

The $append/3$-program can also be used to define, for instance, the membership-relation and the relation between lists and their last elements. This is left as an exercise. One may be willing to compare a definition of the last element of the list based on $append/3$ with the following direct definition:

- $X$ is the last element in the list $[X]$;

- if $X$ is the last element in the list $Tail$ then it is also the last element in the list $[Head|Tail]$.

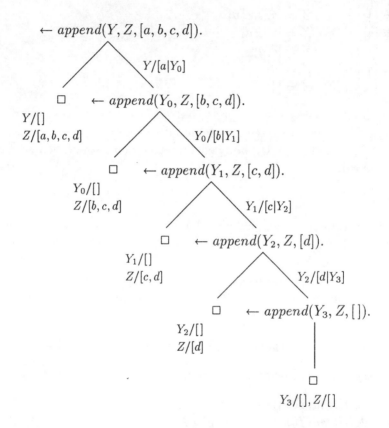

**Figure 7.3: SLD-tree of the goal** $\leftarrow append(Y, Z, [a, b, c, d])$

This can be formalized as follows:

**Example 7.4**

$last(X, [X])$.
$last(X, [Head | Tail]) \leftarrow last(X, Tail)$.

■

All of the programs written so far have a similar structure — the first clause in each of them is a fact and the second clause is a recursive rule. In Examples 7.1 and 7.3 the resemblance is even closer: The program of Example 7.1 can be obtained from that of Example 7.3 by removing the second and third arguments of each atom in the program. This is no coincidence since (almost) every program that operates on lists has a uniform structure. Some programs differ slightly from the general pattern, like examples 7.2 and 7.4 — on the other hand, when removing the first argument from the atoms in these programs, they also closely resemble the $list/1$-program.

Almost all programs in this chapter (also those which follow) are defined by means of a technique which looks like that of *inductive definitions* of sets.

Remember that relations are sets of tuples. The propositions of an inductive definition describe which tuples are in, and outside of this set. The first proposition (usually called the *basic clause*) in the definition is normally unconditional or uses only already fully defined relation(s). It introduces some (one or more) initial tuples in the set. The second proposition (called the *inductive clause*) states that if some tuples are in the set (and possibly satisfy some other, already defined relations) then some other tuples are also in the set. The inductive clause is used to repeatedly "pump up" the set as much as possible. That is, the basic clause gives a set $S_0$. The inductive clause then induces a new set $S_1$ from $S_0$. But since $S_1$ may contain tuples which do not appear in $S_0$, the inductive clause is used on $S_1$ to obtain the set $S_2$ and so on. The basic and inductive clause are sometimes called *direct* clauses.

The direct clauses specify that some tuples are *in* the set (the relation). But that does not exclude the set from also containing other tuples. For instance, saying that 1 is an integer does not exclude Tom and 17 from being integers. Hence, an inductive definition contains also a third clause (called the *extremal clause*) which states that no other tuples are in the set than those which belong to it as a result of the direct clauses. In the definitions above this last statement is omitted. A justification for this is that definite programs describe only positive information and it is not possible to express the extremal clause as a definite clause. However, taking into account the negation-as-failure rule, the third clause becomes explicit when considering the completion of the program. For instance the completion of Example 7.1 contains the formula:

$$list(X) \leftrightarrow X = [] \lor \exists Head, Tail(X = [Head|Tail] \land list(Tail))$$

The "if"-part of this formula corresponds to the direct clauses whereas the "only if"-part is the extremal clause which says that an individual is a list only if it is the empty list or a pair where the tail is a list.

The definition of lists is in some sense prototypical for inductive definitions of relations between lists and other objects. The basic clause states that something holds for the empty list and the inductive clause says that something holds for lists of length $n + 1$ given that something holds for lists of length $n$, $n \geq 0$. By following these principles there is no risk of writing programs like:

> $list([])$.
> $list(Tail) \leftarrow list([Head|Tail])$.

or:

> $list([])$.
> $list(X) \leftarrow list(X)$.

Declaratively, there is nothing wrong with them. All statements are true in the intended model. However, as inductive definitions they are no good. Both of them define the empty list to be the only list. The programs are worthless also operationally — for instance, the goal $\leftarrow list([a])$ yields an infinite loop.

Next some other, more complicated, relations between lists are considered. The first relation is that between lists and their permutations. Informally speaking, a permutation of a list is a reordering of its elements. Consider a list with $n$ elements. What possible reorderings are there? Clearly the first element can be put in $n$ different positions. Consequently there are $n - 1$ positions where the second element may be put. More generally there are $n - m + 1$ positions where the $m$-th element may be put. From this it is easy to see that there are $n!$ different permutations of a list with $n$ elements.

Formally the relation is defined inductively as follows:

- the empty list is a permutation of itself;

- If $W$ is a permutation of $Y$ and $Z$ is the result of inserting $X$ into $W$ then $Z$ is a permutation of $[X|Y]$.

Needless to say this is a definite program. Namely the following one:

**Example 7.5**

> $permutation([], [])$.
> $permutation([X|Y], Z) \leftarrow permutation(Y, W), insert(X, W, Z)$.

$$insert(Y, Xz, Xyz) \leftarrow append(X, Z, Xz), append(X, [Y|Z], Xyz).$$

∎

Operationally the rule of the program states the following — "Remove the first element, $X$, from the list to be permuted, then permute the rest of the list and finally insert $X$ into the permutation". The insertion of an element $Y$ into a list $Xz$ is achieved by first splitting $Xz$ into two parts, $X$ and $Z$. Then the parts are put together with $Y$ in-between.

Now the goal ← $permutation([a, b, c], X)$ may be given, to which Prolog replies with the six possible permutations:

$$X = [a, b, c]$$
$$X = [b, a, c]$$
$$X = [b, c, a]$$
$$X = [a, c, b]$$
$$X = [c, a, b]$$
$$X = [c, b, a]$$

Conceptually this relation is symmetric — that is, if A is a permutation of B then B is a permutation of A. In other words, the goal ← $permutation(X, [a, b, c])$ should return exactly the same answers. So it does (although the order of the answers is different) but after the final answer the program goes into an infinite loop. It turns out that recursive programs with more than one body-literal have to be used with some care. They cannot be called as freely as programs with only a single literal in the body.

If, for some reason, the need arises to call $permutation/2$ with the first argument uninstantiated and still have a finite SLD-tree, the body literals have to be swapped both in the rule of $permutation/2$ and in $insert/3$. After doing this the computation terminates, which means that the SLD-tree of the goal is finite. Hence, when changing the order of the body literals in a clause (or put alternatively, using another computation rule), a completely different SLD-tree is obtained, not just a different traversal of the same tree. As observed above, it is not unusual that one ordering leads to an infinite SLD-tree whereas another ordering results in a finite SLD-tree. Since Prolog uses a fixed computation rule, it is up to the user to make sure that the ordering is "optimal" for the intended use. In most cases this implies that the program only runs efficiently for certain types of goals — for other goals it may be very inefficient or even loop indefinitely (as shown above). If the user wants to run the program in different "directions", it is often necessary to have several versions of the program with different orderings of literals. Needless to say, some programs loop no matter how the body literals are ordered.

The *permutation*/2-program can be used to sort, for instance, lists of natural numbers. The classical specification of the relation between a list and its sorted version says that — "$Y$ is a sorted version of $X$ if $Y$ is a sorted permutation of $X$". Together with the property *sorted*/1 (which holds if a list of integers is sorted in ascending order) the relation may be defined thus (*nsort*/2 stands for naive sort):

**Example 7.6**

$$nsort(X, Y) \leftarrow permutation(X, Y), sorted(Y).$$

$$sorted([\,]).$$
$$sorted([X]).$$
$$sorted([X, Y | Z]) \leftarrow X \leq Y, sorted([Y | Z]).$$

∎

The predicate symbol $\leq$ /2 which is used to compare integers is normally predefined as a so called built-in predicate in most Prolog systems. Needless to say, this program is incredibly inefficient. For more efficient sorting programs the reader is advised to solve exercises 76 – 78. However, the program illustrates quite clearly why the order among the atoms in the body of a clause is important. Consider the goal:

$$\leftarrow nsort([2, 1, 3], X).$$

This reduces to the new goal:

$$\leftarrow permutation([2, 1, 3], X), sorted(X).$$

With the standard computation rule this amounts to finding a permutation of $[2, 1, 3]$ and then checking if this is a sorted list. Not a very efficient way of sorting lists but it is immensely better than first finding a sorted list and then checking if this is a permutation of the list $[2, 1, 3]$ which would be the effect of switching the order among the subgoals. Clearly there are only six permutations of a three-element list but there are infinitely many sorted lists.

The definition of *sorted*/1 differs slightly from what was said above — there are two basic clauses, one for the empty list and one for the list with a single element. It may also happen that there are two or more inductive clauses (cf. exercise 78).

The last example considered here is that of reversing a list. Formally the relation between a list and its reversal is defined as follows:

- the empty list is the reversal of itself;

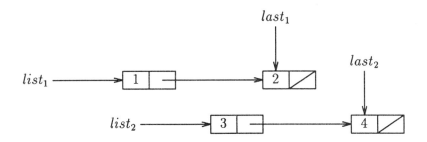

**Figure 7.4: Representation of lists**

- if $W$ is the reversal of $Y$ and $Z$ is the concatenation of $W$ and $[X]$ then $Z$ is the reversal of $[X|Y]$.

This definition results in the following program:

**Example 7.7**

$$reverse([\,],[\,]).$$
$$reverse([X|Y],Z) \leftarrow reverse(Y,W), append(W,[X],Z).$$

Operationally, the second clause says the following — "to reverse $[X|Y]$, first reverse $Y$ into $W$ then concatenate $W$ with $[X]$ to obtain $Z$". Just like in Example 7.5 the goal $\leftarrow reverse([a,b,c],X)$ has a finite SLD-tree whereas $\leftarrow reverse(X,[a,b,c])$ has an infinite one. However, when switching the order of the literals in the body of the recursive clause, the situation becomes the opposite.

## 7.3 Difference-Lists

Computationally the cost of appending two lists in Prolog is typically proportional to the length of the first list. In general a linear algorithm is acceptable but other languages often facilitate concatenation of lists in constant time. The principal idea is to maintain a pointer to the end of the list as shown in figure 7.4. In order to append the two lists the following Pascal-like commands are needed:

$$\vdots$$
$$last_1 \uparrow .pointer := list_2;$$
$$last_1 := last_2;$$
$$\vdots$$

In Prolog the same technique can be adopted by using "variables as pointers". Assume that, in the world of lists, there is a (partial) function which given two lists where the second is a suffix of the first, returns the list obtained by removing the suffix from the first (that is, the result is a prefix of the first list). Now let the functor "$-$" denote this function, then the term:

$$[t_1, \ldots, t_m, t_{m+1}, \ldots, t_{m+n}] - [t_{m+1}, \ldots, t_{m+n}]$$

designates the list denoted by the term $[t_1, \ldots, t_m]$. More generally, the term $[a, b, c | L] - L$ designates the list $[a, b, c]$ for any list assigned to $L$. As a special case the term $L - L$ designates the empty list for any list assigned to $L$. It is now possible to use this to define concatenation of difference-lists:

$$append(X - Y, Y - Z, X - Z).$$

Declaratively this stands for "Appending the difference of $Y$ and $Z$ to the difference of $X$ and $Y$ yields the difference of $X$ and $Z$". The correctness of the statement is easier to see when written as follows:

Using the new definition of $append/3$ it is possible to refute the goal:

$$\leftarrow append([a, b | X] - X, [c, d | Y] - Y, Z)$$

in a single resolution-step and the computed answer substitution becomes:

$$\{X/[c, d|Y], Z/[a, b, c, d|Y] - Y\}$$

which implies that:

$$append([a, b, c, d|Y] - [c, d|Y], [c, d|Y] - Y, [a, b, c, d|Y] - Y)$$

is a logical consequence of the program.

The ability to concatenate lists in constant time comes in quite handy in some programs. Take for instance the program for reversing lists in Example 7.7. The time complexity of this program is $O(n^2)$ where $n$ is the number of elements in the list given as the first argument. That is, to reverse a list of 100 elements approximately 10,000 resolution steps are needed.

However, using difference-lists it is possible to write a program which does the same job in linear time:

**Example 7.8**

$$reverse(X, Y) \leftarrow rev(X, Y - []).$$

$$rev([], X - X).$$
$$rev([X|Y], Z - W) \leftarrow rev(Y, Z - [X|W]).$$

∎

This program reverses lists of $n$ elements in $n + 2$ resolution steps.

Unfortunately, the use of difference-lists is not without problems. Consider the goal:

$$\leftarrow append([a, b] - [b], [c, d] - [d], L).$$

One expects to get an answer that represents the list $[a, c]$. However, Prolog cannot unify the subgoal with the only clause in the program and therefore replies "no". It would be possible to write a new program which handles also this type of goal, but it is not possible to write a program which concatenates lists in constant time (which was the main objective for introducing difference-lists in the first place). Another problem is due to the lack of occur-check in most Prolog systems. A program that specifies what an empty list is may look as follows:

$$empty(L - L).$$

Clearly, $[a|Y] - Y$ is not an empty list (since it denotes the list $[a]$). However, the goal $\leftarrow empty([a|Y] - Y)$ succeeds with $Y$ bound to an infinite term. Yet another problem with difference-lists stems from the fact that "$-$" designates a partial function. So far there is nothing said about the meaning of terms such as $[a, b, c] - [d]$. For instance the goal:

$$\leftarrow append([a, b] - [c], [c] - [b], L)$$

succeeds with the answer $L = [a, b] - [b]$. Again such problems can be solved with additional computational efforts. The $append/3$ program may for instance be written as follows:

$$append(X - Y, Y - Z, X - Z) \leftarrow suffix(Y, X), suffix(Z, Y).$$

But this means that concatenation of lists becomes linear again.

# Exercises

67. Write the following lists as terms with "." (dot) as functor and [] representing the empty list:

   - $[a, b]$
   - $[a \,|\, b]$
   - $[a, [b, c], d]$
   - $[a, b \,|\, X]$

   - $[a \,|\, [b, c]]$
   - $[a, b \,|\, []]$
   - $[[] \,|\, []]$
   - $[a \,|\, [b, c \,|\, []]]$

68. Define a binary relation *last*/2 between lists and their last elements using only the predicate *append*/3.

69. Define the membership-relation by means of the *append*/3-program.

70. Define a binary relation *length*/2 between lists and their lengths (i.e. the number of elements in them).

71. Define a binary relation *lshift*/2 between lists and the result of shifting them (circularly) one step to the left. For example, so that the goal:

   $\leftarrow lshift([a, b, c], X)$

   succeeds with answer $X = [b, c, a]$.

72. Define a binary relation *rshift*/2 between lists and the result of shifting them (circularly) one step to the right. For example, so that the goal:

   $\leftarrow rshift([a, b, c], X)$

   succeeds with answer $X = [c, a, b]$.

73. Define a binary relation *prefix*/2 between lists and all its prefixes. Hint: [], [a] and [a, b] are prefixes of the list [a, b].

74. Define a binary relation *suffix*/2 between lists and all its suffixes. Hint: [], [b] and [a, b] are suffixes of the list [a, b].

75. Define a binary relation *sublist*/2 between lists and their sublists.

76. Implement the insert-sort algorithm for integers in Prolog — informally it can be formulated as follows:

Given a list, remove its first element, sort the rest, and insert the first element in its appropriate place in the sorted list.

77. Implement the quick-sort algorithm for integers in Prolog — informally it can be formulated as follows:

Given a list, split the list into two — one part containing elements less than a given element (e.g. the first element in the list) and one part containing elements greater than or equal to this element. Then sort the two lists and append the results.

78. Implement the merge-sort algorithm for integers in Prolog — informally it can be formulated as follows:

Given a list, divide the list into two halves. Sort the halves and "merge" the two sorted lists.

79. A nondeterministic finite automaton (NFA) is a tuple $\langle S, \Sigma, E, s_1, F \rangle$ where:

- $S$ is a finite set of *states*;
- $\Sigma$ is a finite *input alphabet*;
- $E \subseteq S \times S \times \Sigma$ is a *transition relation*;
- $s_1 \in S$ is an *initial state*;
- $F \subseteq S$ is a set of *final states*.

A string $x_1 x_2 \ldots x_n \in \Sigma^n$ is *accepted* by an NFA if there is a sequence:

$$\langle s_1, s_2, x_1 \rangle \langle s_2, s_3, x_2 \rangle \ldots \langle s_n, s, x_n \rangle \in E^n$$

such that $s \in F$. An NFA is often depicted as a *transition diagram* whose nodes are states and where the transition relation is denoted by labelled edges between nodes. The final states are indicated by double circles. Define the NFA depicted in Figure 7.5 as a logic program (let 1 be the initial state). Use the program to check if strings (represented by lists of a's and b's) are accepted.

80. Informally speaking, a *Turing machine* consists of an infinite tape divided into slots which may be read from/written into by a *tape-head*. In each slot there is exactly one of two symbols called "blank" (denoted by 0) and "nonblank" (denoted by 1). Initially the tape is almost blank — the number of slots from the "leftmost" to the "rightmost" nonblank of the

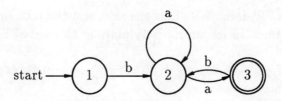

**Figure 7.5: Transition diagram for NFA**

tape is finite. This sequence (string) will be referred to as the *content of the tape*. The machine is always in one of a finite number of *states*, some of which are called *final* and one of which is called *initial*.

The tape-head is situated at exactly one of the slots of the tape. Depending on the contents of this slot and the current state, the machine makes one of a number of possible *moves*:

- It writes 0 or 1 in the slot just read from, and
- changes state, and
- moves the tape-head one slot to the right or to the left.

This can be described through a function, which maps the current state and the symbol in the current slot of the tape into a triple which consists of a new state, the symbol written in the current slot and the direction of the move.

To start with the machine is in the initial state and the tape-head is situated at the "leftmost" nonblank of the tape. A string is said to be accepted by a Turing machine iff it is the initial contents of the tape and there is a finite sequence of moves that take the machine to one of its final states.

Write a Turing machine which accepts a string of $n$ $(n > 0)$ consecutive 1's and halts pointing to the leftmost nonblank in a sequence of $2*n$ 1's. This illustrates another view of Turing machines, not only as language acceptors, but as a function which takes as input a natural number $n$ represented by $n$ consecutive 1's and produces some output represented by the consecutive 1's starting in the slot pointed to when the machine halts.

81. Write a program for multiplying matrices of integers. Obviously the program should succeed only if the number of columns of the first matrix equals the number of rows in the second. Then write a specialized program for multiplying matrices of fixed size.

82. Find some suitable representation of sets. Then define some standard operations on sets, like union, intersection, membership, set-difference.

83. Represent strings by difference lists. Define the property of being a palindrome.

84. Use the concept of difference-lists to implement the quick-sort algorithm in Exercise 77.

85. Use difference-lists to define queues. That is, a first-in-first-out stack. Write relations that describe the effects of adding new objects to and removing objects from queues.

86. Define the property of being a binary tree. Then define what it means for an element to be a member of a binary tree.

87. A binary tree is said to be *sorted* if for every node $N$ in the tree, the nodes in the left subtree are all less than $N$ and all nodes in the right subtree are greater than $N$. Define this by means of a definite program and then define relations for adding and deleting nodes in a sorted binary tree (so that it remains sorted).

# Chapter 8

# Amalgamating Object- and Meta-language

## 8.1 What is a Meta-language?

Generally speaking a *language* is nothing but a, usually infinite, collection of strings. For a language $L$, some existing language has to be used to formulate and reason about the semantics and syntax of the language $L$. Sometimes a language is used to describe itself. This is often the case when reasoning about English (or any natural language for that matter). The following are examples of such sentences:

> *This sentence consists of fiftytwo letters excluding blanks*
> *Rabbit is a noun*

A language which is used to reason about another language (or possibly itself) is called a *meta-language* and the language reasoned about is called the *object-language*. Obviously the meta- and object-languages do not have to be natural languages — they can be any, more or less, formal languages. In the previous chapters English was used to describe the language of predicate logic and in forthcoming chapters logic will be used to formulate rules describing a subset of natural language. Special interest is paid to the use of logic programming as a meta-language for describing other languages, and in particular the use of logic programming to describe itself.

In computer science the word "meta" is used extensively in different contexts, and its meaning is not always very clear. In this book the word "meta-program" will be used for a program which manipulates another program (whatever a program is). With this rather broad definition, programs like compilers, interpreters, debuggers and even language specific editors are considered to be meta-programs.

151

The main topic of this chapter is interpreters but in subsequent chapters other applications are considered.

An interpreter provides a syntactic and semantic description of a language — in a very general sense it takes as input a program and some data, and produces as output some (new) data. The language used to implement the interpreter is the meta-language and the language being interpreted is the object-language. In this chapter some alternative interpreters for "pure" Prolog (i.e. Prolog without built-in predicates) written in Prolog will be presented. Such interpreters are commonly called *meta-circular interpreters*[1] or simply *self-interpreters*.

When writing an interpreter for a language one of the most vital decisions is how to represent programs and data-objects of the object-language in the meta-language. In this chapter some advantages and problems with different representations are discussed. Initially the object-language will be represented by ground terms of the meta-language but later the distinction between meta- and object-language is more or less erased. This may lead to serious problems since it is not always possible to tell the object-language from the meta-language — for example, consider the following sentence of natural language:

*Stockholm is a nine-letter word*

If Stockholm is an object-level word (that is, if Stockholm refers to the word "Stockholm") then the sentence is true. However, if it is part of the meta-language then the sentence is false since Stockholm is the capital of Sweden.

## 8.2   Ground Representation

As discussed in previous chapters logic describes relations between individuals of some universe (domain). Clearly nothing prevents us from describing the world that consists of terms and formulas. For this, all constants, variables, compound terms and formulas of the object-language should be represented uniquely as terms of the meta-language. One possible representation of definite programs may look as follows:

- each constant of the object-language is represented by a unique constant in the meta-language;

- each variable of the object-language is represented by a unique constant of the meta-language;

---

[1]The term *meta*-interpreter is often used as an abbreviation for meta-circular interpreter. However, the word is somewhat misleading since *any* interpreter is a meta-interpreter.

- each $n$-ary functor of the object-language is represented by a unique $n$-ary functor in the meta-language;

- each $n$-ary predicate symbol of the object-language is represented by a unique $n$-ary functor of the meta-language;

- each connective of the object-language is represented by a unique functor in the meta-language (with the corresponding arity).

The representation can be given in terms of a bijective mapping $\phi$ from constants, variables, functors, predicate symbols and connectives of the object-language to a subset of the constants and functors of the meta-language. The meta-language may of course consist of other symbols as well — in particular some predicate symbols. However, leaving them aside for the moment, the domain of the intended interpretation $\Im$ of the meta-language consists of terms and formulas of the object-language. Now the meaning of the constants and functors introduced above are given by the bijection $\phi$, or rather by its inverse $(\phi^{-1})$ as follows:

- The meaning $c_\Im$ of a constant $c$ of the meta-language is the constant or variable $\phi^{-1}(c)$ of the object-language.

- The meaning $f_\Im$ of an $n$-ary functor $f$ of the meta-language is an $n$-ary function which maps:

    1. the terms $t_1, \ldots, t_n$ to the term $\phi^{-1}(f)(t_1, \ldots, t_n)$ if $\phi^{-1}(f)$ is a functor of the object-language;

    2. the terms $t_1, \ldots, t_n$ to the atom $\phi^{-1}(f)(t_1, \ldots, t_n)$ if $\phi^{-1}(f)$ is a predicate letter of the object-language;

    3. the formulas $f_1, \ldots, f_n$ to the formula $\phi^{-1}(f)(f_1, \ldots, f_n)$ if $\phi^{-1}(f)$ is a connective of the object-language.

**Example 8.1** Take as object-language a language with an alphabet consisting of the constants $a$ and $b$, the predicate letters $p/1$ and $q/2$, the connectives $\wedge$ and $\leftarrow$ and an infinite but enumerable set of variables including $X$.

Now assume that the meta-language contains the constants $a$, $b$ and $x$ and the functors $p/1$, $q/2$, $and/2$ and $if/2$ with the obvious intended interpretation. Then the meaning of the meta-language term:

$$if(p(x), and(q(x, a), p(b)))$$

is the object-language formula:

$$p(X) \leftarrow q(X, a) \wedge p(b)$$

∎

It should be noticed that the discussion above avoids some important consid-erations. In particular, the interpretation of meta-language functors consists of partial, not total functions — for instance, there is nothing said about the meaning of the term:

$$if(p(and(a, b)), q(if(a, b)))$$

Intuitively such a term is nothing but garbage. However, predicate logic requires that functors are interpreted as total functions and formally speaking such terms must also have some kind of meaning. There are different methods to deal with the problem; however, these technical considerations are not discussed here.

The coding of object-language expressions given above is of course only one possibility. In fact, in what follows we will not commit ourselves to any particular representation of the object-language. Instead $\ulcorner A \urcorner$ will be used to denote some particular representation of the object-language construction $A$. This is done not to obscure the principal ideas by any particular representation of the object-language.

It is now possible to describe relations between terms and formulas of the object-language in the meta-language. In particular our intention is to describe SLD-resolution and SLD-derivations (in particular SLD-refutations). The first relation considered is that expressed between consecutive goals, $G_i$ and $G_{i+1}$ ($i \geq 0$), in an SLD-derivation:

$$\langle G_0; C_0 \rangle, \ldots, \langle G_i; C_i \rangle, G_{i+1}$$

The relationship between two such goals can be expressed through the following "inference rule" discussed in Chapter 3:

$$\frac{\leftarrow A_1, \ldots, A_{i-1}, A_i, A_{i+1}, \ldots, A_n \qquad H \leftarrow B_1, \ldots, B_m}{\leftarrow (A_1, \ldots, A_{i-1}, B_1, \ldots, B_m, A_{i+1}, \ldots, A_n)\theta}$$

where $\theta$ is the mgu of the two atoms $A_i$ and $H$ and where $H \leftarrow B_1, \ldots, B_m$ is a renamed clause from the program. The relation between the two goals in the rule can be formulated as the following definite clause:

**Example 8.2**

$step(Goal, NewGoal) \leftarrow$
$\qquad select(Goal, Left, SubGoal, Right),$
$\qquad clause(C),$
$\qquad rename(C, Goal, Head, Body),$
$\qquad unify(Head, SubGoal, Mgu),$
$\qquad combine(Left, Body, Right, TmpGoal),$
$\qquad apply(Mgu, TmpGoal, NewGoal).$

∎

Informally the intended interpretation of the used predicate symbols are as follows:

- $select(A, B, C, D)$ describes the relation between a goal $A$ and the selected subgoal $C$ in $A$. $B$ and $D$ are the conjunctions of subgoals to the left and right of the selected one (obviously if $A$ contains only $C$ then $B$ and $D$ are empty);

- $clause(A)$ describes the property of being a clause in the object-language program;

- $rename(A, B, C, D)$ describes the relation between four formulas such that $C$ and $D$ are renamed variants of the head and body of $A$ containing no variables in common with $B$;

- $unify(A, B, C)$ describes the relation between two atoms, $A$ and $B$, and their mgu $C$;

- $combine(A, B, C, D)$ describes the relation between a goal $D$ and three conjunctions which, when combined, form the conjunction $D$;

- $apply(A, B, C)$ describes the relation between a substitution $A$ and two goals such that $A$ applied to $B$ yields $C$;

Some alternative approaches for representing the object-level program have been suggested in the literature. The most general approach is to explicitly carry the program around via an extra argument. Here a more pragmatic approach is employed where each clause $C$ of the object-program is stored as a fact, $clause(\ulcorner C \urcorner)$, of the meta-language. For instance, $clause/1$ may consist of the following four facts:[2]

---

[2]Notice that in many Prolog systems, clause is treated as a predefined predicate symbol which cannot be used to define new relations. This predicate is discussed in Section 8.4

**Example 8.3**

> $clause(\ulcorner grandparent(X,Z) \leftarrow parent(X,Y), parent(Y,Z) \urcorner)$.
> $clause(\ulcorner parent(X,Y) \leftarrow father(X,Y) \urcorner)$.
> $clause(\ulcorner father(adam, bill) \urcorner)$.
> $clause(\ulcorner father(bill, cathy) \urcorner)$.

∎

The task of completing $select/4$ and the other undefined relations is left as an exercise for the reader.

The derives-relation between two goals $G_0$ and $G_i$ of an SLD-derivation (i.e. if there is a derivation whose initial goal is $G_0$ and final goal is $G_i$) can be described as the reflexive and transitive closure of the inference rule above. Thus, an SLD-derivation can be described through the two clauses:

**Example 8.4**

> $derivation(G, G)$.
> $derivation(G0, G2) \leftarrow$
>      $step(G0, G1)$,
>      $derivation(G1, G2)$.

∎

If all undefined relations were properly defined it would be possible to give the goal clause (here $\ulcorner \square \urcorner$ denotes the coding of the empty goal):

> $\leftarrow derivation(\ulcorner \leftarrow grandparent(adam, X) \urcorner, \ulcorner \square \urcorner)$.

which corresponds to the question "Is there a derivation of the object-language goal $\leftarrow grandparent(adam, X)$ which leads to the empty goal?". The meta-language goal reduces to:

> $\leftarrow step(\ulcorner \leftarrow grandparent(adam, X) \urcorner, G), derivation(G, \ulcorner \square \urcorner)$.

The leftmost subgoal is satisfied with $G$ bound to the representation of the object-language goal $\leftarrow parent(adam, Y), parent(Y, X)$ yielding:

> $\leftarrow derivation(\ulcorner \leftarrow parent(adam, Y), parent(Y, X) \urcorner, \ulcorner \square \urcorner)$.

Again this is unified with the second clause of $derivation/2$:

> $\leftarrow step(\ulcorner \leftarrow parent(adam, Y), parent(Y, X) \urcorner, G), derivation(G, \ulcorner \square \urcorner)$.

The computation then proceeds until the goal:

$$\leftarrow derivation(\ulcorner \Box \urcorner, \ulcorner \Box \urcorner).$$

is obtained. This unifies with the fact of $derivation/2$ and Prolog produces the answer "yes". Notice that the answer obtained to the initial goal is only "yes" since the goal contains no variables (only object-language variables which are represented as ground terms in the meta-language). The modified version of the program which also returns a substitution may look as follows:

**Example 8.5**

$$derivation(G, G, \ulcorner \epsilon \urcorner).$$
$$derivation(G0, G2, S0) \leftarrow$$
$$\qquad step(G0, G1, Mgu),$$
$$\qquad derivation(G1, G2, S1),$$
$$\qquad compose(Mgu, S1, S0).$$

$$step(Goal, NewGoal, Mgu) \leftarrow$$
$$\qquad select(Goal, Left, SubGoal, Right),$$
$$\qquad clause(C),$$
$$\qquad rename(C, Goal, Head, Body),$$
$$\qquad unify(Head, SubGoal, Mgu),$$
$$\qquad combine(Left, Body, Right, TmpGoal),$$
$$\qquad apply(Mgu, TmpGoal, NewGoal).$$

∎

Now what is the point in having self-interpreters? Surely it must be better to let an interpreter run the object-language directly, instead of letting the interpreter run a self-interpreter which runs the object-program? The answer is that self-interpreters provide great flexibility for modifying the behaviour of the logical machinery. With a self-interpreter it is possible to write:

- interpreters which employ alternative search strategies — for instance, to avoid using Prolog's depth-first search, an interpreter which uses a breadth-first strategy may be written in Prolog and run on the underlying machine which uses depth-first search;

- debugging facilities — for instance, interpreters which emit traces or collect run-time statistics while running the program;

- interpreters which allow execution of a program which changes during its own execution — desirable in many A.I. applications or in the case of database updates;

- interpreters which collect the actual proof of a satisfied goal — something which is of utmost importance in expert-systems applications;

- interpreters for nonstandard logics or "logic-like" languages — this includes fuzzy logic, nonmonotonic logic, modal logic, Context Free Grammars and Definite Clause Grammars (see Chapter 10).

Applications like compilers and language specific editors have already been mentioned. Furthermore, meta-circular interpreters play a very important role in the area of program transformation, verification and synthesis — topics which are outside the scope of this book.

## 8.3    Nonground Representation

Although the interpreters in the previous section are relatively clear and concise, they suffer severely from efficiency problems. The inefficiency is mainly due to the representation of object-language variables by constants in the meta-language. As a consequence, rather complicated definitions of *renaming, unification* and *application* of substitutions to terms/formulas are needed. In this section a less logical and more pragmatic approach is employed resulting in an extremely short interpreter. The idea is to represent object-language variables by meta-language variables — the whole approach seems straightforward at first sight, but it has severe semantical consequences some of which are raised below.

In addition to representing variables of the object-language by variables of the meta-language, an object-language clause of the form $A_0 \leftarrow A_1, \ldots, A_n$ will be represented in the meta-language by the term[3] $A_0$ *if* $A_1$ *and* $\ldots$ *and* $A_n$ when $n \geq 1$ and $A_0$ *if true* when $n = 0$. A goal $\leftarrow A_1, \ldots, A_n$ of the object-language will be represented by the term $A_1$ *and* $\ldots$ *and* $A_n$ when $n \geq 1$ and *true* when $n = 0$.

The object-language program in Example 8.3 is thus represented by the following collection of meta-language facts:

---

[3]Here it is assumed that *and*/2 is a right-associative functor that binds stronger than *if*/2. That is, the expression *a if b and c and d* is identical to the term *if(a, and(b, and(c, d)))*.

**Example 8.6**

$clause(grandparent(X, Z)$ *if* $parent(X, Y)$ *and* $parent(Y, Z))$.
$clause(parent(X, Y)$ *if* $father(X, Y))$.
$clause(father(adam, bill)$ *if* $true)$.
$clause(father(bill, cathy)$ *if* $true)$.

∎

The interpreter considered in this section simply looks as follows:

**Example 8.7**

$solve(true)$.
$solve(X$ *and* $Y) \leftarrow solve(X), solve(Y)$.
$solve(X) \leftarrow clause(X$ *if* $Y), solve(Y)$.

∎

In what follows we will describe how operations which had to be explicitly spelled out in the earlier interpreters, are now performed automatically on the meta-level. Consider first unification:

Let $\leftarrow parent(adam, bill)$ be an object-language goal. In order to find a refutation of this goal we may instead consider the following meta-language goal:

$\leftarrow solve(parent(adam, bill))$.

The subgoal obviously unifies only with the head of the third clause in Example 8.7. The goal thus reduces to the new goal:

$\leftarrow clause(parent(adam, bill)$ *if* $Y_0), solve(Y_0)$.

Now the leftmost subgoal unifies with the second clause of Example 8.6, resulting in the new goal:

$\leftarrow solve(father(adam, bill))$.

This means that the unification of the object-language atom $parent(adam, bill)$ and the head of the object-language clause $parent(X, Y) \leftarrow father(X, Y)$ is performed automatically on the meta-level. There is no need to provide a definition of unification of object-language formulas as needed in Example 8.2.

The same effect is achieved when dealing with renaming of variables in object-language clauses. Consider the goal:

$\leftarrow solve(parent(X, bill))$.

This reduces to the new goal:

$\quad \leftarrow clause(parent(X, bill) \; if \; Y_0), solve(Y_0).$

Notice that the goal and the second clause of Example 8.6 both contain the variable $X$. However, the variables of the rule are automatically renamed on the meta-level so that the next goal becomes:

$\quad \leftarrow solve(father(X, bill)).$

Finally, application of a substitution to a goal is considered. The goal:

$\quad \leftarrow clause(father(adam, X) \; and \; father(X, Y)).$

which represents the object-language goal $\leftarrow father(adam, X), father(X, Y)$ is resolved with the second clause of Example 8.7 and the goal:

$\quad \leftarrow solve(father(adam, X)), solve(father(X, Y))$

is obtained. This goal is resolved with the third clause of Example 8.7 yielding:

$\quad \leftarrow clause(father(adam, X) \; if \; Y_1), solve(Y_1), solve(father(X, Y)).$

Now the leftmost subgoal unifies with the clause:

$\quad clause(father(adam, bill) \; if \; true).$

and the mgu $\{X/bill, Y_1/true\}$ is obtained. This substitution is used to construct the new goal:

$\quad \leftarrow solve(true), solve(father(bill, Y)).$

Notice that the mgu obtained in this step contains the "object-language substitution" $\{X/bill\}$ and that there is no need to apply it explicitly to the subgoal $father(X, Y)$ as was the case in the previous section.

Hence, by using the interpreter in Example 8.7 instead of that in the previous section, three of the most laborious operations (unification, renaming and application) are no longer explicitly needed. They are of course still performed but all this happens on the meta-level.

Yet another advantage of the interpreter in Example 8.7 is that there is no need to explicitly handle substitutions of the object-language. By giving the goal:

$\quad \leftarrow solve(grandparent(adam, X)).$

Prolog gives the answer $X = cathy$ since the object-language variable $X$ is now represented as a meta-language variable. In the previous section object-language variables were represented by ground terms and to produce a computed answer substitution it was necessary to explicitly represent such substitutions.

Although the program in Example 8.7 works quite nicely, its declarative reading is far from clear. Its simplicity is due to the representation of object-language variables as meta-language variables. But this also introduces problems as pointed out in [74]. Namely, the variables in $solve/1$ and in $clause/1$ range over different domains — the variables in $solve/1$ range over formulas of the object-language whereas the variables in $clause/1$ range over individuals of the intended interpretation of the object-language program (intuitively the persons Adam, Bill and Cathy and possibly some others). The problem can, to some extent, be solved by using a typed language instead of standard predicate logic. However, this discussion is outside the scope of this book.

The interpreter in Example 8.7 can be used for, what is sometimes called, *pure* Prolog. This means that the object-program and goal are not allowed to contain, for instance, negation. However, the interpreter may easily be extended to also take proper care of negation by including the rule:

$$solve(not\ X) \leftarrow not\ solve(X).$$

Similar rules can be added for most built-in predicates of Prolog. One exception is cut (!), which is very difficult to incorporate into the self-interpreter above. However, with some additional effort it is also possible to do this.

## 8.4 Clause/2

To support meta-programming, Prolog provides a number of so called *built-in predicates*. In this section and the following two, some of these are discussed. For a complete list of built-in predicates the reader should consult his/her own Prolog user's manual.

For the interpreter in Example 8.7 to work, the object-program has to be stored as unit-clauses of the form $clause(\ulcorner C \urcorner)$, where $\ulcorner C \urcorner$ is the representation of an object-language clause. The built-in predicate $clause/2$ allows the object-program to be stored directly as a meta-program. The effect of executing $clause/2$ can be described by the following "inference" rule (assuming that Prolog's computation rule is used):

$$\frac{\leftarrow clause(t_1, t_2), A_2, \ldots, A_m \qquad H \leftarrow B_1, \ldots, B_n}{\leftarrow (A_2, \ldots, A_m)\theta}$$

where $m > 0$, $H \leftarrow B_1, \ldots, B_n$ is a (renamed) program clause and $\theta$ is an mgu of $clause(t_1, t_2)$ and $clause(H, (B_1, \ldots, B_n))$. Here comma is treated as a binary functor which is right-associative. That is, the expression $a, b, c$ is the same thing as the term $','(a, ','(b, c))$.

For uniformity, a fact $A$, is treated as if it was a rule of the form $A \leftarrow true$. Notice that there may be many clauses which unify with the arguments of $clause/2$, which means that there may be several possible derivations. For instance, consider the program:

$$father(X, Y) \leftarrow parent(X, Y), male(X).$$
$$father(adam, bill).$$

and the goal $\leftarrow clause(father(X, Y), Z)$. In this case Prolog replies with two answers. The first answer leaves $X$ and $Y$ unbound and $Z$ bound to the conjunction $parent(X_0, Y_0), male(X_0)$. The second answer binds $X$ to $adam$, $Y$ to $bill$ and $Z$ to $true$.

Employing this new built-in predicate it is possible to write Examples 8.6 and 8.7 as:

$$solve(true).$$
$$solve((X, Y)) \leftarrow solve(X), solve(Y).$$
$$solve(X) \leftarrow clause(X, Y), solve(Y).$$

$$grandparent(X, Z) \leftarrow parent(X, Y), parent(Y, Z).$$
$$\vdots$$

making the distinction between meta- and object-language none whatsoever.

The use of $clause/2$ is often restricted in that, at the time when the subgoal is selected, the first argument of $clause/2$ must not be a variable. Hence, in most Prolog systems the goal $\leftarrow solve(X)$ would result in a run-time error when given to the program above.

## 8.5   Assert/1

Prolog also provides some built-in predicates which are used to modify the database of clauses. For instance, the built-in predicate $assert/1$ is used to add new clauses to the database while trying to refute a goal. From a proof-theoretic point of view the logical meaning of $assert/1$ can be described as follows:

$$\frac{\leftarrow assert(t), A_2, \ldots, A_n}{\leftarrow A_2, \ldots, A_n}$$

In other words, *assert*/1 can be interpreted as something which is always true. However, the main effect of *assert*/1 is the addition of *t* to the database of clauses. Of course, *t* should be a well-formed "clause" not to cause a failed derivation.[4] Consider the trivial program:

> *parent*(*adam*, *bill*).

When faced with the goal:

> ← *assert*(*parent*(*adam*, *beth*)), *parent*(*adam*, *X*).

Prolog replies with two answers — *X* = *bill* and *X* = *beth* (the order depends on the particular implementation). The reason is that Prolog first adds the clause *parent*(*adam*, *beth*) to the database and then tries to satisfy the second subgoal which now has two solutions.

Notice that changes made to Prolog's database by *assert*/1 are permanent. That is, they are not undone on backtracking. Notice also that it is possible to assert the same clause several times.

Unfortunately, the effect of using *assert*/1 is not always very clear. For instance, if the order among the subgoals in the previous goal is changed into:

> ← *parent*(*adam*, *X*), *assert*(*parent*(*adam*, *beth*)).

some systems would return the single answer *X* = *bill*, since when the call to *parent*/2 is made, Prolog records that its definition contains only one clause. Thus, when backtracking takes place the new clause added to the definition of *parent*/2 remains invisible to the call. However, other systems would return infinitely many answers. First the answer *bill*, and thereafter an infinite repetition of the answer *beth*. This happens if the implementation does not "freeze" the definition of a predicate when a call is made. Every time a solution is found to the leftmost subgoal a new copy of the clause *parent*(*adam*, *beth*) is added to the definition of *parent*/2. Thus, there will always be one clause for the the leftmost subgoal to backtrack to. A similar problem occurs in connection with the clause:

> *void* ← *assert*(*void*), *fail*.

In some implementations the goal ← *void* would succeed, whereas in others it would fail. However, in both cases the resulting program is:

> *void* ← *assert*(*void*), *fail*.
> *void*.

---

[4]The reason for quoting the word clause is that the argument of *assert*/1 formally is a term. However, in most Prolog systems clauses are handled just as if they were terms. That is, the logical connectives "←" and "," are treated like any other functor.

This suggests that *assert*/1 should be used with great care. Just like cut, *assert*/1 is often abused in misguided attempts to improve the efficiency of programs. However, there are cases when usage of *assert*/1 can be motivated. For instance, if a subgoal is solved, the result can be stored in the database as a *lemma*. Afterwards the same subgoal can be solved in a single derivation step. This kind of usage does not cause any declarative problems since the lemma does not add to, or delete information from the program.

Prolog implementations are usually equipped with two variants of *assert*/1 — *asserta*/1 and *assertz*/1 — the former adds its argument textually first in the definition whereas the latter appends its argument to the end of the definition.

## 8.6   Retract/1

*Retract*/1 is used to delete clauses from Prolog's database. The logical meaning of *retract*/1 is similar to that of *clause*/2. It can be described by the inference rule:

$$\frac{\leftarrow retract(s \leftarrow t), A_2, \ldots, A_m \qquad H \leftarrow B_1, \ldots, B_n}{\leftarrow (A_2, \ldots, A_m)\theta}$$

where $m > 0$, $H \leftarrow B_1, \ldots, B_n$ is a renamed program clause such that $s \leftarrow t$ and $H \leftarrow B_1, \ldots, B_n$ have an mgu $\theta$. Like the case with *clause*/2 there may be more than one clause which unify with the argument of *retract*/1 and, as a result, several derivations are possible.

For uniformity, and by analogy to *clause*/2, a fact may be treated as a rule whose body consists of the literal *true*.

As a side-effect *retract*/1 removes the clause $H \leftarrow B_1, \ldots, B_n$ from Prolog's internal database. The effect is permanent — that is, the clause is not restored when backtracking takes place.

For instance, consider the Prolog database:

> *parent*(*adam*, *bill*).
> *parent*(*adam*, *beth*).
> *parent*(*bill*, *cathy*).

In reply to the goal:

> $\leftarrow retract(parent(adam, X) \leftarrow true)$.

Prolog replies with two answers — $X = bill$ and $X = beth$. Then execution terminates and all that is left of the program is the clause:

> *parent*(*bill*, *cathy*).

In most Prolog implementations it is required that the argument of $retract/1$ is not a variable and if it is of the form $s \leftarrow t$ that $s$ is not a variable.

Like $assert/1$, usage of $retract/1$ is controversial and the effect of using it may diverge in different implementations. In general there are both cleaner and more efficient methods for solving problems than resorting to these two. For example, naive users of Prolog often use $assert/1$ and $retract/1$ to implement a form of global variables. This usually has two effects — the program becomes harder to understand and it runs slower since asserting new clauses to the program involve considerable amount of work and book-keeping. This often comes as a big surprise to people who are used to programming in imperative programming languages.

# Exercises

88. Complete the self-interpreter described in Examples 8.2 – 8.4. Either by using the suggested representation of the object-language or invent your own representation.

89. Extend Example 8.7 so that execution is aborted when the number of resolution-steps for solving a subgoal becomes too large.

90. Modify Example 8.7 so that it uses the *depth-first-iterative-deepening* search strategy. The general idea is to explore all paths of length $n$ from the root (where $n$ is initially 1) using a depth-first strategy. Then the whole process is repeated after incrementing $n$ by 1. Using this technique every refutation in an SLD-tree is eventually found.

91. Write a program for differentiating formulas consisting of natural numbers and some variables (but not Prolog ones!). Implement the program by defining some of the most common differentiation-rules. For instance the following ones:

$$\frac{\partial m}{\partial x} = 0 \qquad \frac{\partial x}{\partial x} = 1 \qquad \frac{\partial x^n}{\partial x} = n * x^{n-1}$$

$$\frac{\partial (f + g)}{\partial x} = \frac{\partial f}{\partial x} + \frac{\partial g}{\partial x} \qquad \frac{\partial (f * g)}{\partial x} = g * \frac{\partial f}{\partial x} + f * \frac{\partial g}{\partial x}$$

where $m \geq 0$ and $n > 0$.

92. Write a Prolog program which determines if a collection of formulas of propositional logic is satisfiable.

93. Write a theorem prover for propositional logic using, for instance, the inference rules of natural deduction.

94. Write a tiny pure-Lisp interpreter which incorporates some of the primitive functions (like CAR, CONS etc.) and allows the definition of new functions in terms of these.

# Chapter 9

# Logic and Expert Systems

## 9.1 Expert Systems

Roughly speaking, an expert system is a program that guides the user in the solution of some problem which normally requires intervention of a human expert in the field. Traditionally such systems were implemented in Lisp, but with the recent success of Prolog and logic programming, a number of systems written in Prolog have emerged.

Tasks which typically call for expert level knowledge include, for instance, *diagnosis*, *control* and *planning*. Diagnosis means trying to find the cause of some malfunction, e.g. the cause of an illness. In control-applications the aim is to prevent a system, e.g. an industrial process from entering abnormal states. Planning, finally, means trying to find some sequence of transformation steps which from a given initial state via a sequence of intermediate steps reaches a specified final state. A typical problem consists in finding a plan which assembles a collection of parts into a final product. This chapter illustrates applicability of logic programming for expert systems by a diagnosis example.

Usually an expert system exhibits a number of characteristics:

- It is divided into an *inference engine* and a *knowledge-base*. The knowledge-base contains rules which describe general knowledge about some problem domain. The inference engine is used to infer knowledge from the knowledge-base. Usually, the inference machine is generic in the sense that one can easily plug in a new knowledge-base without any major changes to the inference machine.

- The knowledge-base is not always definite — it may contain rules which

167

are subject to some *uncertainty*.

- The system often runs on modern workstations and much effort is put into the user interface and the dialogue with the user.

- It has the ability not only to infer new knowledge from existing knowledge, but also to explain how/why some conclusion was reached.

- It has support for incremental acquisition of new knowledge.

It is easy to see that the first point above coincides with the objectives of logic programming — namely to separate the logic component (*what* the problem is) from the control (*how* the problem should be solved). This can be expressed by the equation:

$$\text{Algorithm} = \text{Logic} + \text{Control}$$

That is, Kowalski's well-known paraphrase of Wirth's doctrine Program = Algorithm + Data Structure. In the spirit of Kowalski we could write:

$$\text{Expert System} = \text{Knowledge-base} + \text{Control} + \text{User Interface}$$

The last two terms are commonly called an expert-system *shell*.

The knowledge-base of an expert system typically consists of a set of so called *production rules* (or simply rules). Like definite clauses, they have a set of premises and a conclusion. Such rules say that whenever all the premises hold the conclusion also holds. A typical rule found in one of the earliest expert systems called MYCIN may look as follows:

|  |  |
|---|---|
| **IF** | the stain of the organism is gram-positive |
| **AND** | the morphology of the organism is coccus |
| **AND** | the growth conformation of the organism is clumps |
| **THEN** | the identity of the organism is staphylococcus (0.7) |

It is not very hard to express approximately the same knowledge in the form of a definite clause:

$$identity\_of\_organism(staphylococcus) \leftarrow$$
$$stain\_of\_organism(gram\_positive),$$
$$morphology\_of\_organism(coccus),$$
$$growth\_conformation\_of\_organism(clumps).$$

The figure (0.7) given in the conclusion of the MYCIN-rule above is an example of uncertainty of the rules. It says that if the premises hold then the conclusion holds with probability 0.7. In the following we do not consider these figures of uncertainty but assume that they are always 1.0.

To avoid the risk of causing bodily harm to the reader (or his neighbourhood) we consider an application which involves diagnosing starting problems of cars. The following two propositions seem to express some general knowledge about the cause of malfunctioning gadgets:

- if $Y$ is a necessary component for $X$ and $Y$ is malfunctioning then $X$ is also malfunctioning;

- if $X$ exhibits some fault-symptom $Z$ then either $X$ is malfunctioning or there exists another malfunctioning component which is necessary for $X$.

In predicate logic this may be expressed as:

1) $\forall X (\exists Y (needs(X, Y) \wedge malf(Y)) \rightarrow malf(X))$

2) $\forall X, Z (symp(Z, X) \rightarrow (malf(X) \vee \exists Y (needs(X, Y) \wedge malf(Y))))$

The first of these easily transforms into the definite clause:

$malfunctions(X) \leftarrow needs(X, Y), malfunctions(Y).$

However, in order to write the second formula as a definite clause some transformations are needed. This can be done by introducing an auxiliary predicate symbol $indirect/1$ and saying that:

- $X$ has an indirect fault if there exists a component which is necessary for $X$ and which malfunctions.

Now the second formula can be replaced by the following two:

2a) $\forall X, Y (symp(Y, X) \rightarrow (malf(X) \vee indirect(X)))$

2b) $\forall X (\exists Y (malf(Y) \wedge needs(X, Y)) \rightarrow indirect(X))$

These are straightforward to transform into normal clause form:

$malfunctions(X) \leftarrow symptom(Y, X), not\ indirect(X).$
$indirect(X) \leftarrow needs(X, Y), malfunctions(Y).$

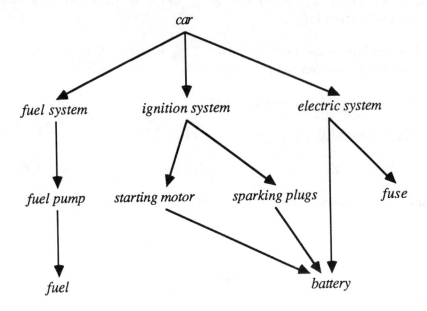

Figure 9.1:  Taxonomy of a car-engine

We must now define the relation *needs*/2 which defines a hierarchy on components and dependencies between them. In this chapter a car-engine is abstracted into the components and dependencies in the taxonomy of Figure 9.1.

The relation described by the figure may be represented by the following definite program:

> *needs*(*car, ignition_system*).
> *needs*(*car, fuel_system*).
> *needs*(*car, electric_system*).
> *needs*(*ignition_system, starting_motor*).
> *needs*(*ignition_system, sparking_plugs*).
> *needs*(*electric_system, fuse*).
> *needs*(*electric_system, battery*).
> *needs*(*fuel_system, fuel_pump*).
> *needs*(*sparking_plugs, battery*).
> *needs*(*starting_motor, battery*).
> *needs*(*fuel_pump, fuel*).

Finally the predicate *symptom*/2 which describes the symptoms of a car (or rather parts of the car) should be defined. However, the symptoms exhibited by a specific car depend on the particular car in a specific moment of time. The description of the symptoms of the car should therefore be added to the database when diagnosing the cause of malfunction of that particular car. How to cope with this is described below.

Hence, the knowledge-base of an expert system can be described as a set of definite or normal clauses, that is, as a logic program. What about the inference engine?

The inference engine is used to infer new knowledge from existing knowledge. This can be done by using two different strategies — (1) either start from what is already known and infer new knowledge from this, or (2) start from the conclusion to be proved and reason backwards until the conclusion depends on what is already known. These methods are called *forward-* and *backward-chaining* respectively. Clearly, SLD-resolution is an example of a backward-chaining proof procedure. There are expert systems which rely on forward-chaining or a mixture of the two, but there are also expert systems which use backward-chaining only. MYCIN is an example of such an expert system.

We have established the close relationship between, on the one hand, the knowledge-base of an expert system and the set of clauses in logic programming and, on the other hand, the inference engines used in some expert systems and SLD-resolution. So what is the main difference between expert systems and logic programming?

Apart from the probabilities of rules and the user interface, an expert system differs from a logic program in the sense that its knowledge-base is usually *incomplete*. As explained above the knowledge-base only contains general knowledge concerning different faults and symptoms. It does not contain information about the specific symptoms of a particular individual. This information has to be added to its knowledge-base whilst diagnosing the individual. That is, while inferring what fault the individual is suffering from, the inference engine asks questions which have to be filled in, in order to complete the knowledge-base.

Another major distinction between logic programming and expert systems is that expert systems have the capability to *explain* their conclusions. If an expert system draws a conclusion concerning the health of a patient it is likely that the doctor (or the patient) wants to know how the system came to that conclusion. Most Prolog systems are not automatically equipped with such a mechanism.

So clearly the knowledge-base may be described as a Prolog program but the Prolog inference engine does not satisfy the requirement needed in an expert system. In order to remedy this we are going to build a new inference engine based on the self-interpreter in Example 8.7 to provide these missing features.

## 9.2   Collecting Proofs

The first refinement made to the program in Example 8.7 is to add the capability of collecting the proof representing the refutation of a goal. As described in Section 3.3 a refutation may be represented as a *proof-* or *derivation-tree*. Referring to Example 8.7 we see that there are three types of goals which need a proof:

- the empty goal (represented by the constant *true*);

- compound goals of the form $X$ *and* $Y$;

- goals consisting of a single literal.

Now in the case of the goal *true* we can simply return the term *void* which represents an empty proof. Furthermore, under the assumption that $X$ has a proof $Px$ and that $Y$ has a proof $Py$, the term $Px + Py$ will represent a proof of the goal represented by $X$ *and* $Y$. Finally, the single literal $X$ has a proof represented by the term $proof(X, P)$ if there is a clause instance $X$ *if* $Y$ and $Y$ has a proof represented by $P$. It is straightforward to convert this into the following definite program:

## Example 9.1

$solve(true, void)$.
$solve((X \ and \ Y), (Px + Py)) \leftarrow$
$\quad\quad solve(X, Px), solve(Y, Py)$.
$solve(X, proof(X, P)) \leftarrow$
$\quad\quad clause(X \ if \ Y), solve(Y, P)$.

∎

Given the goal $\leftarrow solve(grandparent(X, Y), Z)$ and the database:

$clause(grandparent(X, Y) \ if \ parent(X, Z) \ and \ parent(Z, Y))$.
$clause(parent(X, Y) \ if \ father(X, Y))$.
$clause(father(adam, bill) \ if \ true)$.
$clause(father(bill, carl) \ if \ true)$.

Prolog not only finds a refutation and produces the answer $X = adam, Y = carl$ but also returns the term:

$Z = proof(grandparent(adam, carl),$
$\quad\quad\quad proof(parent(adam, bill),$
$\quad\quad\quad\quad\quad proof(father(adam, bill), void))$
$\quad\quad\quad +$
$\quad\quad\quad proof(parent(bill, carl),$
$\quad\quad\quad\quad\quad proof(father(bill, carl), void))$
$\quad\quad )$

which represents the refutation of the goal $\leftarrow grandparent(X, Y)$.

As seen, when proving a positive goal it is rather easy to collect its proof. The situation is more complicated when trying to solve goals containing negative literals. Since the negation-as-failure rule says that $not \ X$ succeeds if $X$ finitely fails (that is, has no refutation) there is no proof to return (except possibly some kind of meta-proof). A naive solution is to add the clause:

$solve(not \ X, proof(not \ X, void)) \leftarrow$
$\quad\quad not \ solve(X, T)$.

to the interpreter. A more satisfactory solution would be to collect the meta-proof which proves that $X$ has no proof but writing an interpreter for doing this is rather complicated.

The discussion concerning the "proof-collecting" interpreter is now temporarily abandoned, but is resumed after the following section which suggests a solution to the problem of the incomplete knowledge-base.

## 9.3   Query-the-User

As explained above the knowledge-base of an expert system is only capable of handling general information valid for every individual. In the case of diagnosing an illness, the symptoms of a specific patient have to be collected during "run-time". This means that when the inference engine encounters certain predicates it should not look for the definition in the knowledge-base but instead *query the user* for information. In the example above the predicate *symptom*/2 is used for this purpose. Such an approach can easily be implemented by means of the interpreter in Example 8.7, if these special predicate symbols are known before-hand.[1]

**Example 9.2**

$$solve(true).$$
$$solve(X \ and \ Y) \leftarrow$$
$$solve(X), solve(Y).$$
$$solve(symptom(X,Y)) \leftarrow$$
$$confirm(X,Y).$$
$$solve(X) \leftarrow$$
$$clause(X \ if \ Y), solve(Y).$$

where *confirm*/2 is defined as:

$$confirm(X,Y) \leftarrow$$
$$write('Is \ the \ '),$$
$$write(Y), tab(1), write(X), write('? \ '),$$
$$read(yes).$$

∎

Now consider the following (trivial) knowledge-base:

$$clause(malfunctions(X) \ if \ possible\_fault(Y,X) \ and \ symptom(Y,X)).$$
$$clause(possible\_fault(flat, tyre) \ if \ true).$$

---

[1]In this and subsequent examples the need for input and output is vital. For this several built-in predicates available in most Prolog implementations are being used. Thus, *write*/1 is used to print a term on the terminal. *read*/1 is used to read a term from the user (a call succeeds if the term unifies with the argument of the call). *nl*/0 prints a newline on the terminal and *tab*/1 is used to print the specified number of blanks on the terminal. Strings of characters enclosed by single quotes are taken to be constants (as is the case in most Prolog systems).

When giving the goal ← *solve(malfunctions(X))* Prolog will print the question "Is the tyre flat?". If the user replies with "yes" the execution succeeds with answer $X = tyre$; if the user answers anything but "yes" (or a variable) the goal simply fails.

## 9.4 Fixing the Car (Extended Example)

Now the principle of implementation of expert systems in Prolog is illustrated by continuing the example discussed in Section 9.1. We do not claim that the result is even close to a real expert system; which is, of course, considerably much more complicated than the program outlined below.

The first step is to describe the knowledge-base as a collection of facts in the meta-language. The predicate symbol *if/2* is used for that purpose; the first argument represents the head of a rule and the second the conjunction of premises. To avoid having to treat unit-clauses of the object-language separately, they will be written in the form $X$ *if true*. The knowledge-base described in Section 9.1 can now be described as follows:

> *malfunctions(X) if needs(X, Y) and malfunctions(Y).*
> *malfunctions(X) if symptom(Y, X) and not indirect(X).*

> *indirect(X) if needs(X, Y) and malfunctions(Y).*

> *needs(car, ignition_system) if true.*
> *needs(car, fuel_system) if true.*
> *needs(car, electric_system) if true.*
> *needs(ignition_system, starting_motor) if true.*
> *needs(ignition_system, sparking_plugs) if true.*
> *needs(electric_system, fuse) if true.*
> *needs(electric_system, battery) if true.*
> *needs(fuel_system, fuel_pump) if true.*
> *needs(sparking_plugs, battery) if true.*
> *needs(starting_motor, battery) if true.*
> *needs(fuel_pump, fuel) if true.*

To construct an inference engine, the interpreters from Examples 9.1 and 9.2 are "joined" into the following one:

$solve(true, void).$
$solve(X \ and \ Y, P1 + P2) \leftarrow$
$\qquad solve(X, P1), solve(Y, P2).$
$solve(not \ X, proof(not \ X, void)) \leftarrow$
$\qquad not \ solve(X, P).$
$solve(symptom(X, Y), proof(symptom(X, Y), void)) \leftarrow$
$\qquad confirm(X, Y).$
$solve(X, proof(X, P)) \leftarrow$
$\qquad (X \ if \ Y), solve(Y, P).$

The program is assumed to interact with a mechanic, exploiting the query-the-user facility. Hence, some easily spotted misbehaviours are characterized:

- one of the sparking plugs does not produce a spark;

- the fuel gauge indicates an empty tank;

- the fuel pump does not feed any fuel;

- a fuse (say number 13) is broken;

- the battery voltage is less than 11 volts;

- the starting motor is silent.

These can be formulated using the predicate symbol $confirm/2$ which poses questions to the mechanic and succeeds if he replies "yes". It may be defined as follows:

$confirm(X, Y) \leftarrow$
$\qquad nl, ask(X, Y), read(yes).$

where $ask(X, Y)$ prints a query asking if $Y$ exhibits misbehaviour $X$ and is defined as:

$ask(worn\_out, sparking\_plugs) \leftarrow$
$\qquad write('Do \ any \ of \ the \ sparking \ plugs \ fail \ to \ produce \ a \ spark?').$
$ask(out\_of, fuel) \leftarrow$
$\qquad write('Does \ the \ fuel \ gauge \ indicate \ an \ empty \ tank?').$
$ask(broken, fuel\_pump) \leftarrow$
$\qquad write('Does \ the \ fuel \ pump \ fail \ to \ feed \ any \ fuel?').$
$ask(broken, fuse) \leftarrow$
$\qquad write('Is \ fuse \ number \ 13 \ broken?').$
$ask(discharged, battery) \leftarrow$
$\qquad write('Is \ the \ battery \ voltage \ less \ than \ 11 \ volts?').$
$ask(broken, starting\_motor) \leftarrow$
$\qquad write('Is \ the \ starting \ motor \ silent?').$

This more or less completes the knowledge-base and inference engine of the expert system. However, the program suffers from operational problems which become evident when giving the goal $\leftarrow solve(malfunctions(car), Proof)$. If the user replies "no" to the question "Is the battery voltage less than 11 volts?", the system immediately asks the same question again. This happens because (see Figure 9.1):

- the car needs the ignition system;

- the ignition-system needs the sparking plugs and the starting motor;

- both the sparking plugs and the starting motor need the battery.

To avoid having to answer the same question several times the system must remember what questions it has already posed and the answers to those questions. This can be achieved by asserting the question/answer to the Prolog database. Before posing a query, the system should look into this database to see if an answer to the question is already there. To implement this facility the predicate $confirm/2$ must be redefined, for instance, in the following way:

$$confirm(X, Y) \leftarrow$$
$$known(X, Y, true).$$
$$confirm(X, Y) \leftarrow$$
$$not\ known(X, Y, Z), nl, ask(X, Y),$$
$$read(A), remember(X, Y, A), A = yes.$$

$$remember(X, Y, yes) \leftarrow$$
$$assertz(known(X, Y, true)).$$
$$remember(X, Y, no) \leftarrow$$
$$assertz(known(X, Y, false)).$$

Note that the second clause is an example of unsafe use of negation. Given a selected subgoal $confirm(a, b)$, the first clause is used (and the subgoal is solved) if the question triggered by $a$ and $b$ was previously confirmed by the user (that is, if $confirm(a, b, true)$ is solved); the second clause is used if the question triggered by $a$ and $b$ was never posed before. This will be the effect since the selected subgoal in the next goal will be the negative literal $not\ known(a, b, Z)$ which succeeds if *there is no Z* such that $known(a, b, Z)$. If neither of these two clauses apply (that is, if the question triggered by $a$ and $b$ has been posed but denied) the call to $confirm/2$ fails.

When calling the program with the goal:

$$\leftarrow solve(malfunctions(car), X).$$

the system first prints the query:

Is the battery voltage less than 11 volts ?

If the user answers "no" the system asks:

Is the starting motor silent?

Under the assumption that the user replies "no", the next question posed by the system is:

Do any of the sparking plugs fail to produce a spark?

If the reply to this question is "yes" the computation stops with the (rather awkward) answer:

$$X = proof(malfunctions(car),$$
$$\qquad proof(needs(car, ignition\_system), void)$$
$$\qquad +$$
$$\qquad proof(malfunctions(ignition\_system),$$
$$\qquad\qquad proof(needs(ignition\_system, sparking\_plugs), void)$$
$$\qquad\qquad +$$
$$\qquad\qquad proof(malfunctions(sparking\_plugs),$$
$$\qquad\qquad\qquad proof(symptom(worn\_out, sparking\_plugs), void)$$
$$\qquad\qquad\qquad +$$
$$\qquad\qquad\qquad proof(not\ indirect(sparking\_plugs), void)$$
$$\qquad\qquad\qquad )$$
$$\qquad\qquad )$$
$$\qquad )$$

Needless to say the answer is rather difficult to overview and there is need for routines that display the proof in a readable form. Some alternative approaches are possible, for instance, by printing the proof as a tree — however such a program would require rather complicated graphics routines. Instead a rather crude approach is employed where the rule-instances that the proof consists of are printed. The "top-loop" of the printing routine looks as follows:

```
print_proof(void).
print_proof(X + Y) ←
        print_proof(X), nl, print_proof(Y).
print_proof(proof(X, void)) ←
        write(X), nl.
print_proof(proof(X, Y)) ←
        Y ≠ void, write(X), write(' BECAUSE'), nl,
        print_children(Y), nl, print_proof(Y).
```

That is, in case of the empty proof nothing is done. If the proof consists of two or more proofs the proofs are printed separately. If the proof is of the form $X$ *if* $Y$ then two possibilities emerge — if $Y$ is the empty proof then $X$ is printed. If $Y \neq void$ then $X$ is printed followed by the word "BECAUSE" and the "top nodes of the constituents of $Y$". Finally the subproofs are printed.

The program for printing the top-nodes of proofs looks as follows:

$$print\_children(proof(X,Y) + Z) \leftarrow$$
$$tab(8), write(X), write(' \text{ AND}'), nl, print\_children(Z).$$
$$print\_children(proof(X,Y)) \leftarrow$$
$$tab(8), write(X), nl.$$

That is, if it is a compound proof then the top of one constituent is printed followed by the word "AND", in turn followed by the top-nodes of the remaining constituents. If the proof is a singleton then the top of that proof is printed.

To complete the program the following "driver"-routine is added:

$$expert \leftarrow$$
$$abolish(known/3),$$
$$solve(malfunctions(car), X),$$
$$print\_proof(X).$$

where $abolish/1$ is a built-in predicate which removes all clauses whose heads have the same predicate symbol and arity as the argument. When faced with the goal $\leftarrow expert$ the following dialogue may appear (with user input in bold-face):

Is the battery voltage less than 11 volts? **no.**

Is the starting motor silent? **no.**

Do any of the sparking plugs fail to produce a spark? **yes.**

malfunctions(car) BECAUSE
        needs(car, ignition_system) AND
        malfunctions(ignition_system)

needs(car, ignition_system)

malfunctions(ignition_system) BECAUSE
        needs(ignition_system, sparking_plugs) AND
        malfunctions(sparking_plugs)

needs(ignition_system, sparking_plugs)

malfunctions(sparking_plugs) BECAUSE
        symptom(worn_out, sparking_plugs) AND
        not indirect(sparking_plugs)

symptom(worn_out, sparking_plugs)

not indirect(sparking_plugs)

In conclusion, the complete listing of this tiny expert-system shell and the particular knowledge-base for diagnosing starting problems of cars is depicted below. (Lines preceded by the symbol "%" are comments.)

```
% Top level routine
expert ←
        abolish(known/3),
        solve(malfunctions(car), X),
        print_proof(X).

% Inference engine
solve(true, void).
solve(X and Y, P1 + P2) ←
        solve(X, P1), solve(Y, P2).
solve(not X, proof(not X, void)) ←
        not solve(X, P).
solve(symptom(X, Y), proof(symptom(X, Y), void)) ←
        confirm(X, Y).
solve(X, proof(X, P)) ←
        (X if Y), solve(Y, P).

% Query-the-user
confirm(X, Y) ←
        known(X, Y, true).
confirm(X, Y) ←
        not known(X, Y, Z), nl, ask(X, Y),
        read(A), remember(X, Y, A), A = yes.

remember(X, Y, yes) ←
        assertz(known(X, Y, true)).
remember(X, Y, no) ←
        assertz(known(X, Y, false)).
```

$ask(worn\_out, sparking\_plugs) \leftarrow$
 $\quad write(\text{'Do any of the sparking plugs fail to produce a spark?'}).$
$ask(out\_of, fuel) \leftarrow$
 $\quad write(\text{'Does the fuel gauge indicate an empty tank?'}).$
$ask(broken, fuel\_pump) \leftarrow$
 $\quad write(\text{'Does the fuel pump fail to feed any fuel?'}).$
$ask(broken, fuse) \leftarrow$
 $\quad write(\text{'Is fuse number 13 broken?'}).$
$ask(discharged, battery) \leftarrow$
 $\quad write(\text{'Is the battery voltage less than 11 volts?'}).$
$ask(broken, starting\_motor) \leftarrow$
 $\quad write(\text{'Is the starting motor silent?'}).$

% Explanations
$print\_proof(void).$
$print\_proof(X + Y) \leftarrow$
 $\quad print\_proof(X), nl, print\_proof(Y).$
$print\_proof(proof(X, void)) \leftarrow$
 $\quad write(X), nl.$
$print\_proof(proof(X, Y)) \leftarrow$
 $\quad Y \neq void, write(X), write(\text{' BECAUSE'}), nl,$
 $\quad print\_children(Y), nl, print\_proof(Y).$

$print\_children(proof(X, Y) + Z) \leftarrow$
 $\quad tab(8), write(X), write(\text{' AND'}), nl, print\_children(Z).$
$print\_children(proof(X, Y)) \leftarrow$
 $\quad tab(8), write(X), nl.$

% Knowledge-base
$malfunctions(X) \text{ if } needs(X, Y) \text{ and } malfunctions(Y).$
$malfunctions(X) \text{ if } symptom(Y, X) \text{ and not } indirect(X).$

$indirect(X) \text{ if } needs(X, Y) \text{ and } malfunctions(Y).$

$needs(car, ignition\_system) \text{ if true.}$
$needs(car, fuel\_system) \text{ if true.}$
$needs(car, electric\_system) \text{ if true.}$
$needs(ignition\_system, starting\_motor) \text{ if true.}$
$needs(ignition\_system, sparking\_plugs) \text{ if true.}$
$needs(electric\_system, fuse) \text{ if true.}$

*needs*(*electric_system, battery*) *if true.*
*needs*(*fuel_system, fuel_pump*) *if true.*
*needs*(*sparking_plugs, battery*) *if true.*
*needs*(*starting_motor, battery*) *if true.*
*needs*(*fuel_pump, fuel*) *if true.*

# Exercises

95. Improve the printing of the proof. For instance, instead of printing the whole proof at once the system may print the top of the proof and then let the user decide which branch to explain further. Another possibility is the use of natural language. Thus a possible interaction may look as follows:

> The car malfunctions BECAUSE
>> (1) the car needs the ignition-system AND
>> (2) the ignition-system malfunctions

> Explore? **2.**

> The ignition-system malfunctions BECAUSE
>> (1) the ignition-system needs the sparking-plugs AND
>> (2) the sparking-plugs malfunction

> Explore?

96. Write an inference engine which exploits probabilities of rules so that it becomes possible to draw conclusions together with some measurement of their belief.

97. Extend the shell so that the user may give the query "why?" in reply to the system's questions. In such cases the system should explain the conclusions possible if the user gives a particular answer to the query.

# Chapter 10

# Logic and Grammars

## 10.1 Context Free Grammars

A language can be viewed as a (usually infinite) set of *sentences/strings* of finite length. Such strings are composed of symbols of some alphabet (not necessarily the Latin alphabet). However, not all combinations of symbols are well-formed strings. Thus, when defining a new, or describing an existing language, be it a natural or an artificial one (for instance, a programming language), the specification should contain only well-formed strings. A number of formalisms have been suggested to facilitate such systematic descriptions of languages — most notably the formalism of Context Free Grammars (CFGs). This section contains a brief recapitulation of basic definitions from formal language theory (for details see e.g. [78]).

Formally a context free grammar is a 4-tuple $\langle N, T, P, S \rangle$, where $N$ and $T$ are finite, disjoint sets of identifiers called the nonterminal- and terminal-alphabets respectively. $P$ is a finite subset of $N \times (N \cup T)^*$. $S$ is a nonterminal symbol called the *start symbol*.

As usual $(N \cup T)^*$ denotes the set of all strings (sequences) of terminals and nonterminals. Traditionally the empty string is denoted by the symbol $\epsilon$. Elements of the relation $P$ are usually written in the form:

$$A \rightarrow B_1 \cdots B_n \quad \text{when } n > 0$$
$$A \rightarrow \epsilon \quad \text{when } n = 0$$

Each such an element is called a *production rule*. To distinguish between terminals and nonterminals the latter will be written within angle brackets. As an example, consider the production rule:

$$\langle statement \rangle \; \rightarrow \; \texttt{if} \; \langle condition \rangle \; \texttt{then} \; \langle statement \rangle$$

This rule states that a string is a statement if it begins with the symbol " `if` "
followed in turn by; a string which is a condition, the symbol "`then`" and finally
a string which is a statement. A CFG may contain several production rules with
the same left-hand side.

Now let $\alpha$, $\beta$ and $\gamma$ be arbitrary strings from the set $(\mathsf{N} \cup \mathsf{T})^*$. We say that
the string $\alpha\beta\gamma$ is *directly derivable* from $\alpha A\gamma$ iff $A \rightarrow \beta \in \mathsf{P}$. The relation is
denoted by $\alpha A\gamma \Rightarrow \alpha\beta\gamma$.

Let $\overset{*}{\Rightarrow}$ be the reflexive and transitive closure of the relation $\Rightarrow$ and let $\alpha$,
$\beta \in (\mathsf{N} \cup \mathsf{T})^*$. Then $\beta$ is said to be *derived* from $\alpha$ iff $\alpha \overset{*}{\Rightarrow} \beta$. The sequence
$\alpha \Rightarrow \cdots \Rightarrow \beta$ is called a *derivation*.

**Example 10.1** Consider the following set of production rules:

| | | |
|---|---|---|
| $\langle sentence \rangle$ | $\rightarrow$ | $\langle noun\text{-}phrase \rangle$ $\langle verb\text{-}phrase \rangle$ |
| $\langle noun\text{-}phrase \rangle$ | $\rightarrow$ | `the` $\langle noun \rangle$ |
| $\langle verb\text{-}phrase \rangle$ | $\rightarrow$ | `runs` |
| $\langle noun \rangle$ | $\rightarrow$ | `engine` |
| $\langle noun \rangle$ | $\rightarrow$ | `rabbit` |

For instance, $\langle sentence \rangle$ derives the string `the rabbit runs` since:

| | | |
|---|---|---|
| $\langle sentence \rangle$ | $\Rightarrow$ | $\langle noun\text{-}phrase \rangle$ $\langle verb\text{-}phrase \rangle$ |
| | $\Rightarrow$ | `the` $\langle noun \rangle$ $\langle verb\text{-}phrase \rangle$ |
| | $\Rightarrow$ | `the rabbit` $\langle verb\text{-}phrase \rangle$ |
| | $\Rightarrow$ | `the rabbit runs` |

∎

The *language* of a nonterminal $A$ is the set $\{\alpha \in \mathsf{T}^* \mid A \overset{*}{\Rightarrow} \alpha\}$. The language
of a CFG is the language of its start-symbol. However, no specific start-symbol
will be used below.

**Example 10.2** The language of $\langle sentence \rangle$ in the previous example is the set
{ `the rabbit runs` , `the engine runs` }.                                        ∎

The derivation of a terminal string $\alpha$ from a nonterminal $A$ can also be
described by means of a so called derivation-tree (or parse-tree) constructed as
follows:

- the root of the tree is labelled by $A$;

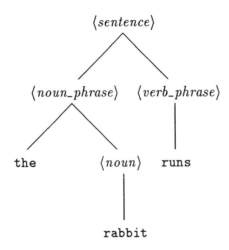

Figure 10.1: Derivation tree for CFG

- the leaves of the tree are terminals;

- concatenation of the leaves from left to right yields the string $\alpha$;

- an internal node $X$ has the children $X_1, \ldots, X_n$ (from left to right) only if there is a production rule of the form $X \to X_1 \ldots X_n$.

For instance, the derivation in Example 10.1 is contained in Figure 10.1. Notice that the derivation tree in general represents many derivations depending on what nonterminal one selects in each step. There is an analogy to the "independence of computation rule" which is reflected in the derivation- or proof-trees for definite programs (see Chapter 3).

By describing the two relations "$\Rightarrow$" and "$\overset{*}{\Rightarrow}$" it is possible to construct an "interpreter" for context free grammars, which behaves as a parser that recognizes strings defined by the grammar. To do this, terminals and nonterminals will be represented by constants, strings will be represented by lists and each production rule will be represented by the clause:

$prod\_rule(X, Y).$

where $X$ and $Y$ represent the left- and right-sides of the rule.

**Example 10.3** The CFG in Example 10.1 may be represented by the definite program:

$prod\_rule(sentence, [noun\_phrase, verb\_phrase])$.
$prod\_rule(noun\_phrase, [the, noun])$.
$prod\_rule(verb\_phrase, [runs])$.
$prod\_rule(noun, [rabbit])$.
$prod\_rule(noun, [engine])$.

It is now straightforward to define the relation "$\Rightarrow$":

$derives\_directly(X, Y) \leftarrow$
$\qquad append(Left, [Lhs], Right, X),$
$\qquad prod\_rule(Lhs, Rhs),$
$\qquad append(Left, Rhs, Right, Y).$

where $append/4$ is defined either using $append/3$:

$append(X, Y, Z, W) \leftarrow append(X, Y, Tmp), append(Tmp, Z, W).$

or more efficiently as:

$append([], [], X, X)$.
$append([], [Head|Y], Z, [Head|W]) \leftarrow append([], Y, Z, W).$
$append([Head|X], Y, Z, [Head|W]) \leftarrow append(X, Y, Z, W).$

Since "$\overset{*}{\Rightarrow}$" is the reflexive and transitive closure of "$\Rightarrow$" it is defined as follows (cf. Chapter 6):

$derives(X, X)$.
$derives(X, Z) \leftarrow$
$\qquad derives\_directly(X, Y),$
$\qquad derives(Y, Z).$

■

Presented with the goal $\leftarrow derives([sentence], X)$ Prolog succeeds with all possible (non-)terminal strings which may be derived from ⟨*sentence*⟩ including the two terminal strings $X = [the, rabbit, runs]$ and $X = [the, engine, runs]$.

As shown in the next section there are more efficient ways of describing context free languages than the program in Example 10.3. However, the specification works nicely as a provisional prototype and it has the following interesting properties:

- The program is extremely general — to describe another context free language it suffices to rewrite the definition of $prod\_rule/1$. The rest of the program may be used for any context free grammar.

- When comparing Example 10.3 and Examples 8.2 – 8.4 one realizes that the programs are very similar — $derives\_directly/2$ and $step/2$ both describe a relation between two expressions where the second is obtained by rewriting the first using some kind of rule. The relations $derives/2$ and $derivation/2$ are the reflexive and transitive closures of these relations. Finally, $prod\_rule/1$ and $clause/1$ are used to represent rules of each formalism.

- The program operates either as a *top-down* or a *bottom-up* parser depending on how the subgoals in the clauses are ordered. As presented in Example 10.3 it behaves as a traditional recursive descent parser under Prolog's computation rule, but if the subgoals in $derives/2$ and $derives\_directly/2$ are swapped the program behaves as a (quite inefficient) bottom-up parser.

## 10.2  Logic Grammars

Although Example 10.3 provides a very general specification of the derivability-relation for context free grammars it is a rather inefficient program. In this section a more direct approach is employed which avoids the extra interpreter-layer and results in parsers with better efficiency than the one above.

As already noticed there is a very close resemblance between logic programs and context free grammars. It is not hard to see that logic programs can be used directly to specify exactly the same language as a CFG, without resorting to explicit definitions of the two relations "$\Rightarrow$" and "$\overset{*}{\Rightarrow}$". Consider the following clause:

$$sentence(Z) \leftarrow append(X, Y, Z), noun\_phrase(X), verb\_phrase(Y).$$

Declaratively it reads "For any $X, Y, Z$ — $Z$ is a sentence if $X$ is a noun-phrase, $Y$ is a verb-phrase and $Z$ is the concatenation of $X$ and $Y$". By representing strings as lists of ground terms the whole grammar in Example 10.1 can be formulated as the following Prolog program:

**Example 10.4**

$$sentence(Z) \leftarrow append(X, Y, Z), noun\_phrase(X), verb\_phrase(Y).$$

$$noun\_phrase([the|X]) \leftarrow noun(X).$$

$$verb\_phrase([runs]).$$

$$noun([engine]).$$
$$noun([rabbit]).$$

$$append([\,], X, X).$$
$$append([X|Y], Z, [X|W]) \leftarrow append(Y, Z, W).$$

∎

The program is able to refute goals like:

$$\leftarrow sentence([the, rabbit, runs]).$$
$$\leftarrow sentence([the, X, runs])$$

In reply to the second goal Prolog would give the answers $X = rabbit$ and $X = engine$. It is even possible to give the goal:

$$\leftarrow sentence(X).$$

In this case Prolog returns all (=both) sentences of the language before going into an infinite loop (incidentally, this loop can be avoided by moving the call to $append/3$ to the very end of the first clause).

Unfortunately the program in Example 10.4 is also rather inefficient. The $append/3$ procedure will blindly generate all partitions of the list and it may take some time to find the correct splitting (at least in the case when the list is very long). To remedy this problem the concept of *difference lists* may be used.

Using difference lists the first clause of Example 10.4 can be written as:

$$sentence(X_0 - X_2) \leftarrow noun\_phrase(X_0 - X_1), verb\_phrase(X_1 - X_2).$$

Declaratively it reads — "The difference between $X_0$ and $X_2$ is a sentence if the difference between $X_0$ and $X_1$ is a noun-phrase and the difference between $X_1$ and $X_2$ is a verb-phrase". The statement is evidently true — consider the string:

$$\underbrace{\overbrace{x_1 \ldots x_i\, x_{i+1} \ldots x_j\, \underbrace{x_{j+1} \ldots x_k}_{X_2}}^{X_1}}_{X_0}$$

If the difference between $X_1$ and $X_2$ (that is, the string $x_{i+1} \ldots x_j$) is a verb-phrase and the difference between $X_0$ and $X_1$ (the string $x_1 \ldots x_i$) is a noun-phrase then the string $x_1 \ldots x_i x_{i+1} \ldots x_j$ (that is the difference between $X_0$ and $X_2$) is a sentence.

Using this approach, Example 10.4 can be reformulated as follows:

**Example 10.5**

$$sentence(X_0 - X_2) \leftarrow noun\_phrase(X_0 - X_1), verb\_phrase(X_1 - X_2).$$

$$noun\_phrase(X_0 - X_2) \leftarrow diff(X_0, X_1, [the]), noun(X_1 - X_2).$$

$$verb\_phrase(X_0 - X_1) \leftarrow diff(X_0, X_1, [runs]).$$

$$noun(X_0 - X_1) \leftarrow diff(X_0, X_1, [engine]).$$
$$noun(X_0 - X_1) \leftarrow diff(X_0, X_1, [rabbits]).$$

$$diff([X|Y], Y, [X]).$$

∎

Although the intended interpretation of the functor $-/2$ is a function which produces the difference between two lists, the Prolog interpreter has no knowledge about this particular interpretation. As a consequence the goal:

$$\leftarrow sentence([the, rabbit, runs]).$$

does not succeed (simply because $[the, rabbit, runs]$ does not unify with the term $X_0 - X_2$). In order to get a positive answer the goal must contain, as its argument, a difference list. For instance:

$$\leftarrow sentence([the, rabbit, runs] - []).$$

Intuitively, this goal has the same declarative reading as the previous one since the difference of the list denoted by $[the, rabbit, runs]$ and the empty list is equivalent to the intended meaning of the term $[the, rabbit, runs]$.

Other examples of goals which succeed are:

$$\leftarrow sentence([the, rabbit, runs|X] - X).$$
$$\leftarrow sentence([the, rabbit, runs, quickly] - [quickly]).$$
$$\leftarrow sentence(X - []).$$
$$\leftarrow sentence(X).$$

For instance, the third goal produces two answers. On the one hand $X = [the, rabbit, runs]$ and on the other hand $X = [the, engine, runs]$.

Notice the way terminals of the grammar are treated — an auxiliary predicate $diff/3$ is used to check if the difference of the first and second argument is identical to the one-element list containing the terminal. Actually, this auxiliary predicate can be done away with by performing some *partial evaluation* of the program — consider the clause:[1]

$$noun\_phrase(X_0 - X_2) \leftarrow diff(X_0, X_1, [the]), noun(X_1 - X_2).$$

Now "evaluate" the leftmost atom in the body — unifying $diff(X_0, X_1, [the])$ with the clause $diff([X|Y], Y, [X])$ yields the mgu:

$$\{X_0/[the|X_1], X/the, Y/X_1\}$$

Replacing the subgoal by the body of the clause (which is empty) and applying the mgu to the whole clause yields the new clause:

$$noun\_phrase([the|X_1] - X_2) \leftarrow noun(X_1 - X_2).$$

Partial evaluation of all the other clauses in Example 10.5 yields a new program which does not make use of the predicate $diff/3$:

**Example 10.6**

$$sentence(X_0 - X_2) \leftarrow noun\_phrase(X_0 - X_1), verb\_phrase(X_1 - X_2).$$

$$noun\_phrase([the|X_1] - X_2) \leftarrow noun(X_1 - X_2).$$

$$verb\_phrase([runs|X_1] - X_1).$$

$$noun([engine|X_1] - X_1).$$
$$noun([rabbit|X_1] - X_1).$$

∎

---

[1]Partial evaluation is a simple but yet powerful technique for transforming (logic) programs. Roughly speaking the method can be formulated as follows — let $C$ be the clause:

$$A_0 \leftarrow A_1, \ldots, A_{i-1}, A_i, A_{i+1}, \ldots, A_n$$

and let:

$$B_0 \leftarrow B_1, \ldots, B_m$$

be a clause whose head unifies with $A_i$ (with the mgu $\theta$). Then $C$ may be replaced by the new clause:

$$(A_0 \leftarrow A_1, \ldots, A_{i-1}, B_1, \ldots, B_m, A_{i+1}, \ldots, A_n)\theta$$

It is easy to prove that this transformation does not add to the set of formulas which follow logically from the program. That is, the transformation is "sound". Under certain restrictions one can also prove that the technique is "complete" in the sense that the set of all logical consequences of the old program is exactly the same as the set of logical consequences of the new program.

## 10.3   Context Dependent Languages

Although CFGs are often used to specify the syntax of programming languages
they have many limitations — in particular, very few useful languages are actually context free. That is, it is not possible to specify the language by means
of a CFG. A very simple example is the language which contains only strings of
the form a$^n$ b$^n$ c$^n$ where $n \in \{0, 1, 2, \ldots\}$ — that is, all strings which are built
from equal number of a's, b's and c's. Consider the grammar:

$$
\begin{aligned}
\langle abc \rangle &\rightarrow \langle a \rangle \, \langle b \rangle \, \langle c \rangle \\
\langle a \rangle &\rightarrow \epsilon \\
\langle a \rangle &\rightarrow \text{a} \, \langle a \rangle \\
\langle b \rangle &\rightarrow \epsilon \\
\langle b \rangle &\rightarrow \text{b} \, \langle b \rangle \\
\langle c \rangle &\rightarrow \epsilon \\
\langle c \rangle &\rightarrow \text{c} \, \langle c \rangle
\end{aligned}
$$

The language of $\langle abc \rangle$ certainly contains the language a$^n$ b$^n$ c$^n$ but also other
strings — like abbccc . To describe languages like a$^n$ b$^n$ c$^n$ more powerful
formalisms are called for. For instance, the property of being a string in the
language a$^n$ b$^n$ c$^n$ is described by the following definite program:

**Example 10.7**

$$abc(X_0 - X_3) \leftarrow a(N, X_0 - X_1), b(N, X_1 - X_2), c(N, X_2 - X_3).$$

$$a(0, X_0 - X_0).$$
$$a(s(N), [a|X_1] - X_2) \leftarrow a(N, X_1 - X_2).$$

$$b(0, X_0 - X_0).$$
$$b(s(N), [b|X_1] - X_2) \leftarrow b(N, X_1 - X_2).$$

$$c(0, X_0 - X_0).$$
$$c(s(N), [c|X_1] - X_2) \leftarrow c(N, X_1 - X_2).$$

∎

Here the first clause reads "The string $X_0 - X_3$ is a member of a$^n$ b$^n$ c$^n$ if
$X_0 - X_1$ is a string of $N$ a's and $X_1 - X_2$ is a string of $N$ b's and $X_2 - X_3$ is
a string of $N$ c's". The restriction to equal number of a's, b's and c's is thus
obtained through the extra argument of the predicate symbols $a/2$, $b/2$ and $c/2$.

As an additional example consider the following excerpt from a natural language description:

$$\begin{array}{lcl}
\langle sentence \rangle & \rightarrow & \langle noun\text{-}phrase \rangle \; \langle verb \rangle \\
\langle noun\text{-}phrase \rangle & \rightarrow & \langle pronoun \rangle \\
\langle noun\text{-}phrase \rangle & \rightarrow & \text{the } \langle noun \rangle \\
\langle noun \rangle & \rightarrow & \text{rabbit} \\
\langle noun \rangle & \rightarrow & \text{rabbits} \\
\langle pronoun \rangle & \rightarrow & \text{it} \\
\langle pronoun \rangle & \rightarrow & \text{they} \\
\langle verb \rangle & \rightarrow & \text{runs} \\
\langle verb \rangle & \rightarrow & \text{run}
\end{array}$$

Unfortunately the language of $\langle sentence \rangle$ includes strings like "the rabbit run", "they runs" and "it run" — ill-formed strings which should not be part of the language. Again, this can be fixed reasonably easy by defining the grammar by means of a logic program and by adding extra arguments to the predicate symbols which correspond to nonterminals:

## Example 10.8

$$sentence(X_0 - X_2) \leftarrow noun\_phrase(Y, X_0 - X_1), verb(Y, X_1 - X_2).$$

$$noun\_phrase(Y, X_0 - X_1) \leftarrow pronoun(Y, X_0 - X_1).$$
$$noun\_phrase(Y, X_0 - X_2) \leftarrow diff(X_0, X_1, [the]), noun(Y, X_1 - X_2).$$

$$noun(singular(3), X_0 - X_1) \leftarrow diff(X_0, X_1, [rabbit]).$$
$$noun(plural(3), X_0 - X_1) \leftarrow diff(X_0, X_1, [rabbits]).$$

$$pronoun(singular(3), X_0 - X_1) \leftarrow diff(X_0, X_1, [it]).$$
$$pronoun(plural(3), X_0 - X_1) \leftarrow diff(X_0, X_1, [they]).$$

$$verb(plural(Y), X_0 - X_1) \leftarrow diff(X_0, X_1, [run]).$$
$$verb(singular(3), X_0 - X_1) \leftarrow diff(X_0, X_1, [runs]).$$

∎

Now the goal:

$$\leftarrow sentence([the, rabbits, runs] - []).$$

reduces to:

$$\leftarrow noun\_phrase(Y, [the, rabbits, runs] - X_1), verb(Y, X_1 - []).$$

The leftmost goal eventually succeeds with the bindings $Y = plural(3)$ and $X_1 = [runs]$ but the remaining goal:

$$\leftarrow verb(plural(3), [runs] - [\,]).$$

fails. Thus, the string is not included in the language defined by the program.

The extra arguments added to some predicate symbols serve essentially two purposes — as demonstrated above, they can be used to propagate constraints between subgoals corresponding to nonterminals of the grammar and they may also be used to construct some alternative (structured) representation of the string being analysed. For instance, as a parse-tree or some other form of intermediate code.

## 10.4 Definite Clause Grammars (DCGs)

Many Prolog systems employ special syntax for language specifications. When such a description is encountered, the system automatically compiles it into a Prolog program. Such specifications are called *Definite Clause Grammars* (DCGs). There are two possible views of such grammars — either they are viewed simply as a "syntactic sugar" for Prolog. That is, the grammar is seen as a convenient shorthand for a Prolog program. Alternatively they are viewed as an independent formalism on its own merits. In this book the latter view is adopted.

Assume that an alphabet similar to that in Chapter 1 is given. Then a DCG is a triple $\langle \mathsf{N}, \mathsf{T}, \mathsf{P} \rangle$ where:

- $\mathsf{N}$ is a possibly infinite set of atoms;

- $\mathsf{T}$ is a possibly infinite set of terms;

- $\mathsf{P} \subseteq \mathsf{N} \times (\mathsf{N} \cup \mathsf{T})^*$ is a finite set of (production) rules.

By analogy to CFGs $\mathsf{N}$ and $\mathsf{T}$ are assumed to be disjoint and are called *nonterminals* and *terminals* respectively.

DCGs are generalizations of CFGs and it is therefore possible to generalize the concept of direct derivability. Let $\alpha$, $\alpha'$, $\beta \in (\mathsf{N} \cup \mathsf{T})^*$ and let $p(t_1, \ldots, t_n) \to \beta \in \mathsf{P}$ (where variables are renamed so that no name clashes occur with variables in $\alpha$). Then $\alpha'$ is directly derivable from $\alpha$ iff:

- $\alpha$ is of the form $\alpha_1 p(s_1, \ldots, s_n)\alpha_2$;

- $p(t_1, \ldots, t_n)$ and $p(s_1, \ldots, s_n)$ unify with mgu $\theta$;

- $\alpha'$ is of the form $(\alpha_1 \beta \alpha_2)\theta$.

Also the concept of *derivation* is a generalization of the CFG-counterpart. The derivability-relation for DCGs is the reflexive and transitive closure of the direct-derivability-relation. A string of terminals $\beta \in \mathbf{T}^*$ is in the language of $A \in \mathbf{N}$ iff $\langle A; \beta \rangle$ is in the derivability-relation.

To illustrate these notions consider the following example:

### Example 10.9

$$\begin{array}{rcl}
sentence(s(X,Y)) & \rightarrow & np(X,N)\ vp(Y,N)\\
np(john, singular(3)) & \rightarrow & \texttt{john}\\
np(they, plural(3)) & \rightarrow & \texttt{they}\\
vp(run, plural(X)) & \rightarrow & \texttt{run}\\
vp(runs, singular(3)) & \rightarrow & \texttt{runs}
\end{array}$$

∎

From the nonterminal $sentence(X)$ the following derivation may be constructed:

$$\begin{array}{rcl}
sentence(X) & \Rightarrow & np(X_0, N_0)\ vp(Y_0, N_0)\\
& \Rightarrow & \texttt{john}\ vp(Y_0, singular(3))\\
& \Rightarrow & \texttt{john runs}
\end{array}$$

Thus, the string "`john runs`" is in the language of $sentence(X)$. But more than that, the mgu's of the derivation together produce a binding for the variables used in the derivation — in the first step $X$ is bound to the term $s(X_0, Y_0)$. Later on $X_0$ is bound to *john* and $Y_0$ is bound to *runs*. However, this derivation is not the only one starting with the nonterminal $sentence(X)$. For instance, in step two above the second nonterminal may be selected instead, and in the same step the third production rule may be used instead of the second. It turns out that the choice of nonterminal is of no importance, but that the choice of production rule is. This is yet another similarity between DCGs and logic programs. The choice of nonterminal corresponds to the selection of subgoal. In fact, the collection of all derivations starting with a nonterminal under a fixed "computation rule" can be depicted as an "SLD-tree". For instance, all possible derivations originating from the nonterminal $sentence(X)$ (where the left-most nonterminal is always selected) is depicted in Figure 10.2.

As discussed above many Prolog systems support usage of DCGs by automatically translating them into Prolog programs. In order to discuss combining DCGs and Prolog we need to settle some notational conventions for writing DCGs:

- since Prolog systems cannot tell terms from atoms, terminals are enclosed by list-brackets;

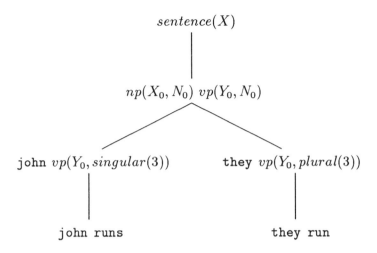

**Figure 10.2: "SLD-tree" for DCGs**

- nonterminals are written as ordinary compound terms or constants except that they are not allowed to use certain reserved symbols (e.g. ./2) as principal functors;

- the functor ','/2 (comma) separates terminals and nonterminals in the right-hand side of rules;

- the functor '-->'/2 separates the left- and right-hand sides of a production rule;

- the empty string is denoted by the empty list.

This means that DCGs can be represented as terms. For instance, the rule:

$$np(X) \rightarrow \textbf{the}\ noun(X)$$

will be written as the term:

$$np(X) \texttt{ --> } [the], noun(X).$$

or using standard syntax:

$$\texttt{'-->'}(np(X), \texttt{','}([the], noun(X)))$$

In addition Prolog often allows special treatment of nonterminals which always derive the empty string. Consider the language where each string consists of an even number of a's followed by the same number of b's in turn followed by the same number of c's. This language can be specified as follows using DCGs with Prolog syntax:

**Example 10.10**

$$
\begin{array}{lll}
abc & \texttt{-->} & a(N), b(N), c(N), even(N). \\
a(0) & \texttt{-->} & []. \\
a(s(N)) & \texttt{-->} & [a], a(N). \\
b(0) & \texttt{-->} & []. \\
b(s(N)) & \texttt{-->} & [b], b(N). \\
c(0) & \texttt{-->} & []. \\
c(s(N)) & \texttt{-->} & [c], c(N). \\
even(0) & \texttt{-->} & []. \\
even(s(s(N))) & \texttt{-->} & even(N).
\end{array}
$$

&#9632;

In this example the occurrence of $even(N)$ in the first rule always derives the empty string. In this respect it can be removed from the rule. However, the primary function of this nonterminal is to constrain bindings of $N$ to terms representing even numbers. That is, it not only defines the language consisting solely of the empty string but also defines a relation (in this case the property of being an even natural number). To distinguish such nonterminals from those which derive nonempty strings they are written within curly brackets, and the definition of the relation is written directly in Prolog. Thus, in Prolog it is possible to write the rule:

$$abc \texttt{-->} a(N), b(N), c(N), \{even(N)\}.$$

together with the definite program:

$$
\begin{array}{l}
even(0). \\
even(s(s(N))) \leftarrow even(N).
\end{array}
$$

replacing the first and the two final production rules of the DCG in Example 10.10. It should be noted that the notation $\{even(N)\}$ is not allowed in some Prolog systems. In fact, the notation is merely a syntactic sugar for the term '{}'($even(N)$). That is, a compound, unary term whose principal functor is '{}'/1.

Now since calls to Prolog may be inserted into a DCG it is also possible to utilize the built-in predicates of Prolog in a DCG. This is illustrated by the following example, which is a grammar that recognizes arithmetic expressions but, more than that, also computes the value of the expression:

**Example 10.11**

$$expr(X) \quad \text{-->} \quad term(Y), [+], expr(Z), \{X \ is \ Y + Z\}.$$
$$expr(X) \quad \text{-->} \quad term(Y), [-], expr(Z), \{X \ is \ Y - Z\}.$$
$$expr(X) \quad \text{-->} \quad term(X).$$
$$term(X) \quad \text{-->} \quad factor(Y), [*], term(Z), \{X \ is \ Y * Z\}.$$
$$term(X) \quad \text{-->} \quad factor(Y), [/], term(Z), \{X \ is \ Y/Z\}.$$
$$term(X) \quad \text{-->} \quad factor(X).$$
$$factor(X) \quad \text{-->} \quad [X], \{integer(X)\}.$$

■

For instance, the last rule states that any string which consists of a single terminal which is an integer is a factor with the same value as the terminal. Similarly, the first rule states that any string which starts with a term of value $Y$ followed by "+" followed by an expression of value $Z$ is an expression of value $Y + Z$.

As already discussed, when a DCG is loaded into a Prolog system it is usually compiled into a Prolog program similar in style to those in Section 10.2. This transformation is quite simple and it is discussed in the next section. Some implementations of Prolog do not include this feature. Fortunately, it is not very hard to write an *interpreter* for DCGs similar to the Prolog-interpreter in Example 8.7.

For this purpose, view a DCG-rule as a binary fact with predicate symbol '-->'/2 where the first and second arguments consist of the left- and right-side of the production rule. The relationship between strings of terminals/nonterminals and the derivable terminal strings can then be defined as follows:

**Example 10.12**

$$derives([], S - S).$$
$$derives([X], [X|S] - S).$$
$$derives(\{X\}, S - S) \leftarrow$$
$$\quad call(X).$$
$$derives((X, Y), S_0 - S_2) \leftarrow$$
$$\quad derives(X, S_0 - S_1), derives(Y, S_1 - S_2).$$
$$derives(X, S_0 - S_1) \leftarrow$$
$$\quad (X \text{ -->} Y), derives(Y, S_0 - S_1).$$

■

The interpreter is surprisingly simple. Declaratively the clauses state the following:

- the empty string derives itself. That is, the difference between $S$ and $S$ for any $S$;

- the second clause says that the terminal string $[X]$ derives itself. That is, the difference between $[X|S]$ and $S$ for any $S$;

- a nonterminal $X$ in curly brackets derives the empty string if the goal $\leftarrow X$ has a refutation;

- if the string $X$ derives the terminal string $S_0 - S_1$ and the string $Y$ derives the terminal string $S_1 - S_2$ then the string $(X, Y)$ (that is, $Y$ appended to $X$) derives the terminal string $S_0 - S_2$;

- if there is a rule $(X \dashrightarrow Y)$ such that $Y$ derives the terminal string $S_0 - S_1$ then the nonterminal $X$ derives the same terminal string.

For instance, in the presence of the DCG of Example 10.9 the goal:

$$\leftarrow derives(sentence(X), [john, runs] - [\,]).$$

succeeds with answer $X = s(john, runs)$. Similarly the grammar in Example 10.11 and the goal:

$$\leftarrow derives(expr(X), [2, +, 3, *, 4] - [\,]).$$

result in the answer $X = 14$.


# 10.5    Compilation of DCGs into Prolog

The standard treatment of DCGs in most Prolog systems is to compile them directly into Prolog clauses. Since each production rule translates into one clause, the transformation is relatively simple. The clause obtained as a result of the transformations described below may differ slightly from what is obtained in some Prolog systems but the principle is the same.

The general idea is the following — consider a production rule of the form:

$$p(t_1, \ldots, t_n) \dashrightarrow T_1, \ldots, T_m$$

Assume that $X_0, \ldots, X_m$ are distinct variables which do not appear in the rule. Then the rule translates into the clause:

$$p(t_1, \ldots, t_n, X_0, X_m) \leftarrow T_1', \ldots, T_m'.$$

where each $T_i'$, $(1 \leq i \leq m)$, is of the form:

$$q(s_1, \ldots, s_j, X_{i-1}, X_i) \quad \text{if } T_i \text{ is of the form} \quad q(s_1, \ldots, s_j)$$
$$diff(X_{i-1}, X_i, [X]) \quad \text{if } T_i \text{ is of the form} \quad [X]$$
$$T, X_{i-1} = X_i \quad \text{if } T_i \text{ is of the form} \quad \{T\}$$
$$X_{i-1} = X_i \quad \text{if } T_i \text{ is of the form} \quad []$$

For instance, the first rule of Example 10.11 is transformed as follows:

$$expr(X) \texttt{ --> } \qquad\qquad\qquad expr(X, X_0, X_4) \leftarrow$$
$$term(Y), \qquad\qquad\qquad\qquad term(Y, X_0, X_1),$$
$$[+], \qquad\qquad \Rightarrow \qquad\qquad diff(X_1, X_2, [+]),$$
$$expr(Z), \qquad\qquad\qquad\qquad expr(Z, X_2, X_3),$$
$$\{X \text{ is } Y + Z\}. \qquad\qquad\qquad X \text{ is } Y + Z, X_3 = X_4.$$

Some improvements can be made to the final result — in particular, subgoals of the form $X = Y$ may be omitted if all occurrences of $Y$ are replaced by the variable $X$. This means that the result obtained above can be simplified into:

$$expr(X, X_0, X_3) \leftarrow$$
$$term(Y, X_0, X_1),$$
$$diff(X_1, X_2, [+]),$$
$$expr(Z, X_2, X_3),$$
$$X \text{ is } Y + Z.$$

The final program must be extended by the definition of $diff/3$. When all rules are translated in this way, the resulting program can be used to refute goals like $\leftarrow expr(X, [2, +, 3, *, 4], [])$, with the expected answer $X = 14$.

A CFG (which is a special case of a DCG) like the one in Example 10.1 translates into the program of Example 10.5 except that arguments of the form $X - Y$ are split into two arguments and that the names of the variables may differ.

**Example 10.13** As a final example the translation of Example 10.9 results in the following program:

$$sentence(s(X, Y), X_0, X_2) \leftarrow$$
$$np(X, N, X_0, X_1),$$
$$vp(Y, N, X_1, X_2).$$

$$np(john, singular(3), X_0, X_1) \leftarrow$$
$$diff(X_0, X_1, [john]).$$
$$np(they, plural(3), X_0, X_1) \leftarrow$$
$$diff(X_0, X_1, [they]).$$

$$vp(run, plural(X), X_0, X_1) \leftarrow$$
$$diff(X_0, X_1, [run]).$$
$$vp(runs, singular(3), X_0, X_1) \leftarrow$$
$$diff(X_0, X_1, [runs]).$$

$$diff([X|Y], Y, [X]).$$

Given the goal $\leftarrow sentence(X, [john, runs], [])$ Prolog replies with the answer $X = s(john, runs)$.  ∎

## Exercises

98. Write a DCG which describes the language of strings of octal numbers. Extend the grammar so that the decimal value of the string is returned. For instance, the goal $\leftarrow octal(X, [4, 6], [])$ should succeed with $X = 38$.

99. Write a Prolog program or a DCG which accepts strings in the language $a^m\ b^n\ c^m\ d^n$ , $(n, m \geq 0)$.

100. Consider the following CFG:

$$\langle bleat \rangle \quad \rightarrow \quad b\ \langle aaa \rangle$$
$$\langle aaa \rangle \quad \rightarrow \quad a$$
$$\langle aaa \rangle \quad \rightarrow \quad a\ \langle aaa \rangle$$

Describe the same language using DCG notation. Then "compile" the specification into a Prolog program and write an SLD-refutation which proves that the string "b a a" is in the language of $\langle bleat \rangle$ .

101. Explain the usage of the following DCG:

$$x([], X, X) \qquad \text{-->} \quad [].$$
$$x([X|Y], Z, [X|W]) \quad \text{-->} \quad x(Y, Z, W).$$

102. Write an interface to a database that facilitates communication in natural language.

103. Write a DCG which describes a subset of some Pascal-like programming language. The grammar should return some structured representation of the accepted programs suitable e.g. for an interpreter.

# Chapter 11

---

# Searching in a State-Space

## 11.1   State-Graphs and Transitions

Many problems in computer science can be formulated as a possibly infinite set $S$ of *states* and a binary transition-relation $T$ over this *state-space*. Given some *start*-state $s \in S$ and a set $G \subseteq S$ of *goal*-states such problems consist in determining whether there exists a sequence:

$$\langle s; s_1 \rangle \langle s_1; s_2 \rangle \langle s_2; s_3 \rangle \cdots \langle s_{n-1}; s_n \rangle \in T^*$$

such that $s_n \in G$. More informally the states can be seen as nodes in a graph whose edges represent the pairs in the transition-relation. Then the problem reduces to that of finding a path from the start-state to one of the goal-states.

Example 6.7 embodies an instance of such a problem — the state-space consisted of a finite set of states named by $a$, $b$, $c$, $d$, $e$, $f$ and $g$. The predicate symbol $edge/2$ was used to describe the transition relation and $path/2$ described the transitive and reflexive closure of the transition relation. Hence, the existence of a path from, for instance, the state $a$ to $e$ is checked by giving the goal $\leftarrow path(a, e)$. Now this is by no means the only example of such a problem. The following ones are all examples of similar "worlds":

- *Planning* amounts to finding a sequence of worlds where the initial world is transformed into some desired final world. For instance, the initial world may consist of a robot and some pieces of material. The objective is to find a world where the pieces are assembled in some desirable way. Here the description of the world are states and the transformations which transform one world to another can be seen as a transition relation.

- The derivation of a string of terminals $\alpha$ from a nonterminal $A$ can also be viewed in this way. The state-space consists of all strings of terminals/nonterminals. The string $A$ is the start-state and $\alpha$ the goal-state. The relation "$\Rightarrow$" is the transition relation and the problem amounts to finding a sequence $A \Rightarrow \cdots \Rightarrow \alpha$.

- Also SLD-derivations may be formulated in this way — the states are goals and the transition relation consists of the SLD-resolution principle which produces a goal $G_{i+1}$ out of another goal $G_i$ and some program clause $C_i$. In most cases the start-state is the initial goal and the goal-state is the empty goal.

Consider the following two clauses of Example 6.7 again:

$$path(X, X).$$
$$path(X, Z) \leftarrow edge(X, Y), path(Y, Z).$$

Operationally the second clause reads as follows if Prolog's computation rule is employed — "To find a path from $X$ to $Z$, first find an edge from $X$ to $Y$ and then find a path from $Y$ to $Z$". That is, first try to find a node adjacent to the start-state, and then try to find a path from the new node to the goal-state. In other words, the search proceeds in a forward direction — from the start-state to the goal-state. However, it is easy to modify the program to search in the opposite direction assuming that Prolog's computation rule is used — simply rewrite the second clause as:

$$path(X, Z) \leftarrow edge(Y, Z), path(X, Y).$$

The decision whether to search in a forward or backward direction depends on what the search space looks like. Such considerations will not be discussed here, but the reader is referred, for instance, to any book on A.I.

The $path/2$-program above does not work without modifications if there is more than one goal-state. For instance, if both $f$ and $g$ are goal-states one has to give two goals. An alternative solution is to extend the program with the property of being a goal-state:

$$goal\_state(f).$$
$$goal\_state(g).$$

Now the problem of finding a path from $a$ to one of the goal-states reduces to finding a refutation of the goal:

$$\leftarrow path(a, X), goal\_state(X).$$

The program above can be simplified if the goal-state is known in advance. In this case it is not necessary to use the second argument of *path*/2. Instead the program may be simplified into:

$$path(\ulcorner goal \urcorner).$$
$$path(X) \leftarrow edge(X, Y), path(Y).$$

where $\ulcorner goal \urcorner$ is a term representing the goal-state (if there are several goal-states there will be one such fact for each state).

## 11.2 Loop Detection

One problem mentioned in connection with Example 6.7, appears when the graph defined by the transition relation is cyclic. Consider the program:

**Example 11.1**

$$path(X, X).$$
$$path(X, Z) \leftarrow edge(X, Y), path(Y, Z).$$

$$edge(a, b). \quad edge(b, a). \quad edge(a, c).$$
$$edge(b, d). \quad edge(b, e). \quad edge(c, e).$$
$$edge(d, f). \quad edge(e, f). \quad edge(e, g).$$

∎

As pointed out in Chapter 6 the program may go into an infinite loop for certain goals — from state $a$ it is possible to go to state $b$ and from this state it is possible to go back to state $a$ via the cycle in the transition relation. One simple solution to such problems is to keep a *log* of all states already visited. Before moving to a new state it should be checked that the new state has not already been visited. This extension can be made rather easily to the program above:

**Example 11.2**

$$path(X, Y) \leftarrow$$
$$\qquad path(X, Y, [X]).$$

$$path(X, X, \mathit{Visited}).$$
$$path(X, Z, \mathit{Visited}) \leftarrow$$
$$\qquad edge(X, Y),$$
$$\qquad not\ member(Y, \mathit{Visited}),$$
$$\qquad path(Y, Z, [Y \mid \mathit{Visited}]).$$

$member(X, [X|Y])$.
$member(X, [Y|Z]) \leftarrow$
$\qquad member(X, Z)$.

■

Declaratively the recursive clause of $path/3$ says that — "there is a path from $X$ to $Z$ if there is an edge from $X$ to $Y$ and a path from $Y$ to $Z$ such that $Y$ has not already been visited".

At first glance the solution may look a bit inelegant and there certainly *are* more sophisticated solutions around. However, carrying the log around is not such a bad thing after all — in many problems similar to the one above, it is not sufficient just to answer "yes" or "no" to the question of whether there is a path between two states. Often it is necessary that the actual path is returned as an answer to the goal. As an example, it is not much use to know that there *is* a plan which assembles some pieces of material into a gadget; in general one wants to see the actual plan. This extension can be implemented through the following modification of Example 11.2:

**Example 11.3**

$path(X, Y, Path) \leftarrow$
$\qquad path(X, Y, [X], Path)$.

$path(X, X, Visited, Visited)$.
$path(X, Z, Visited, Path) \leftarrow$
$\qquad edge(X, Y)$,
$\qquad not\ member(Y, Visited)$,
$\qquad path(Y, Z, [Y|Visited], Path)$.

■

With these modifications the goal $\leftarrow path(a, d, X)$ succeeds with the answer $X = [d, b, a]$ which says that the path from $a$ to $d$ goes via the intermediate state $b$. Intuitively, $path(A, B, C, D)$ can be interpreted as follows — "The difference between $D$ and $C$ constitutes a path from $A$ to $B$".

## 11.3   Water-Jug Problem (Extended Example)

The discussion above will be illustrated with the well-known water-jug problem often encountered in the A.I.-literature. The problem is formulated thus:

Two water jugs are given, a 4-gallon and a 3-gallon jug. Neither of them has any type of marking on it. There is an infinite supply of water (a tap?) nearby. How can you get exactly 2 gallons of water into the 4-gallon jug? Initially both jugs are empty.

The problem can obviously be described as a state-space traversal — a state is described by a pair $\langle x; y \rangle$ where $x$ represents the amount of water in the 4-gallon jug and $y$ represents the amount of water in the 3-gallon jug. The start-state then is $\langle 0; 0 \rangle$ and the goal-state is any pair where the first component equals 2. First of all some transformations between states must be formulated. The following is by no means a complete set of transformations but it turns out that there is no need for additional ones:

- empty the 4-gallon jug if it is not already empty;

- empty the 3-gallon jug if it is not already empty;

- fill up the 4-gallon jug if it is not already full;

- fill up the 3-gallon jug if it is not already full;

- if there is enough water in the 3-gallon jug, use it to fill up the 4-gallon jug until it is full;

- if there is enough water in the 4-gallon jug, use it to fill up the 3-gallon jug until it is full;

- if there is room in the 4-gallon jug, pour all water from the 3-gallon jug into it;

- if there is room in the 3-gallon jug, pour all water from the 4-gallon jug into it.

It is now possible to express these actions as a binary relation between two states. The binary functor :/2 (written in infix notation) is used to represent a pair:

$$action(X : Y, 0 : Y) \leftarrow X > 0.$$
$$action(X : Y, X : 0) \leftarrow Y > 0.$$
$$action(X : Y, 4 : Y) \leftarrow X < 4.$$
$$action(X : Y, X : 3) \leftarrow Y < 3.$$
$$action(X : Y, 4 : Z) \leftarrow X < 4, Z \text{ is } Y - (4 - X), Z \geq 0.$$
$$action(X : Y, Z : 3) \leftarrow Y < 3, Z \text{ is } X - (3 - Y), Z \geq 0.$$
$$action(X : Y, Z : 0) \leftarrow Y > 0, Z \text{ is } X + Y, Z \leq 4.$$
$$action(X : Y, 0 : Z) \leftarrow X > 0, Z \text{ is } X + Y, Z \leq 3.$$

The definition of a path is based on the program in Example 11.3. However, since the goal-state is known to be $\langle 2; X \rangle$ for any value of $X$ (or at least $0 \leq X \leq 3$) there is no need for the second argument of $path/4$. With some minor additional changes the final version looks as follows:

$path(X) \leftarrow$
$\qquad path(0 : 0, [0 : 0], X).$

$path(2 : X, Visited, Visited).$
$path(State, Visited, Path) \leftarrow$
$\qquad action(State, NewState),$
$\qquad not\ member(NewState, Visited),$
$\qquad path(NewState, [NewState|Visited], Path).$

$member(X, [X|Y]).$
$member(X, [Y|Z]) \leftarrow$
$\qquad member(X, Z).$

Given this program and the goal $\leftarrow path(X)$ several answers are obtained some of which are rather naive. One answer is $X = [2 : 0,0 : 2,4 : 2,3 : 3,3 : 0,0 : 3,0 : 0]$. That is, first fill the 3-gallon jug and pour this water into the 4-gallon jug. Then the 3-gallon jug is filled again, and the 4-gallon jug is filled with water from the 3-gallon jug. The last actions are to empty the 4-gallon jug and then pour the content of the 3-gallon jug into it. Another answer is $X = [2 : 0,0 : 2,4 : 2,3 : 3,3 : 0,0 : 3,4 : 3,4 : 0,0 : 0]$. In all 27 answers are produced.

## 11.4   Blocks World (Extended Example)

A similar problem is the so-called *blocks world*. Consider a table with three distinct positions. On the table are a number of blocks which may be stacked on top of each other. The aim is to move the blocks from a given start-state to a goal-state. Only blocks which are free (that is, with no other block on top of them) can be moved.

The first step towards a program that solves such problems is to agree on some representation of the state. A reasonable solution is to use a ternary functor $state/3$ to represent the three positions of the table. Furthermore, use the constant *table* to denote the table. Finally represent by $on(X, Y)$ the fact that $X$ is positioned on top of $Y$. That is, $state(on(c, on(b, on(a, table))), table, table)$ represents the state:

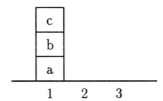

The following are possible actions to transform the state:

- if the first position is nonempty the topmost block can be moved to either the second or the third position;

- if the second position is nonempty the topmost block can be moved to either the first or the third position;

- if the third position is nonempty the topmost block can be moved to either the first or the second position.

The first action is expressible through the two clauses:

$$move(state(on(X, NewX), OldY, Z), state(NewX, on(X, OldY), Z)).$$
$$move(state(on(X, NewX), Y, OldZ), state(NewX, Y, on(X, OldZ))).$$

The remaining two actions may be expressed in a similar way. Finally the program is completed by adding the path-program from Example 11.3 (where $edge/2$ is renamed into $move/2$). It is now possible to find the path from the start-state above to the following goal-state:

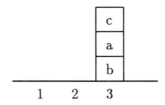

by giving the goal:

$$\leftarrow path(\quad state(on(c, on(b, on(a, table))), table, table),$$
$$state(table, table, on(c, on(a, on(b, table))))), \quad X).$$

One answer to the goal is:

$$X = [\quad state(table, table, on(c, on(a, on(b, table)))),$$
$$state(table, on(c, table), on(a, on(b, table))),$$
$$state(on(a, table), on(c, table), on(b, table)),$$
$$state(on(b, on(a, table)), on(c, table), table),$$
$$state(on(c, on(b, on(a, table))), table, table) \quad ]$$

That is, first move $c$ to position 2. Then move $b$ to position 3 and $a$ on top of $b$. Finally move $c$ on top of $a$.

## 11.5   Alternative Search Strategies

For many problems the depth-first traversal of a state-space is sufficient as shown above — the depth-first strategy is relatively simple to implement and the memory-requirements are relatively modest. However, sometimes there is need for alternative search strategies — the depth-first traversal may be stuck on an infinite path in the state-space although there are finite paths which lead to (one of) the goal-states. Even worse, sometimes the branching of the state-space is so huge that it is simply not feasible to try all possible paths — instead one has to rely on heuristic knowledge to reduce the number of potential paths. When describing such problems by means of logic programming there are two solutions to this problem — either the logic program (for instance that in Example 11.1) is given to an inference system which employs the desired search strategy; or one writes a Prolog program which solves the problem using the desired strategy (however, this program is of course executed using the standard depth-first technique of Prolog). In this section an example of a Prolog program which searches a (simple) tree using a breadth-first traversal is shown.

**Example 11.4** Consider the following tree:

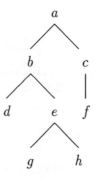

To look for a path in a tree (or a graph) using a breadth-first strategy means first looking at all paths of length 1 from the start-state (or *to* the goal-state). Then all paths of length 2 are investigated. The process is repeated until a complete path from the start- to a goal-state is found.

The tree above will be represented using a binary predicate symbol $children/2$ where the first argument is the name of a node of the tree and the second argument is the names of the children of that node. Hence the tree above is represented as follows:

$$children(a, [b, c]).$$
$$children(b, [d, e]).$$
$$children(c, [f]).$$
$$children(e, [g, h]).$$

In order to realize the breadth-first strategy paths will be represented by "reversed" lists of nodes. For instance, $[d, b, a]$ represents the path which starts at the root of the tree and proceeds to $d$ via the intermediate node $b$. Given all paths of length $n$ from a start-state the problem of finding a path to a goal-state reduces to finding a path from the end of one of these paths to the goal-state. Initially this amounts to finding a path from the empty branch $[X]$ (where $X$ is the start-state) to a goal-state. That is:

$$path(X, Y) \leftarrow bf\_path([[X]], Y).$$

The first argument of $bf\_path/2$ consists of a collection of paths (represented by a list) and the second argument is the goal-state (this may easily be generalized to several goal-states):

$$bf\_path([[leaf|Branch]|Branches], leaf).$$
$$bf\_path([[leaf|Branch]|Branches], Goal) \leftarrow$$
$$\quad children(leaf, Adjacent),$$
$$\quad expand([leaf|Branch], Adjacent, Expanded),$$
$$\quad append(Branches, Expanded, NewBranches),$$
$$\quad bf\_path(NewBranches, Goal).$$
$$bf\_path([[leaf|Branch]|Branches], Goal) \leftarrow$$
$$\quad not\ children(leaf, Leaves),$$
$$\quad bf\_path(Branches, Goal).$$

The last clause exploits unsafe use of negation and applies when a path cannot be expanded any further. Notice, that in order to implement a breadth-first search, it is vital that $Expanded$ is appended $to\ Branches$. The other way around would lead to a depth-first search. Thus, the first argument of $bf\_path/2$ behaves as a FIFO-queue where a prefix contains paths of length $n$ and where the rest of the queue contains paths of length $n + 1$. $expand/3$ describes the relation between a path $X$, the children $X_1, \ldots, X_n$ of the final node in $X$ and the paths obtained by adding $X_1$, $X_2$, etc. to the end of $X$:

$expand(X, [\,], [\,])$.
$expand(X, [Y|Z], [[Y|X]|W]) \leftarrow$
$\quad expand(X, Z, W)$.

For instance, the goal $\leftarrow expand([b, a], [d, e], X)$ succeeds with the answer $X = [[d, b, a], [e, b, a]]$.

When extended with the usual definition of $append/3$ the goal $\leftarrow path(a, X)$ yields all eight possible solutions. That is, $a$, $b$, $c$, $d$, $e$, $f$, $g$ and $h$. ∎

# Exercises

104. A chessboard of size $N \times N$ is given — the problem is to move a knight across the board in such a way that every square on the board is visited exactly once. The knight may move only in accordance with the standard chess rules.

105. A farmer, a wolf and a goat are standing on the same river-bank accompanied by a cabbage-head (a huge one!). A boat is available for transportation. Unfortunately, it has room for only two individuals including the cabbage-head. To complicate things even worse (1) the boat can be operated only by the farmer and (2) if the wolf is left alone with the goat it will be eaten. Similarly if the goat is left alone with the cabbage-head. Is there some way for them to cross the river without anyone being eaten?

106. Three missionaries and three cannibals are standing on the same side of a river. A boat with room for two persons is available. If the missionaries on either side of the river are outnumbered by cannibals they will be done away with. Is there some way for all missionaries and cannibals to cross the river without anyone being eaten?

107. (Towers of Hanoi) Three pins are available together with $N$ disks of different sizes. Initially all disks are stacked (smaller on top of bigger) on the leftmost pin. The task is to move all disks to the rightmost pin. However, at no time may a disk be on top of a smaller one. Hint: there is a very simple and efficient algorithmic solution to this puzzle. However, it may be solved also with the techniques described above.

# Part III

# Alternative
# Logic Programming Schemes

# Chapter 12

# Logic Programming and Concurrency

## 12.1 Algorithm = Logic + Control

The construction of a computer program can be divided into two steps (which are usually interleaved) — the formulation of the actual problem (*what* the problem is) and the description of *how* to solve the problem. Together they make up an algorithm. This idea constitutes the core of logic programming — the logic gives a description of the problem and SLD-resolution provides the means for executing the description. However, the logic has a meaning in itself — its declarative semantics — which is independent of any particular execution-strategy. This means that, as long as the inference mechanism is sound, the behaviour of the algorithm may be altered by selecting different inference systems. We do not have to go as far as abandoning SLD-resolution — the behaviour of the execution can be altered simply by choosing different computation rules as illustrated by the following example:

**Example 12.1** The following execution illustrates the impact of a more versatile computation rule than the one used in, for instance, Prolog. Consider the following program:

1)  *append*([], X, X).
2)  *append*([X|Y], Z, [X|W]) ← *append*(Y, Z, W).

3)  *succlist*([], []).
4)  *succlist*([X|Y], [Z|W]) ← *succlist*(Y, W), Z is X + 1.

Now consider the following SLD-derivation whose initial goal consists of two components (subgoals). Each of the subsequent goals in the derivation can be divided into two parts originating from the components of the initial goal as visualized by the frames:

$$G_0 \quad \leftarrow \quad \boxed{append([4,5],[3],X)} \quad \boxed{succlist(X,Res)}$$

Selecting $append([4,5],[3],X)$ and 2) yields the binding $[4|W_0]$ for $X$ and:

$$G_1 \quad \leftarrow \quad \boxed{append([5],[3],W_0)} \quad \boxed{succlist([4|W_0],Res)}$$

Selecting $succlist([4|W_0],Res)$ and 4) yields the binding $[Z_1|W_1]$ for $Res$:

$$G_2 \quad \leftarrow \quad \boxed{append([5],[3],W_0)} \quad \boxed{succlist(W_0,W_1), Z_1 \ is \ 4+1}$$

Selecting $append([5],[3],W_0)$ and 2) yields the binding $[5|W_2]$ for $W_0$:

$$G_3 \quad \leftarrow \quad \boxed{append([\,],[3],W_2)} \quad \boxed{succlist([5|W_2],W_1), Z_1 \ is \ 4+1}$$

Selecting $Z_1 \ is \ 4+1$ binds $Z_1$ to 5 and, thus, $Res$ to $[5|W_1]$:

$$G_4 \quad \leftarrow \quad \boxed{append([\,],[3],W_2)} \quad \boxed{succlist([5|W_2],W_1)}$$

Selecting $succlist([5|W_2],W_1)$ and 4) yields the binding $[Z_4|W_4]$ for $W_1$:

$$G_5 \quad \leftarrow \quad \boxed{append([\,],[3],W_2)} \quad \boxed{succlist(W_2,W_4), Z_4 \ is \ 5+1}$$

Selecting $append([\,],[3],W_2)$ and 1) binds $W_2$ to $[3]$:

$$G_6 \quad \leftarrow \quad \boxed{\phantom{xx}} \quad \boxed{succlist([3],W_4), Z_4 \ is \ 5+1}$$

Selecting $Z_4 \ is \ 5+1$ binds $Z_4$ to 6 and $Res$ is bound to $[5,6|W_4]$:

$$G_7 \quad \leftarrow \quad \boxed{\phantom{xx}} \quad \boxed{succlist([3],W_4)}$$

In the next step $W_4$ is bound to $[Z_7|W_7]$ yielding:

$$G_8 \quad \leftarrow \quad \boxed{\phantom{xx}} \quad \boxed{succlist([\,],W_7), Z_7 \ is \ 3+1}$$

Selecting $succlist([\,],W_7)$ binds $W_7$ to $[\,]$:

$$G_9 \quad \leftarrow \quad \boxed{\phantom{xx}} \quad \boxed{Z_7 \ is \ 3+1}$$

Finally $Z_7$ is bound to 4 yielding a refutation where the binding for $Res$ is the list $[5,6,4]$. ∎

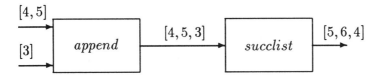

**Figure 12.1: Process-interpretation of $G_0$**

To refute the initial goal, 10 SLD-steps are needed. Notice that it is not possible to improve on this by choosing an alternative computation rule — no matter what rule is used the refutation will be of length 10.

With this versatile computation rule the two subgoals in $G_0$ may be viewed as two *processes* which communicate with each other using the (shared) variable $X$. The frames in the derivation capture the internal behaviour of the processes and the shared variable acts as a "communication channel" where a stream of data flows — namely the elements of the list to which the shared variable $X$ is (incrementally) bound to (first 4 then 5 and finally 3). See Figure 12.1.

Notice that there is no parallelism in this example. The executions of the two processes are only interleaved with each other. The control is merely shifted between them and there is no real gain in performance. This type of control is commonly known as *coroutining*.

The possibility of viewing subgoals as *processes* and goals as *nets* of processes connected via shared variables implies yet another interpretation of logic programs in addition to its operational and declarative meaning. This new view of logic programming extends the possible application areas of logic programming to include also process programming (like operating systems, simulators or industrial process control systems).

## 12.2 AND-Parallelism

Instead of solving the subgoals in a goal in sequence (using SLD-resolution) it is possible to use an operational semantics where some of the subgoals are solved in parallel. This is commonly called AND-parallelism. However, since the subgoals may contain shared variables it is not always feasible to solve them independently. Consider the following goal and program:

$\leftarrow do\_this(X), do\_that(X).$
$do\_this(a).$
$do\_that(b).$

Here the goal would fail using SLD-resolution. However, the two subgoals are solvable independently. The leftmost binds $X$ to $a$ and the rightmost binds $X$ to $b$. When two subgoals contain a common variable special care must be taken so that the different occurrences of the variable do not get bound to inconsistent values. For this some form of *communication/synchronization* between the subgoals is needed. However there are some special cases when two/more derivation-steps may go on in parallel:

- when the subgoals have no common variable, and

- when not more than one of the subgoals bind a shared variable.

Consider the derivation in Example 12.1 again. Notice that the selected subgoals in $G_1$ and $G_2$ can be executed in parallel since the only shared variable ($W_0$) is bound only in one of the derivation steps. Similarly the selected subgoals in $G_3$ – $G_5$, $G_6$ – $G_7$ and $G_8$ – $G_9$ may be executed in parallel. Thus, by exploiting AND-parallelism the goal may be solved in only five steps reducing the (theoretical) time of execution by 50%.

## 12.3    Producers and Consumers

One thing worth noticing about Example 12.1 is that the execution is completely determinate — no selected subgoal unifies with more than one clause-head. However, this is not necessarily the case if some other computation rule is employed. For instance, the rightmost subgoal in $G_0$ unifies with two different clauses. To reduce the search-space it is desirable to have a computation rule which is "as determinate as possible". Unfortunately it is rather difficult (if at all possible) to implement a computation rule which always selects the "best" subgoal. However, the user in most cases has some idea how the program should be executed to obtain good efficiency (although not always optimal). Hence we may allow the user to provide additional information describing how the program should be executed.

The subgoal $append([4,5],[3],X)$ in $G_0$ may be viewed as a *process* which consumes input from two streams ($[4,5]$ and $[3]$) and acts as a *producer* of bindings for the variable $X$. Similarly $succlist(X, Res)$ may be viewed as a *process* which *consumes* bindings for the variable $X$ and produces a stream of output for the variable $Res$. Since, in general, it is not obvious which subgoals are intended to act as consumers and producers of shared variable-occurrences the user normally has to provide a declaration. For instance, to say that the first two arguments of *append*/3 act as consumers and the third as producer. There are several ways to provide such information. In what follows we will use a notion of *read-only* variables which very closely resembles that employed in for instance Concurrent Prolog (one of the first and most influential languages based on a concurrent execution model).

Roughly speaking, each clause (including the goal) may contain several occurrences of a variable. On the other hand, variables can be bound at most once in an SLD-derivation. This implies that at most one of the atoms in a clause acts as a producer of a binding for that variable whereas all remaining atoms containing some occurrence of the variable act as consumers. The idea employed for instance in Concurrent Prolog is that the user annotates variable-occurrences appearing in consumer atoms by putting a question-mark immediately after each occurrence. As an example $G_0$ may be written as follows:

$$\leftarrow append([4,5],[3],X), succlist(X?, Res).$$

This means that the call to *append*/3 acts as a producer of values for $X$ and that *succlist*/2 acts as a consumer of values for $X$ and producer of values for *Res*. Variables annotated by '?' are called *read-only* variables. Variables which are not annotated are said to be *write-enabled*.

Now what is the meaning of a read-only variable? From a declarative point of view they are not different from write-enabled occurrences of the same variable. That is, the question-mark can be ignored. Therefore $X$ and $X?$ denote the very same variable. However, from an operational point of view $X$ and $X?$ behave differently. The rôle of $X?$ is to *suspend* unification temporarily if it is not possible to unify a subgoal with a clause head without producing a binding for $X?$. The unification can be resumed only when the variable $X$ is bound to a nonvariable by some other process containing a write-enabled occurrence of the variable. For instance, unification of $X?$ and $p(Y)$ suspends whereas unification of $p(Y?)$ and $p(X)$ succeeds with mgu $\{X/Y?\}$.

Application of a substitution $\theta$ to a term or a formula is defined in the same way as before except that $X?\theta = (X\theta)?$. As a result of this, the read-only annotation may appear after nonvariable terms. In this case it has no effect and can simply be removed. For instance:

$$p(X?, Y, Z?)\{X/f(W), Y/f(W?)\} = p(f(W)?, f(W?), Z?)$$

However, since the occurrence of '?' in $f(W)?$ has no effect, the term is normally simplified into $p(f(W), f(W?), Z?)$.

**Example 12.2** Consider the following (nonterminating) program for solving the producer-consumer problem with an unbounded buffer. That is, there is a producer which produces data and a consumer which consumes data and we require that the consumer does not attempt to consume data which is not there:

$$producer([X|Y]) \leftarrow prod(X), producer(Y).$$

$$consumer([X|Y]) \leftarrow print(X?), consumer(Y?).$$

We do not specify exctly how $prod/1$ and $print/1$ are defined but only assume that the call $prod(X)$ suspends until some data (e.g. a text file) is available from outside whereas $print(X)$ is a printer-server which prints the file $X$. To avoid some technical problems we assume that a call to $producer/1$ ($consumer/1$) does not proceed until $prod/1$ ($print/1$) succeeds.                               ∎

Now consider the goal:

$$\leftarrow producer(X), consumer(X?).$$

Because of the read-only annotation the second subgoal suspends. The first subgoal unifies with $producer([X_0|Y_0])$ resulting in the mgu $\{X/[X_0|Y_0]\}$ and the new goal:

$$\leftarrow prod(X_0), producer(Y_0), consumer([X_0|Y_0]).$$

At this point only the third subgoal may proceed. (The first subgoal suspends until some data becomes available from outside and the second subgoal suspends until the first subgoal succeeds.)

$$\leftarrow prod(X_0), producer(Y_0), print(X_0?), consumer(Y_0?).$$

At this point we assume that a job is received (to avoid having to consider how jobs are represented we just denote it by $\ulcorner job1 \urcorner$):

$$\leftarrow producer(Y_0), print(\ulcorner job1 \urcorner), consumer(Y_0?).$$

Now assume that the $producer/1$-process reduces to:

$$\leftarrow prod(X_1), producer(Y_1), print(\ulcorner job1 \urcorner), consumer([X_1|Y_1]).$$

and that a new job arrives from outside while the first is being printed:

$$\leftarrow producer(Y_1), print(\ulcorner job1 \urcorner), consumer([\ulcorner job2 \urcorner|Y_1]).$$

The $producer/1$-process can now be reduced to:

$$\leftarrow prod(X_2), producer(Y_2), print(\ulcorner job1\urcorner), consumer([\ulcorner job2\urcorner, X_2|Y_2]).$$

Now the whole process suspends until either (1) a new job arrives (in which case the new job is enqueued after the second job) or (2) printing of the first job ends (in which case the second job can be printed). As pointed out above the program does not terminate.

Notice that it may happen that all subgoals in a goal become suspended. A trivial example is:

$$\leftarrow consumer(X?).$$

This situation is called *deadlock*.

## 12.4  Don't Care Nondeterminism

The Prolog computation consists of a traversal of the SLD-tree. The branching of the tree occurs when the selected subgoal matches several clause heads. To be sure that no success-nodes are disregarded a backtracking strategy is employed. Informally the system "does not know" how to obtain the answers so all possibilities are tried (unless, of course, the search gets stuck on some infinite branch). This is sometimes called "don't know nondeterminism".

The traversal of the tree may be carried out in parallel. This is commonly called *OR-parallelism*. Notice that OR-parallelism does not necessarily speed up the discovery of a particular answer.

Although full OR-parallelism may be combined with AND-parallelism this is seldom done because of implementation difficulties. Instead a form of limited OR-parallelism is employed. The idea is to *commit* to a single clause as soon as possible when trying to satisfy a literal. This means that all other attempts to solve a subgoal are abandoned as soon as the subgoal unifies with a clause head and some of the subgoals in that clause are solved. For this the concept of *commit-operator* is introduced. It divides the body of a clause into a *guard-* and *body*-part. The commit-operator may be viewed as a generalized cut operator in the sense that it cuts off all other attempts to solve a subgoal. This scheme is usually called "don't care nondeterminism". Intuitively this can be understood as follows — assume that a subgoal can be solved using several different clauses all of which lead to the same solution. Then it does not matter which clause to pick. Hence, it suffices to pick *one* of the clauses and not to care about the others. Of course, in general it is not possible to tell whether all attempts will lead to the same solution and the responsibility has to be left to the user.

## 12.5  Concurrent Logic Programming

The concepts discussed above provide a basis for a class of programming languages based on logic programming. They are commonly called Concurrent Logic Programming languages or Committed Choice Languages. For the rest of this chapter the principles of these languages are discussed. To illustrate the principles we use a language similar to Shapiro's Concurrent Prolog.

By analogy to definite programs, the programs considered here are finite sets of *guarded clauses*. The general scheme for a guarded clause looks as follows:

$$H \leftarrow G_1, \ldots, G_m \mid B_1, \ldots, B_n \qquad m \geq 0, n \geq 0$$

where $H, G_1, \ldots, G_m, B_1, \ldots, B_n$ are atoms possibly containing read-only annotations. $H$ is called the *head* of the clause. $G_1, \ldots, G_m$ and $B_1, \ldots, B_n$ are called the *guard* and the *body* of the clause. The symbol "|" which divides the clause into a guard- and body-part is called the *commit operator*. If the guard is empty the commit operator is not written out. To simplify the operational semantics of the language, guards are only allowed to contain certain predefined *test-predicates* — typically (arithmetic) comparisons. Such guards are usually called *flat* and the restriction of Concurrent Prolog which allows only flat guards is called Flat Concurrent Prolog (FCP).

Like definite programs, FCP-programs are used to produce bindings for variables in goals given by the user. The initial goal is not allowed to contain any guard.

**Example 12.3** The following are two examples of FCP-programs for merging lists and deleting elements from lists:

$merge([\,], [\,], [\,])$.
$merge([X|Y], Z, [X|W]) \leftarrow merge(Y?, Z, W)$.
$merge(X, [Y|Z], [Y|W]) \leftarrow merge(X, Z?, W)$.

$delete(X, [\,], [\,])$.
$delete(X, [X|Y], Z) \leftarrow delete(X, Y?, Z)$.
$delete(X, [Y|Z], [Y|W]) \leftarrow X \neq Y \mid delete(X, Z?, W)$.

∎

Like definite clauses, guarded clauses have a logical reading:

- all variables in a guarded clause are implicitly universally quantified — the read-only annotations have no logical meaning;

- "←" denotes logical implication;

- "|" and "," denote conjunctions.

Each clause of the program must contain exactly one commit operator (although usually not explicitly written when the guard-part is empty). Operationally it divides the right-hand side of a clause into two parts which are solved in sequence. Before starting solving the body the whole guard must be solved. Literals in the guard and body are separated by commas. Operationally this means that the literals may be solved in parallel.

The notion of derivation basically carries over from definite programs. However, the read-only annotations and commit operators impose certain restrictions on the selection of subgoal in a derivation step. This is because some subgoals may be temporarily suspended. There are three reasons for this — either because (1) unification of a subgoal with a clause head cannot be performed without binding read-only variables or (2) the subgoal appears in the body of a guarded clause whose guard is not yet satisfied or (3) the subgoal is a nonground test-predicate.

To describe the basic derivation-step taking these restrictions into account the goal will be partitioned into groups of guards and bodies. To emphasize this the goal will be written as follows:

$$\leftarrow \boxed{G_1 \mid B_1}, \ldots, \boxed{G_i \mid B_i}, \ldots, \boxed{G_n \mid B_n}.$$

where both $G_j$ and $B_j$, $(1 \le j \le n)$, are possibly empty conjunctions of atoms (in case of $G_j$ containing only test-predicates). A single reduction of the goal then amounts to selecting some subgoal $A$ such that either:

1. $A$ is a test-predicate in $G_i$ or $B_i$ (if $G_i$ is empty) which is both ground and true. The new goal is obtained simply by removing $A$ from the goal.

2. $G_i$ is empty, $A$ appears in $B_i$ and is a user-defined predicate and there is a (renamed) guarded clause of the form:

$$H \leftarrow G_m \mid B_m.$$

such that $A$ and $H$ unify (with mgu $\theta$) without binding any read-only variables. The new goal obtained is:

$$(\leftarrow \boxed{G_1 \mid B_1}, \ldots, \boxed{B_i \setminus A}, \boxed{G_m \mid B_m}, \ldots, \boxed{G_n \mid B_n})\theta.$$

where $B_i \setminus A$ denotes the result of removing $A$ from $B_i$.

A successful derivation is one where the final goal is empty.

Like SLD-resolution this scheme contains several nondeterministic choices — several subgoals may be selected and if the subgoal selected is user-defined there may be several guarded clauses which unify with it. In the latter case the commit operator has an effect similar to that of cut. In order to solve a subgoal several clauses are tried in parallel. However, as soon as the subgoal unifies with *one* of the clauses and succeeds in solving its guard, all other attempts to solve the subgoal are abandoned. Thus, in this respect the commit operator behaves as a kind of symmetric cut. For instance, take Example 12.3 and the goal:

$$\leftarrow merge([a, b], [c, d], X).$$

This goal has many solutions in Prolog. In FCP there is only one solution to the goal. Which answer one obtains depends on what clauses the refutation commits to.

Since each clause is required to contain exactly one commit operator no goal can have more than one solution. For instance, it is not possible to use $append/3$ to generate splittings of a list. At most one solution will be found. This is one of the main disadvantages of this class of languages. However, this is the price which has to be paid in order to be able to implement these languages efficiently. Because of this, it is vital to test for inequality in the guard of the last clause of the $delete/3$-program. If the test is moved to the body it may happen that goals fail because of committing to the third clause instead of the second.

The execution model given above is somewhat simplified since at each step only one subgoal is selected. As already mentioned, languages like FCP support AND-parallelism which means that several subgoals may be selected simultaneously. However, incorporating this extra dimension into the execution model above makes it rather complicated and we will therefore stick to the sequential version which simulates parallelism through coroutining.

The chapter is concluded with an outline of a simple database system with a fixed number of clients.

**Example 12.4** Consider an application involving a database transaction system. Such a system consists of some processes where customers (users) input transactions and a database management system (DBMS) performs the transactions using a database and outputs the results to the user. See Figure 12.2.

To create such a system of processes the following goal may be given (if we restrict ourselves to two users of the database system):

$$\leftarrow user(tty1, X), user(tty2, Y), merge(X?, Y?, Z), dbms(Z?, []).$$

A formal definition of the $user/2$-process will not be provided. Informally the process $user(tty, X)$ is assumed to behave as follows:

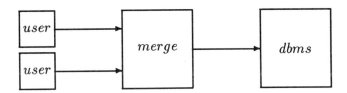

**Figure 12.2: Transaction system**

- it reads a message from the terminal named *tty* (the set of possible messages are listed below);

- binds $X$ to the pair $[T|Msgs]$ where $T$ is a term representing the message read from the terminal and *Msgs* is a new variable;

- suspends until $T$ becomes ground;

- then prints a message on *tty* and finally

- reduces to the new process $user(tty, Msgs)$.

The messages which can be read from the terminal are the following ones:

- "Add *value* under *key* to the database". This message will be represented by the term $add(key, value, Reply))$. The first two arguments are assumed to be ground and the last argument is assumed to be a variable which "returns" the result of the transaction.

- "Delete the *value* (and *key*) associated with *key* from the database". This message will be represented by the term $del(key, Reply)$ where *key* is ground.

- "What is the value associated with *key*?" which is represented by the term $in(key, Reply)$ where *key* is assumed to be ground.

Hence, the *user*/2-processes generate an (infinite) stream of transactions which are merged nondeterministically by the *merge*/3-process and the resulting stream is processed by the *dbms*/2-system.

For the sake of simplicity, assume that the database consists of a list of pairs of the form $item(key, value)$ where *key* is a unique identifier and *value* is the data associated with the key. Three different transactions are to be considered — a pair may be (1) added to the database, (2) deleted from the database, and

(3) retrieved from the database. On the top level the data base management system may be organized as follows (the first clause is not needed in this version of the program but is added as a hint to exercise 110):

> $dbms([kill|Nxt], Db).$
> $dbms([in(Key, Reply)|Nxt], Db) \leftarrow$
> $\qquad retrieve(Key, Db, Reply),$
> $\qquad dbms(Nxt?, Db).$
> $dbms([add(Key, Val, Reply)|Nxt], Db) \leftarrow$
> $\qquad insert(Key, Val, Db?, NewDb, Reply),$
> $\qquad dbms(Nxt?, NewDb?).$
> $dbms([del(Key, Reply)|Nxt], Db) \leftarrow$
> $\qquad delete(Key, Db?, NewDb, Reply),$
> $\qquad dbms(Nxt?, NewDb?).$

If the first transaction appearing in the stream is a request to retrieve information from the database, $dbms/2$ invokes the procedure $retrieve/3$. The first argument is the key sought for, the second argument is the current database and the third argument is the value associated with the key (or $not\_found$ if the key does not appear in the database).

> $retrieve(Key, [\,], not\_found).$
> $retrieve(Key, [item(Key, X)|Db], X).$
> $retrieve(Key, [item(K, Y)|Db], X) \leftarrow$
> $\qquad Key \neq K \mid retrieve(Key, Db, X).$

On the other hand, if the first transaction is a request to add a new pair to the database the data is stored in the database by means of the predicate $insert/5$. The first and second arguments are the key and its associated value, the third argument is the current database, the fourth argument is the new database after adding the pair and the final argument returns a reply to the user (since the operation always succeeds the reply is always $done$).

> $insert(Key, X, [\,], [item(Key, X)], done).$
> $insert(Key, X, [item(Key, Y)|Db], [item(Key, X)|Db], done).$
> $insert(Key, X, [item(K, Y)|Db], [item(K, Y)|NewDb], Reply) \leftarrow$
> $\qquad Key \neq K \mid insert(Key, X, Db, NewDb, Reply).$

Notice that $insert/5$ either adds the pair at the very end of the database or, if the key is already used in the database, replaces the old value associated with the key by the new value. If the latter is not wanted an error message may be returned instead by simple modifications of the second clause.

The last transaction supported is removal of pairs from the database. This is handled by the predicate *delete*/4. The first argument is the key of the pair to be removed from the database which is available in the second argument. The third argument holds the new database and the fourth argument records the result of the transaction (*done* if the key was found and *not_found* if not):

$delete(Key, [], [], not\_found).$
$delete(Key, [item(Key, Y)|Db], Db, done).$
$delete(Key, [item(K, Y)|Db], [item(K, Y)|NewDb], Reply) \leftarrow$
$\qquad Key \neq K \mid delete(Key, Db, NewDb, Reply).$

We conclude the example by considering an outline of a possible execution of the goal:

$\leftarrow user(tty1, X), user(tty2, Y), merge(X?, Y?, Z), dbms(Z?, []).$

Initially, the *merge*/3 and *dbms*/2-processes are suspended. Now assume that the first *user*/2-process binds $X$ to $[add(k10, john, R)|X_0]$:

$\leftarrow \ldots, merge([add(k10, john, R)|X_0], Y?, Z), dbms(Z?, []).$

Then *merge*/3 can be resumed binding $Z$ to $[add(k10, john, R)|W_1]$ and the new goal becomes:

$\leftarrow \ldots, merge(X_0?, Y?, W_1), dbms([add(k10, john, R)|W_1], []).$

At this point *dbms*/2 may be resumed reducing the goal to:

$\leftarrow \ldots, merge(\ldots), insert(k10, john, [], D, R), dbms(W_1?, D?).$

The call to *insert*/5 succeeds binding $D$ to $[item(k10, john)]$ and $R$ to *done* (the reply *done* is echoed on *tty1*):

$\leftarrow \ldots, merge(X_0?, Y?, W_1), dbms(W_1?, [item(k10, john)]).$

At this point both *merge*/3 and *dbms*/2 are suspended waiting for new messages from one of the terminals. Assume that the second user wants to know the value associated with the key $k10$. Then $Y$ is bound to $[in(k10, R)|Y_2]$:

$\leftarrow \ldots, merge(X_0?, [in(k10, R)|Y_2], W_1), dbms(W_1?, [item(k10, john)]).$

Next $W_1$ is bound to $[in(k10, R)|W_3]$ and the goal is reduced to:

$\leftarrow \ldots, merge(X_0?, Y_2?, W_3), dbms([in(k10, R)|W_3], [item(k10, john)]).$

Thereafter *dbms*/2 is resumed and unified with the second clause yielding the goal:

$$\leftarrow \ldots, merge(\ldots), retrieve(k10, [item(k10, john)], R), dbms(W_3?, \ldots).$$

The call to $retrieve/3$ succeeds with $R$ bound to $john$ and the goal reduces to:

$$\leftarrow \ldots, merge(X_0?, Y_2?, W_3), dbms(W_3?, [item(k10, john)]).$$

At this point the whole system is suspended until one of the users supplies another transaction.                                                                      ∎

The example above illustrates one fundamental difference between sequential SLD-resolution for definite programs and concurrent execution. In the former case computations are normally finite and the program computes relations. However, in the latter case, computations may be infinite and the meaning of the program is not so easily defined in terms of relations. For instance, when giving a goal:

$$\leftarrow A_1, \ldots, A_n$$

we normally want this goal to succeed with some answer substitution. However, the goal in Example 12.4 does not terminate, yet the execution results in some useful output via side-effects (supplying transactions to the terminal and obtaining answers echoed on the screen). This fundamental difference makes more complicated to give a declarative semantics to concurrent logic programming languages like FCP.

## Exercises

108. Write a concurrent logic program for checking if two binary trees have the same set of labels associated with the nodes of the tree. Note that the labels associated with corresponding nodes do not have to be the same.

109. Write a concurrent program for multiplying $N \times N$-matrices of integers (for arbitrary $N$'s).

110. Suggest a way of including a "kill"-process in Example 12.4. Such a process is initially suspended but should, when it is activated, terminate all other processes in the transaction system in a controlled way.

111. Write a concurrent program which takes as input a stream of letters (represented by constants) and replaces all occurrences of the sequence "aa" by "a" and all occurrences of "–" by the empty string. All other letters should appear as they stand in the input.

112. Give a solution to the producer-consumer problem with a bounded buffer.

# Chapter 13

# Logic Programs with Equality

As emphasized in the previous chapters, logic programs describe relations. Of course, since a function may be viewed as a special case of a relation it is also possible to define functions as relations using logic programs. However, in this case it is usually not clear whether the described relation is a function or not. Furthermore, this kind of description associates functions with predicate symbols, while it would be more desirable to have functions associated with functors.

In this chapter we present a mechanism that allows us to incorporate such functional definitions into logic programming. The idea is to introduce a special binary predicate symbol "$\doteq$" — called the equality — which is to be interpreted as the identityrelation on the domain of any interpretation of logic programs.

The notion of equality thus makes it possible to restrict attention to interpretations where certain terms are identified. For instance the factorial function may be defined by the equations:

$factorial(0) \doteq s(0).$
$factorial(s(X)) \doteq s(X) * factorial(X).$

$0 + X \doteq X.$
$s(X) + Y \doteq s(X + Y).$

$0 * X \doteq 0.$
$s(X) * Y \doteq X * Y + Y.$

In any model of these formulas the meanings of the terms $factorial(0)$ and $s(0)$ are the same. The use of such equations may be exploited to extend the notion of unification. Consider the definite program:

$odd(s(0))$.
$odd(s(s(X))) \leftarrow odd(X)$.

The formula $odd(factorial(0))$ certainly is true in the intended interpretation. However, since SLD-resolution is based on the notion of syntactic equality it is not powerful enough to produce a refutation from the definite goal:

$\leftarrow odd(factorial(0))$.

In section 13.3 we will see how definite programs with equality can be used to extend the notion of unification into so-called $E$-unification. However, before involving definite programs we study the meaning of equality axioms similar to those used above.

## 13.1   Equations and Equality

In what follows an *equation* will be a formula of the form $s \doteq t$ where $s$ and $t$ are terms from a given alphabet. This kind of unconditional equation may be extended to *conditional* ones. That is, formulas of the form:

$$f(\ldots) \doteq g(\ldots) \leftarrow P(\ldots)$$

where $f(\ldots)$ and $g(\ldots)$ are terms and $P(\ldots)$ is some formula possibly containing other predicate symbols than "$\doteq$". In this chapter attention is restricted to unconditional equations.

At first glance the restriction to unconditional equations may seem to be a serious limitation. But from a theoretical point of view unconditional equations are sufficient to define any computable function (cf. [142]). Hence, the restriction is solely syntactic.

The intuition behind introducing the new predicate symbol "$\doteq$", is to identify terms which denote the same individual in the domain of discourse, regardless of the values of their variables. Hence, for two terms $s$ and $t$, the formula $s \doteq t$ is true in an interpretation $\Im$ and valuation $\varphi$ iff $s$ and $t$ have identical interpretations in $\Im$ and $\varphi$. $\Im$ is said to be a model of $s \doteq t$ if $s \doteq t$ is true in $\Im$ under any valuation $\varphi$. This extends to sets $E$ of equations: $\Im$ is a model of the equation-set $E$ iff $\Im$ is a model of each equation in $E$.

The concept of logical consequence carries over from Chapter 1 with the modification that only such interpretations are considered that associate "$\doteq$" with the identity relation. That is, given a set of equations $E$, $s \doteq t$ is said to be a logical consequence of $E$ (denoted by $E \models s \doteq t$) iff $s \doteq t$ is true in any model of $E$.

Now take a possibly infinite collection $E$ of equations. This set induces an equivalence relation, $\equiv_E$, called an *equality theory*, on the set of all terms: Let $\equiv_E$ be the smallest relation which is:

- *stable* — for any $s \doteq t \in E$ and substitution $\theta$, $s\theta \equiv_E t\theta$;

- *reflexive* — for any term $s$, $s \equiv_E s$;

- *symmetric* — if $s \equiv_E t$ then $t \equiv_E s$;

- *transitive* — if $r \equiv_E s$ and $s \equiv_E t$ then $r \equiv_E t$;

- *compatible* — if $s_1 \equiv_E t_1, \ldots, s_n \equiv_E t_n$ then $f(s_1, \ldots, s_n) \equiv_E f(t_1, \ldots, t_n)$ for any functor $f/n$.

The fact that $E \models s \doteq t$ iff $s \equiv_E t$ is often referred to as "completeness of the equational calculus" and was first proved by G. Birkhoff in 1935.

The notion of $E$-unification will be defined relative to the equality theory induced by $E$. Two (possibly nonground) terms, $s$ and $t$, are said to be $E$-*unifiable* if there exists some substitution $\theta$ such that $s\theta \equiv_E t\theta$. The substitution $\theta$ is called an $E$-unifier of $s$ and $t$.

Notice, that in the case of the empty equality theory, $\equiv_\emptyset$ relates terms to themselves only. This implies that two terms, $s$ and $t$ are $\emptyset$-unifiable iff there is some substitution $\theta$ such that $s\theta$ is identical to $t\theta$. Hence, the notion of $E$-unification encompasses "standard" unification as a special case.

**Example 13.1** Let $E$ be the following equalities defining addition among natural numbers:

1) $sum(0, X) \doteq X$.
2) $sum(s(X), Y) \doteq s(sum(X, Y))$.

From the definition of $E$-unification it follows that the terms $sum(s(X), Y)$ and $s(s(0))$ are $E$-unifiable since, for the substitution $\{X/0, Y/s(0)\}$:

$$sum(s(0), s(0)) \equiv_E s(s(0))$$

In order to see why, it suffices to note that:

$$sum(s(0), s(0)) \equiv_E s(sum(0, s(0)))$$

since $sum(s(0), s(0)) \doteq s(sum(0, s(0)))$ is a substitution instance of 2). Moreover:

$$sum(0, s(0)) \equiv_E s(0)$$

for the same reason but using 1). And since $\equiv_E$ is compatible we know that:

$$s(sum(0, s(0))) \equiv_E s(s(0))$$

Finally we note that $\equiv_E$ is an equivalence relation. This means that it is transitive and that $sum(s(0), s(0)) \equiv_E s(s(0))$. ∎

## 13.2   E-unification

As observed above, standard unification as defined in Chapter 3 is a special case of $E$-unification for the degenerate case when $E = \varnothing$ . This suggests that it may be possible to generalize SLD-resolution into something more powerful by replacing standard unification by $E$-unification. Such an extension is discussed in the next section but first a number of questions are raised concerning the practical problems of $E$-unification.

First of all, an $E$-unification algorithm must be provided. For the case when $E = \varnothing$ there are efficient unification algorithms available as discussed in Chapter 3. The algorithm given there has some nice properties — it always terminates and if the terms given as input to the algorithm are unifiable, it returns a most general unifier of the terms; otherwise it fails. For arbitrary $E$'s these properties are not carried over. For instance, $E$-unification is undecidable. That is, given an arbitrary set $E$ of equations and two terms $s$ and $t$, it is not in general possible to determine whether $s \equiv_E t$.[1]

In addition, the algorithm of Chapter 3 is *complete* in the sense that if $s$ and $t$ are unifiable, then any of their unifiers can be obtained by composing the output of the algorithm with some other substitution. This is because existence of a unifier implies the existence of a *most general* one. This is not true for arbitrary sets of equations. Instead a set of unifiers must be considered. Before resorting to an example, some preliminaries are needed to formulate this more precisely.

A term $s$ is said to *subsume* the term $t$ iff there is a substitution $\sigma$ such that $s\sigma \equiv_E t$. This is denoted by $s \preceq_E t$. The relation can be extended to substitutions as follows — let $V$ be a set of variables and $\sigma$, $\theta$ substitutions. Then $\sigma$ subsumes $\theta$ relative to $V$ (denoted $\sigma \preceq_E \theta[V]$) iff $X\sigma \preceq_E X\theta$ for all $X \in V$. If $V$ is the set of all variables in $s$ and $t$, then the set $S$ of substitutions is a *complete set of E-unifiers* of $s$ and $t$ iff:

- every $\theta \in S$ is an $E$-unifier of $s$ and $t$;

- for every $E$-unifier $\sigma$ of $s$ and $t$, there exists $\theta \in S$ such that $\theta \preceq_E \sigma[V]$.

---

[1]This can be shown by letting $E$ be Peano's axioms. Then $E$-unification is precisely Hilbert's tenth problem which is known to be undecidable (for details see [112]).

For the case when $E = \varnothing$ the standard unification algorithm produces a complete set of $E$-unifiers. This set is either empty (if the terms are not unifiable) or consists of a single mgu. Unfortunately, for nonempty sets $E$ of equations, complete sets of $E$-unifiers may be arbitrary large. In fact, there are cases when two terms only have an infinite complete set of $E$-unifiers.

    The following example shows two terms with two $E$-unifiers where the first $E$-unifier is not subsumed by the other and vice versa.

**Example 13.2** Consider the equations in Example 13.1 again. The substitution $\theta := \{X/0, Y/s(0)\}$ is an $E$-unifier of the terms $sum(X, Y)$ and $s(0)$. This follows trivially since:

$$sum(0, s(0)) \equiv_E s(0)$$

However, also $\sigma = \{X/s(0), Y/0\}$ is a unifier since:

$$sum(s(0), 0) \equiv_E s(sum(0, 0))$$

and:

$$sum(0, 0) \equiv_E 0$$

and since $\equiv_E$ is both compatible and transitive.

    It is easy to see that neither $\theta \preceq_E \sigma[\{X, Y\}]$ nor $\sigma \preceq_E \theta[\{X, Y\}]$. However, it can be shown that any other $E$-unifier of the two terms is subsumed by one of these two substitutions. Thus, the set $\{\theta, \sigma\}$ constitutes a complete set of $E$-unifiers of the two terms. ∎

An $E$-unification algorithm is said to be *sound* if, for arbitrary terms $s$ and $t$, its output is a set of $E$-unifiers of $s$ and $t$. The algorithm is *complete* if the set in addition is a complete set of $E$-unifiers. Needless to say, it is desirable to have an $E$-unification algorithm which is at least sound and preferably complete. However, as already pointed out, there are sets of equations and pairs of terms which do not have finite sets of $E$-unifiers. For such cases we cannot find a complete $E$-unification algorithm. Thus, one must weaken the notion of completeness by saying that an algorithm is complete if it *enumerates* a complete set of $E$-unifiers (for arbitrary pairs of terms). Under this definition there are both sound and complete $E$-unification algorithms for arbitrary sets $E$ of equations. Unfortunately they are of little practical interest because of their tendency to loop.

    Thus, instead of studying general-purpose algorithms, research has concentrated on trying to find algorithms for restricted classes of equations, much like research on logic programming started with the restricted form of definite programs. Standard unification is a trivial example where no equations whatsoever are allowed.

The most well-known approach based on restricted forms of equations is called *narrowing* which, in many ways, resembles SLD-resolution. It has been shown to be both sound and complete for a nontrivial class of equational theories. Characterizing this class more exactly is outside the scope of this book.

Unfortunately narrowing also suffers from termination problems. The reason is that the algorithm does not know when it has found a complete set of unifiers. It may of course happen that this set is infinite in which case there is no hope for termination whatsoever. But even if the set is finite, the algorithm often loops since it is not possible to say whether the set found so far is a complete set of $E$-unifiers. Hence, in practice one has to impose some form of restrictions not only on the form of the equations but also on the terms to be $E$-unified. One simple case occurs when both terms are ground. In this case either $\emptyset$ or the singleton $\{\epsilon\}$ is a complete set of $E$-unifiers of the terms.

## 13.3　　Logic Programs with Equality

In this section we review the integration of definite programs and equations. It turns out that the proof-theoretic and model-theoretic semantics of this language are natural extensions of the corresponding concepts for definite programs alone. But before describing the nature of these extensions the syntax of definite programs with equations is given. Thereafter weaknesses of definite programs alone are discussed to motivate the extensions.

A *definite program with equality* is a pair P, $E$ where:

- P is a finite set of definite clauses which do not make use of the predicate symbol "$\doteq$";

- $E$ is a possibly infinite set of equations.

One sometimes sees different extensions of this idea where $E$ may contain e.g. conditional equations or where "$\doteq$" may appear in the bodies of clauses in P. What is described below can also be generalized to such programs with some additional effort.

Now, consider the following definite program P where the symbols have their natural intended interpretations:

$$odd(1).$$
$$odd(X + 2) \leftarrow odd(X).$$

Although $odd(2+1)$ is true in the intended model it is not a logical consequence of the program because the program has at least one model (for instance the least Herbrand model $M_P$) where $odd(2+1)$ is false. It may thus be argued that the least Herbrand model is "incompatible" with the intended interpretation since the two terms $1+2$ and $2+1$ have distinct interpretations in $M_P$ — recall that any ground term denotes itself in any Herbrand interpretations.

As pointed out above equations may be used to focus attention on certain models — namely those where some terms denote the same object. For instance, by adding to P the equation $E$:

$$2+1 \doteq 1+2$$

(or more generally $X + Y \doteq Y + X$) it is possible to exclude certain unwanted interpretations from being models of P and $E$. In particular, $M_P$ is no longer a model of both P and $E$. (In fact, no Herbrand interpretation of P is a model of P and $E$ since the terms $1+2$ and $2+1$ denote distinct objects.)

We recall that the model-theoretic semantics of definite programs without equality enjoys some attractive properties: To characterize the meaning of a program (i.e. its set of ground, atomic logical consequences) it is sufficient to consider the set of all Herbrand models. In fact, attention may be focused on a single *least* Herbrand model. Evidently, this is not applicable to definite programs with equality. However, there is a natural extension of these ideas: Instead of considering interpretations where the domain consists of ground terms one may consider interpretations where the domain consists of *sets* of ground terms. More precisely one may consider the quotient set of $U_P$ with respect to a congruence relation. Such a set will be called an $E$-universe. In what follows, it will be clear from the context what congruence relation is intended, and we will just write $\bar{s}$ to denote the equivalence class which contains $s$.

By analogy to definite programs the $E$-base will be the set:

$$\{p(t_1, \ldots, t_n) \mid t_1, \ldots, t_n \in E\text{-universe and } p/n \text{ is a predicate symbol}\}$$

and an $E$-interpretation will be a subset of the $E$-base. The intuition behind an $E$-interpretation is as follows: (1) the meaning of a ground term $t$ is the equivalence class $\bar{t}$ and (2) if $s$ and $t$ are ground terms, then $s \doteq t$ is true in the interpretation iff $s$ and $t$ are members in the same equivalence class of the domain (i.e. if $\bar{s} = \bar{t}$).

To characterize the set of all ground, atomic logical consequences of a program P, $E$ we first define a set of $E$-interpretations which are models of $E$. Then we consider $E$-interpretations which are also models of P. The following theorem shows that it is reasonable to restrict attention to $E$-interpretations whose domain is $U_P/\equiv_E$ (the set of all equivalence-classes of $U_P$ wrt the relation $\equiv_E$), since they characterize the set of all ground equations which are logical consequences of $E$:

**Theorem 13.3** Let $E$ be a set of equations, $s$, $t$ ground terms and $\Im$ an $E$-interpretation whose domain is $U_P/\equiv_E$. Then:

$$\models_\Im s \doteq t \quad \text{iff} \quad \bar{s} = \bar{t}$$
$$\text{iff} \quad s \equiv_E t$$
$$\text{iff} \quad E \models s \doteq t$$

∎

Such $E$-interpretations are called *canonical*. Notice that if $E = \emptyset$ then $\bar{s} = \{s\}$ for any ground term $s$, and $\Im$ reduces to a Herbrand interpretation (except that the domain consists of singleton sets of ground terms).

**Example 13.4** Consider the following set $E$ of equations:

    *father(sally)* $\doteq$ *robert.*
    *father(bruce)* $\doteq$ *adam.*
    *father(simon)* $\doteq$ *robert.*

Then $U_P/\equiv_E$ contains for instance the following elements:

$$
\begin{aligned}
\overline{robert} &= \{robert, father(sally), father(simon)\} \\
\overline{adam} &= \{adam, father(bruce)\} \\
\overline{sally} &= \{sally\} \\
\overline{bruce} &= \{bruce\}
\end{aligned}
$$

∎

Most of the results from Chapter 2 can be carried over to canonical $E$-interpretations. For instance (see [85] or [84] for details):

- if $P, E$ has a model then it also has a canonical $E$-model;

- the intersection of all canonical $E$-models of $P, E$ is a canonical $E$-model;

- there is a least canonical $E$-model (denoted by $M_{P,E}$).

Moreover, $M_{P,E}$ characterizes the set of all ground, atomic logical consequences of $P, E$. In what follows let $\overline{p(t_1, \ldots, t_n)}$ be an abbreviation of $p(\overline{t_1}, \ldots, \overline{t_n})$. If $t_1, \ldots, t_n$ are ground terms, then:

$$P, E \models p(t_1, \ldots, t_n) \quad \text{iff} \quad \overline{p(t_1, \ldots, t_n)} \in M_{P,E}$$

An alternative characterization of this set can be given by a fixpoint-operator similar to the $T_P$-operator for definite programs. The operator — denoted by $T_{P,E}$ — is defined as follows:

$$T_{P,E}(x) := \{ \overline{A} \mid A \leftarrow B_1, \ldots, B_n \in ground(P) \wedge \overline{B_1}, \ldots, \overline{B_n} \in x \}$$

It has been shown (cf. [84]) that $M_{P,E} = T_{P,E} \uparrow \omega$.

**Example 13.5** Let $P, E$ be the program:

$proud(father(X)) \leftarrow newborn(X).$
$newborn(sally).$
$newborn(bruce).$

$father(sally) \doteq robert.$
$father(bruce) \doteq adam.$
$father(simon) \doteq robert.$

In this case:

$$M_{P,E} = \{ proud(\overline{robert}), proud(\overline{adam}), newborn(\overline{sally}), newborn(\overline{bruce}) \}$$

∎

As observed above the model-theoretic semantics of definite programs with equality is a generalization of the model-theoretic semantics of definite programs. This is not particularly strange since a definite program also has a set of equations, albeit empty. One might expect that a similar situation would crop up for the proof-theoretic semantics and, indeed, it does. In principle, the only modification which is needed to SLD-resolution is to replace ordinary unification by $E$-unification. In what follows we presuppose the existence of a complete $E$-unification algorithm. However, we do not spell out how it works. The following informal description describes the principles of the proof-theory.

Let $P$ be a definite program, $E$ a set of equations and $G$ the definite goal:

$$\leftarrow A_1, \ldots, A_{m-1}, A_m, A_{m+1}, \ldots, A_n$$

Now assume that $C$ is the (renamed) program clause:

$$H \leftarrow B_1, \ldots, B_j \qquad (j \geq 0)$$

and that $A_m$ and $H$ have a nonempty, complete set of $E$-unifiers $\Theta$. Then $G$ and $C$ resolve into the new goal:

$$\leftarrow (A_1, \ldots, A_{m-1}, B_1, \ldots, B_j, A_{m+1}, \ldots, A_n)\theta$$

if $\theta \in \Theta$.

To avoid confusing this with ordinary SLD-resolution it will be called the *SLDE-resolution* principle. The notion of SLDE-derivation, refutation etc. carry over from Chapter 3. SLDE-resolution introduces one extra level of nondeterminism — since two atoms may have several $E$-unifiers none of which subsume the others, it may happen that a given computation rule, a goal and a clause with a head that $E$-unifies with the selected subgoal, result in several new goals. This was not the case for SLD-resolution since the existence of a unique mgu allowed only one new goal to be derived.

**Example 13.6** Consider again the following definite program and equations:

> $proud(father(X)) \leftarrow newborn(X).$
> $newborn(sally).$
> $newborn(bruce).$

> $father(sally) \doteq robert.$
> $father(bruce) \doteq adam.$
> $father(simon) \doteq robert.$

Let $G_0$ be the goal:

> $\leftarrow proud(robert).$

Since $\{\{X_0/sally\}, \{X_0/simon\}\}$ is a complete set of $E$-unifiers of $proud(robert)$ and $proud(father(X_0))$, $G_1$ is either of the form:

> $\leftarrow newborn(sally).$

which results in a refutation; or of the form:

> $\leftarrow newborn(simon).$

which fails since *simon* $E$-unifies neither with *sally* nor with *bruce*.  ∎

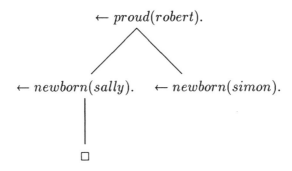

**Figure 13.1: SLDE-tree for the goal** ← *proud(robert)*

By analogy to SLD-resolution all (complete) SLDE-derivations under a given computation rule may be depicted in a single SLDE-tree (cf. Figure 13.1). Notice in contrast to SLD-trees, that the root of the tree has two children despite the fact that the definition of *proud*/1 contains only one clause. Since the complete set of *E*-unifiers of two terms may be infinite, a node in the SLDE-tree may have infinitely many children — something which is not possible in ordinary SLD-trees. This, of course, may cause operational problems since a breadth-first traversal is, in general, not sufficient for finding all refutations in the SLDE-tree. However, soundness and completeness results similar to those for SLD-resolution can and have been proved also for SLDE-resolution described above.

# Chapter 14

# Constraint Logic Programming

Logical inference consists of symbolic manipulations of formulas without any particular knowledge about the meaning of the symbols. On the one hand this makes it a very general mechanism for deductive reasoning. On the other hand it makes it rather weak, since it takes all of a program's models into account, not just the intended one. Indeed, sometimes the intended model cannot even be represented as the least model of some program (take e.g. the real numbers). Consider the domain of natural numbers and the obvious interpretation of the symbols. Then the goal:

$$\leftarrow X < 4, 2 < X.$$

has a simple solution (namely $X = 3$). However, to prove that it is a logical consequence of some set of axioms is a rather elaborate task. On the other hand, if the domain and the interpretation of $<$, 2 and 4 are known there are specialized algorithms for finding the answer(s) to such goals. The predicate symbol "$\doteq$" introduced in the previous chapter is an example of such a predicate symbol.

Another shortcoming of SLD-resolution is the form of the answers produced in refutations. Answers are of the form $X = t$ where $t$ is some term. This is fine as long as the set of answers can be finitely represented. Let the intended interpretation of $zero$, $s/1$ and $\neq/2$ be the usual one. Even if the set of answers to the goal:

$$\leftarrow X \neq s(zero).$$

is infinite, it can be represented by a finite number of terms. Namely $X = zero$ and $X = s(s(Y))$. However, if the "normal" notation (0, 1, 2 etc.) is used for natural numbers the answers to the goal:

$$\leftarrow X \neq 1.$$

cannot be finitely represented in the form $X = t$. These problems have motivated the development of a new logic programming scheme where some constants, functors and predicate symbols are allowed to have a fixed and known interpretation. The scheme considered here is called *constraint logic programming* and consists in extending logic programs with dedicated predicate symbols, functors and constants over some specified domain. The remaining functors of the program are then interpreted as constructors of structures (possibly including the elements of this domain). The remaining predicate symbols are to be interpreted as relations over the domain of such stuctures. Thus the domain of the intended interpretation of the program includes the predefined domain as a proper subdomain. Operationally it amounts to extending SLD-resolution with special-purpose algorithms to check that subgoals built from this alphabet are *solvable*. The semantics of this new language can be formally defined. However, for the formal presentation of its declarative semantics the reader is referred to e.g. [82] and [175]

## 14.1   Logic Programs with Constraints

The general idea of constraint logic programming is quite simple — syntactically it amounts to extending the alphabet of the language by certain reserved symbols (constants, functors and predicate symbols) with fixed meaning. Typically, a logic program may be extended with constants denoting real numbers, functors like $+$, $-$, $*$ and $/$ and predicate symbols like $=$, $<$ etc. Atoms built from these additional symbols will be referred to as *constraints*. Terms built solely from the extra symbols are called *interpreted terms* in contrast to *uninterpreted* ones which are built from the remaining alphabet. Terms may, in general, contain arbitrary functors and variables but if they contain a subterm starting with an interpreted functor that subterm must not contain any uninterpreted symbols.

Roughly speaking, the operational semantics is a generalization of SLD-resolution including notions like derivations and refutations. Let:

$$\leftarrow C_1, \ldots, C_m, A_1, \ldots, A_n.$$

be a definite goal where $C_1, \ldots, C_m$ are constraints and $A_1, \ldots, A_n$ are atoms with ordinary predicate symbols but which may contain interpreted subterms. Then a derivation-step amounts to picking an ordinary subgoal, for instance $A_1$ (say that $A_1$ is of the form $p(t_1, \ldots, t_k)$) and finding a program clause:

$$p(s_1, \ldots, s_k) \leftarrow C_1', \ldots, C_i', B_1, \ldots, B_j$$

where $C'_1, \ldots, C'_i$ are constraints. Then the derived goal is of the form:

$$\leftarrow C_1, \ldots, C_m, C'_1, \ldots, C'_i, t_1 = s_1, \ldots, t_k = s_k, B_1, \ldots, B_j, A_2, \ldots, A_n.$$

*if* the constraints and the equalities are *solvable*. Intuitively, solvable means that there exists a valuation which makes the constraints and equalities (which are a special kind of constraint) true in the intended interpretation of the language.

For instance, consider the goal:

$$\leftarrow equal(pair(2 + 5, 7)), p(X).$$

where $0, 1, 2, \ldots, +/2$ and $= /2$ are interpreted symbols. Using the clause:

$$equal(pair(X_0, Y_0)) \leftarrow X_0 = Y_0.$$

the goal may be reduced to:

$$\leftarrow pair(2 + 5, 7) = pair(X_0, Y_0), X_0 = Y_0, p(X).$$

In practice such goals can be simplified considerably without loosing any solutions. For instance, equations of the form:

$$f(t_1, \ldots, t_n) = f(s_1, \ldots, s_n)$$

where $f$ is an uninterpreted functor may be replaced by the equalities:

$$t_1 = s_1, \ldots, t_n = s_n$$

For instance, the derived goal above can be simplified into:

$$\leftarrow 2 + 5 = X_0, 7 = Y_0, X_0 = Y_0, p(X).$$

Moreover, the first two constraints may be done away with if all occurrences of $X_0$ and $Y_0$ are replaced by $2 + 5$ and $7$ respectively. Since the only remaining constraint $(2 + 5 = 7)$ is trivially satisfied the goal can be simplified into:

$$\leftarrow p(X).$$

A "refutation" is obtained when the goal contains only solvable constraints. These constraints constitute an answer to the initial goal. This definition encompasses SLD-resolution as a special case in which constraints are atoms of the form $s = t$ where $s$ and $t$ are (unifiable) terms. However, by allowing other interpreted predicate symbols more expressive answers can be produced. For instance, inequality and — in the case of ordered domains — symbols like $<, \leq$ etc.

To illustrate the above-mentioned ideas, consider the following example from elementary electrical engineering:

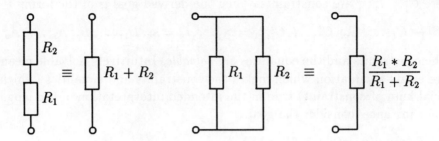

**Figure 14.1: Equivalent nets**

**Example 14.1** Assume that the domain of real numbers is given, let $*$, $+$ etc. be operations over this domain and assume that $=$ expresses equality. The symbols $r/1$, $cell/1$, $serial/2$ and $parallel/2$ are all uninterpreted functors:

$res(r(X), X).$
$res(cell(X), 0).$
$res(serial(X, Xs), R + Rs) \leftarrow$
$\qquad res(X, R), res(Y, Rs).$
$res(parallel(X, Xs), (R * Rs)/(R + Rs)) \leftarrow$
$\qquad res(X, R), res(Xs, Rs).$

■

These clauses describe some elementary laws concerning the resistance of simple electronic circuits and components. For instance:

- the resistance of an ideal voltage-cell is $0\Omega$;

- the resistance of two serial-coupled circuits is the sum of resistances of each individual circuit (see Figure 14.1);

- the resistance of two parallel-coupled circuits is the product divided by the sum of resistances of each individual circuit (see Figure 14.1).

The program can be used to calculate the resistance of a given circuit. For instance, imagine two resistors ($10\Omega$ and $20\Omega$) coupled in series. The total resistance of this circuit is obtained by giving the goal:

$\qquad \leftarrow res(serial(r(10), r(20)), X).$

to which the system answers $X = 30$. However, the program can also be used to design a circuit with some desired resistance. For instance, the goal:

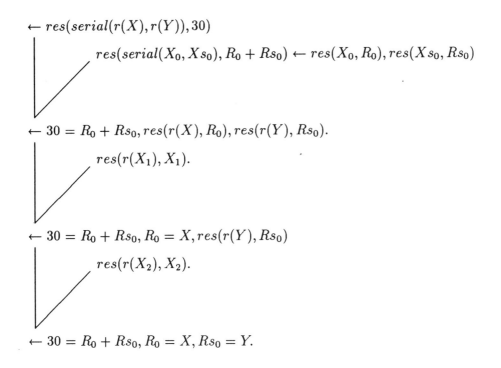

$\leftarrow res(serial(r(X), r(Y)), 30)$

$res(serial(X_0, Xs_0), R_0 + Rs_0) \leftarrow res(X_0, R_0), res(Xs_0, Rs_0)$

$\leftarrow 30 = R_0 + Rs_0, res(r(X), R_0), res(r(Y), Rs_0).$

$res(r(X_1), X_1).$

$\leftarrow 30 = R_0 + Rs_0, R_0 = X, res(r(Y), Rs_0)$

$res(r(X_2), X_2).$

$\leftarrow 30 = R_0 + Rs_0, R_0 = X, Rs_0 = Y.$

**Figure 14.2: Derivation with constraints**

$\leftarrow res(serial(r(X), r(Y)), 30).$

produces the answer $X = 30 - Y$. The derivation which leads to this answer is shown in Figure 14.2. In the first step the constraint $30 = R_0 + Rs_0$ is obtained. Then in the following two steps the additional constraints $R_0 = X$ and $Rs_0 = Y$ are produced after which the goal contains solely (solvable) constraints and a refutation is obtained. The solution presented to the user consists of some simplifications of these three constraints. Exactly what the answer looks like depends on the particular implementation.

The following are other examples of goals and the answers produced in $CLP(\Re)$ (an implementation made at Monash University, Australia, of constraint logic programming over real numbers):

The goal:

$\leftarrow res(parallel(serial(r(X), cell(5)), r(Y)), 5).$

yields the answer $5 * X + 5 * Y = X * Y$ and the goal:

$\leftarrow res(parallel(serial(r(X), cell(5)), r(Y)), 5), X = 10.$

produces the answer $X = 10, Y = 10$.
Finally consider the tax-program from Section 5.2:

**Example 14.2** Assume that $<$ and $\leq$ are interpreted symbols in addition to
the symbols above:

$tax(X, 0.5 * X) \leftarrow X > 150000.$
$tax(X, 0.25 * (X - 30000)) \leftarrow X \leq 150000.$

∎

In order to find out how much tax to pay out of an income of 160,000 the correct
answer is obtained by giving the goal:

$\leftarrow tax(160000, X).$

$X = 80000$

If, on the other hand, the aim is to infer how much to earn in order to pay exactly
25,000 in tax the appropriate goal looks as follows:

$\leftarrow tax(X, 25000).$

$X = 130000$

Finally, in order to find out how much to earn in order not to pay more than
20,000 in tax the following goal will do:

$\leftarrow tax(X, Y), Y < 20000.$

$X = 30000 + 4 * Y$
$20000 > Y$

Notice that in the last case the system does not answer with an explicit answer
of the form $s = t$. Instead, the answer says that "in order to pay less than 20,000
in tax your income should be $30,000 + 4 * Y$ where $Y$ is less than $20,000$".
    In the examples above all constraints range over the real numbers. However,
by using other special-purpose algorithms to check for solvability of constraints
other languages can be defined. For instance, with constraints using strings, sets
or integers.

# Exercises

113. Solve the "SEND MORE MONEY" puzzle using logic programs with constrains similar to those above. The puzzle consists in associating with each letter a number from 0 to 9 such that the equation:

$$
\begin{array}{ccccc}
  & S & E & N & D \\
+ & M & O & R & E \\
\hline
M & O & N & E & Y \\
\end{array}
$$

is satisfied.

114. Write a constraint logic program which solves the $N$-queens problem. That is, given are $N$ chess-queens and a board of size $N \times N$. The goal is to position the queens in such a way that no queen is attacked by another queen.

# Appendix A

# Bibliographical Notes

## A.1 Foundations

**Logic:**   Logic is the science of valid inference and its history dates back to 300-400 B.C. and the work of Aristotle. His work predominated for over 2000 years until logic finally begun to take its current shape around 100 years ago. That is, long before the era of electronic computers. In this historical perspective it is not so strange that logic programming, in many ways, builds on fundamentally different principles than most existing (algorithmic) programming languages. In fact, many of the results which constitute the core of logic programming (including some used in this book) actually date back to the early 20th century. For instance, the name *Herbrand interpretation* is given in honour to the French logician J. Herbrand. However, the ideas were first introduced around 1920 by the Norwegian T. Skolem. Theorem 2.12 is a consequence of the so called Skolem-Lövenheim-theorem.

There are many introductory textbooks on mathemetical logic. For example J. Shoenfield [153], D. van Dalen [171] and C. L. Chang and R. C. T. Lee [29] may be recommended. For readers already familiar with the basic concepts of predicate logic the book by G. Boolos and R. Jeffrey [19] provides a good starting point for further studies. An account of the early history of mathematical logic and its influence on computer science by M. Davis can be found in [155].

With the introduction of electronic computers it was widely believed that it was only a matter of time before computers were able to reason intelligently by means of logic. Much research was devoted to this field (commonly called *automated theorem proving* or *automated reasoning*) during the 1960s. Many of the most influential papers from this era are collected in [155,156]. Good

introductions to theorem proving and different kinds of resolution methods are
provided e.g. by Chang and Lee [29] and J. A. Robinson [140]. The basis for both
these books (and for logic programming) is the early work of Robinson [139] from
1965 where he introduced the notion of unification and the resolution principle
for predicate logic.

**Definite programs:**  Logic programming emerged with the motivation to improve the efficiency of theorem proving. As already stated the proposed solution
was to take a subset of the language of predicate logic and to use the simplified
inference rule known as the SLD-resolution principle.

The observation that every definite programs has a unique minimal Herbrand
model (expressed in the Theorems 2.13, 2.15 and 2.19) originates from M. van
Emden and R. Kowalski's landmark paper [172] from 1976. Proofs similar to
those provided in Chapter 2 can be found also in [5] and [105].

The name *immediate consequence operator* was coined by K. Clark [31]. It
uses results of the theory of fixpoints due to A. Tarski [165] and D. Scott [145].
M. Van Emden and R. Kowalski [172] showed that the least fixpoint of $T_P$ is
identical to the model-theoretic meaning of definite programs (Theorem 2.19).
A corresponding result relating the greatest fixed point of $T_P$ to the subset of
the Herbrand base whose members finitely fails (that is, has a finite SLD-tree
without any refutations) was provided by K. Apt and M. van Emden [7]. For
a comprehensive account of the fixpoint semantics of definite programs, see [5]
and [105].

**SLD-resolution:**  *SLD-resolution* is an offspring from SL-resolution described
by Kowalski and Kuehner [92]. It was originally called LUSH-resolution [76]
(Linear resolution with Unrestricted Selection for Horn clauses). However, it
was first described (without being named) by R. Kowalski [91]. The formulation
of soundness for SLD-resolution (Theorem 3.25) is due to K. Clark [31]. Versions
of this proof can be found in, for instance, [5] and [105]. The first completeness
theorem for SLD-resolution was reported by R. Hill [76] but the formulation of
the stronger theorem given in Theorem 3.27 is due to Clark [31]. The actual
proof is not very difficult and can be found in [5] and [105].

The core of the resolution principle is the *unification* algorithm. The algorithm as we know it today is usually attributed to the 1965 landmark paper by
Robinson [139]. Although the origin is not entirely clear the concept of unification goes back to results from J. Herbrand [73] and later D. Prawitz [131]. Several
attempts have been made to come up with algorithms which are not (worst case)
exponential — some of these are reported to have linear time complexity (see
[111,125]). Nevertheless most Prolog implementations use approximately the

original version of the algorithm but sacrifice the occur-check (for details about the consequences of this approach see e.g. [14,109,130]). Some important results concerning unification are described by J-L. Lassez, M. Maher and K. Marriott [96] and E. Eder [54]. A general introduction to unification is provided by J. Siekmann [154].

**Negation:** As discussed in Chapter 2 definite programs and SLD-resolution cannot be used to infer negative knowledge. In a sense this is useful since it guarantees that definite programs always are consistent. On the other hand it means that definite programs cannot fully express state of affairs. The solution to this shortcoming is similar to that adopted in relational databases — if something is not inside the definition of a relation it is assumed to be outside of the relation. This approach works only as long as the definition of the relation is complete and finite. This assumption is commonly called the *closed world assumption* and is due to R. Reiter [137]. However, since the closed world assumption is undecidable for logic programs, K. Clark suggested a weaker notion called the *negation-as-failure* rule [30]. Clark provided a logical justification of the this rule by introducing the notion of *completion* and showed the soundness (Theorem 4.6) of the rule. As pointed out, the negation-as-failure rule is not complete in the general case. However, some results on the completeness of the rule are nevertheless provided by Jaffar, Lassez and Lloyd [83] who prove that if $\neg A$ is a *ground* literal which is a logical consequence of comp(P) then there *exists* a computation rule such that the goal $\leftarrow A$ finitely fails. In practice this means that a *fair* computation rule must be used in addition to the restriction to ground atoms. However, the computational overhead of fair computation rules is not negligible and since Prolog's computation rule is not fair the result is normally not applicable.

As pointed out in Chapter 3 negation, as implemented in Prolog, is not sound. In particular, the subgoal $\neg A$ fails when the goal $\leftarrow A$ succeeds. In a sound implementation it is necessary to check that the computed answer substitution for $\leftarrow A$ is empty. Still there are implementations — such as NU-Prolog [166] — which incorporate sound versions of negation. In addition NU-Prolog allows variables to be existentially quantified within the scope of "$\neg$". Hence, NU-Prolog also solves the potential ambiguity of meaning of clauses such as:

$$orphan(Y) \leftarrow \neg parent(X,Y).$$

This, and other features of NU-Prolog, are reported by L. Naish in e.g. [121] and [122].

A more fundamental question concerns the validity of viewing comp(P) as the "intended meaning" of P. Some problems which arise in this setting are

discussed by T. Flannagan [58] and by J. Shepherdson [151,150]. However, some
anomalies can be avoided by restricting the form of normal programs.

The notion of *stratified* programs was introduced in an article by K. Apt,
H. Blair and A. Walker [6]. They showed that each stratified program has a
well-defined minimal model. This model is called the *standard* model and in the
case of definite programs it coincides with the least Herbrand model. They also
showed that the standard model does not depend on different stratifications of
the program. The notion of stratification was also put forward independently by
A. van Gelder [173]. However, both papers build on results by A. Chandra and
D. Harel [28]. A completeness result for a limited class of stratified programs is
provided by L. Cavedon and J. Lloyd [25].

Several attempts have been made to extend the class of "meaningful" normal
programs to include also some programs which are not stratified in the sense
of [6]. In particular, T. Przymusinski [132,134] suggested the notion of *locally
stratified* programs. Roughly speaking, a program is locally stratified if the
Herbrand base can be partitioned in such a way that for every ground clause-
instance, the head appears in higher strata than all positive literals in the body
and strictly higher strata than negative literals in the body. Unfortunately, the
property of being locally stratified is not decidable whereas ordinary stratification
is. M. Gelfond and V. Lifschitz [64] suggested a notion of *stable models* which
are also generalizations of the semantics for stratified programs. A similar notion
of *well-founded models* was introduced by A. Van Gelder, K. Ross and J. Schlipf
[174].

The negation problem is not an isolated problem which affects only the logic
programming community — many related problems arise in the area of *non-
monotonic logic*. For an introduction see the textbook by M. Genesereth and
N. Nilsson [65]. In several papers (e.g. [100] and [133]) the relationship between
negation-as-failure and approaches to nonmonotonic logic — like McCarthy's *circumscription* and Reiter's *default logic* — is discussed. Under certain restrictions
it is even possible to implement circumscription through logic programming (as
described e.g. by M. Gelfond and V. Lifschitz [63]).

An alternative approach to providing a semantics to logic programs with negation consists in using three-valued logic (see e.g. [57,135,94,93,152]). Roughly
speaking the extra truth value corresponds to ground atoms which have neither
refutations nor finitely failing SLD-trees.

One of the main shortcomings of the negation-as-failure rule is the disability
to fully handle existentially quantified negative subgoals — that is, goals which
intuitively read "is there an $X$ such that $\neg p(X)$?". This restriction has motivated
a number of techniques with the ability of producing answers (roughly speaking,
bindings for $X$) to this type of goals. This area of research is commonly called

*constructive* negation and recent results are published in e.g. [12,13,26,107].

# A.2  Programming in Logic

**Databases:**  As already pointed out in Chapter 6 there are many similarities between relational databases (as first defined by E. F. Codd [39]) and logic programming in that they are both used to describe relations between objects. There has been a growing interest in the database community to use logic programs as a *language* for representing *data*, *integrity constraints*, *views* and *queries* in a single uniform framework. However, in many cases SLD-resolution is inappropriate as the operational semantics of deductive databases because of the enormous amount of data that must be handled. Much of the research therefore concentrates on characterizing subsets of logic programs where it is possible to apply alternative and special-purpose algorithms for computing relations as efficiently as possible. Many of the existing algorithms are based on bottom-up computations which start from the extensional database and then compute relations defined by the intensional database in contrast to SLD-resolution. Research in this area is represented, for instance, by the NAIL!-project led by J. D. Ullman [168,120]. Related work is reported for instance in [4,9,10,15,27,136].

Several survey articles of the field of deductive databases are available. For instance, both H. Gallaire, J. Minker and J-M. Nicolas [60] and R. Reiter [138] provide extensive comparison between logic and relational databases, but use a richer logical language than that normally found in logic programming literature. In [169] and [170] J. D. Ullman provides a thorough introduction both to traditional database theory and the use of logic programming for describing relational databases.

In [119] J. Minker gives a historical account of the field of deductive databases and discusses its relation to negation. A whole collection of selected papers on negation and deductive databases are available in the book [118]. An early collection of papers is also available in [59].

Several suggestions have been put forward on how to increase the expressive power of logic programs. In a series of papers J. Lloyd and R. Topor [102,103,104] suggest several extensions to logic programs. The main idea is to extend logic programs to include a notion of *program clauses* which are formulas of the form $\forall(A \leftarrow W)$ where $A$ is an atom and $W$ is an arbitrary *typed* formula of predicate logic. It is shown how to compile program clauses into Prolog programs. They also raise the problem of *integrity constraints*. Roughly speaking, an integrity constraint is a formula which constrains the information which may be stored in the database. The validity of the constraints must be checked every time updates are made to the database. Lloyd, Sonenberg and Topor [101] provide a method for checking the validity of integrity constraints in the case of stratified databases. A recapitulation of these results is also available in [105].

The notion of integrity constraints concerns *updates* in databases. The semantics of database updates is a major problem, not only in logic programming systems, but in any system which must maintain consistent information. The problems become particularly difficult when the updates are made while making deductions from the database, since adding information to or deleting information from the database may invalidate conclusions already made. These are problems which have engaged quite a number of researchers in different fields. Unfortunately the results so far seem not to provide any realistic solution. One common suggestion is to treat the database as a collection of theories and to specify, explicitly, in which theory to prove subgoals. Some alternative approaches are available for instance in [8,20,21,56,75,178].

**Recursive data-structures:**  Most of the programs in Chapter 7 have appeared elsewhere. Many of them are simple adaptations of, for instance, functional programs. *Difference lists* were discussed together with several other data-structures by K. Clark and S-Å. Tärnlund [37]. Ways of transforming programs operating on lists into programs operating on difference lists were discussed by Å. Hansson and S-Å. Tärnlund [69], J. Zhang and P. W. Grant [181] and by K. Marriott and H. Søndergaard [110].

**Meta-logical reasoning:**  The idea to describe a language in itself is not very new. Many of the most important results on computability and incompleteness of predicate logic are based on this idea. For instance, Gödel's incompleteness theorem and the undecidability of the halting problem (see e.g. Boolos and Jeffrey [19] for a good account of these results). K. Bowen and R. Kowalski [21] raised the possibility of amalgamating the object- and meta-language in the case of logic programming. The self-interpreter based on the ground representation presented in Chapter 8 is influenced by their interpreter. However, in contrast to our interpreter they keep explicit track of the database using an extra argument, something which makes it easier to perform updates. A continuation of [21] is described in [22] and [20].

The self-interpreter in Example 8.7 which works on a nonground representation appeared for the first time in [129]. R. O'Keefe [124] described an extension of the self-interpreter which handles cut.

Recently P. Hill and J. Lloyd showed several deficiencies of existing attempts to formalize meta-level reasoning in Prolog. Their solution is to use a language of typed predicate logic and a ground representation of the object language [74]. The solution makes it possible to give a clean logical meaning to some of Prolog's built-in predicates. In [75] they try to give a clean semantics for the predicates *assert*/1 and *retract*/1. Some other meta-logical predicates of Prolog are discussed by D. H. D. Warren [177].

Meta-logical reasoning is closely related to the area of *program transformation* — an area which has gained substantial interest lately. On the one hand program transformation is a special case of meta-level reasoning. On the other hand program transformation can be used to improve the efficiency of meta-level programs. In particular *partial evaluation* plays an important role here. The notion of partial evaluation was suggested in the 1970s and was introduced into logic programming by J. Komorowski [87]. The approach has gained considerable interest lately because of its ability to "compile away" the overhead introduced by having one extra level of interpretation. Several papers on partial evaluation of logic programs are collected in [55] and annotated bibliographies are available in [17,55].

For additional readings in the area of meta-logical reasoning see the collection of papers from the Meta88 workshop [2].

**Expert systems:** *Expert systems* as described in Chapter 9, are particular applications of meta-logical reasoning. An early account of the application of logic programming in the field of expert systems was provided by K. Clark and F. McCabe [35]. The example in Chapter 9 is based on the technique of composing self-interpreters which is suggested by L. Sterling and A. Lakhotia [95,161]. Similar expert-system shells are described e.g. in [159,160,162,163].

Techniques for explaining not just the proof of a goal but also the *failure* of a goal are provided e.g. by Ü. Yalçinalp and L. Sterling [179] and by A. Bruffaerts and E. Henin [24].

**Grammars:** One of the earliest applications of logic programming is that of describing natural- and programming languages. In fact, the very first implementation of Prolog — made by A. Colmerauer's group in Marseilles in 1972 [143] — was primarily used for processing of natural language [45]. Since then several results concerning the relationship between logic programming and different grammatical formalisms have been published. For instance, between logic programming and respectively (1) *two-level grammars* [108,106] and (2) *attribute grammars* [50]. For an extensive account of the field see P. Deransart and J. Małuszyński[49].

The notion of DCGs was introduced by D. H. D. Warren and F. Pereira [127] and incorporated into the DEC-10 Prolog system developed at the University of Edinburgh. However, the basic idea is an adaptation of A. Colmerauer's *Metamorphosis Grammars* [43]. The form of DCGs described in Chapter 10 may deviate somewhat from that implemented in most Prolog systems. In most implementations DCGs are merely viewed as a syntactic sugar for Prolog and, as a consequence, all of Prolog built-in features (including cut, negation etc.) may be inserted into the grammar rules. Our objective was to visualize the underlying principles of DCGs without obscuring these by implementation-specific features of particular Prolog systems. Any user's manual of specific Prolog systems that support DCGs can fill in the remaining gaps.

The simple translation of DCGs into Prolog clauses shown in Section 10.5 is by no means the only possibility:

- Y. Matsumoto et. al. [113] describe a left-corner bottom-up strategy;

- U. Nilsson [123] showed how to translate an arbitrary DCG into a Prolog program which embodies the $LR(k)$ parsing technique;

- J. Cohen and T. Hickey [40] describe a whole range of parsing techniques and their use in compiler construction.

A large number of formalisms similar to DCGs have been suggested. Some of the most noteworthy are H. Abramson's *Definite Clause Translation Grammars* (see [1]) which are closely related to attribute grammars and *Gapping Grammars* by V. Dahl and H. Abramson [47]. These, and other formalisms, are surveyed in [46].

For an extensive account of the use of Prolog in natural language processing, see textbooks by F. Pereira and S. Shieber [126] (who also make extensive use of partial evaluation techniques) and by G. Gazdar and C. Mellish [62].

**Searching:** Chapter 11 presents some fundamental concepts related to the problem of searching in a state space. Several other, more advanced techniques can be found, for instance, in textbooks by I. Bratko [23], L. Sterling and E. Shapiro [163], W. Clocksin and C. Mellish [38] and in [114] edited by A. Walker.

# A.3   Alternative Logic Programming Schemes

**Concurrency:** There exists a number of logic programming languages based on a concurrent execution model. The most well-known are *PARLOG*, *Guarded Horn Clauses* and *Concurrent Prolog*, but several others have been suggested. They all originate from the experimental language *IC-Prolog* developed around 1980 at Imperial College, London [36]. The main feature of this language was its execution model based on pseudo-parallelism and coroutining as suggested e.g. by Kowalski [89,90]. In IC-Prolog this was achieved by associating control-annotations to variables in the clauses. The language also had a concept of *guards* but no *commit operator* in the sense of Chapter 12. IC-Prolog was succeeded by the *Relational Language* [32] which introduced guards and the commit operator in the spirit of E. W. Dijkstra [52] and C. A. R. Hoare's CSP [77]. The synchronization between subgoals was specified by means of *mode-declarations* — that is, annotations which describe how arguments of calls to predicates are to be instantiated in order for the call to go ahead. Unfortunately, the modes were so restricted that programs in the language more or less behaved as functional programs with relational syntax. However, some of these restrictions were relaxed in the successor language called PARLOG (see e.g. [33,34,68]).

Concurrent Prolog (see e.g. [146,147]) was developed by E. Shapiro as a direct descendant of the Relational Language. The language is closely related to PARLOG but differs in some respects — in Concurrent Prolog synchronization between subgoals is achieved by means of *read-only* annotations as opposed to PARLOG where the same effect is obtained by means of mode-declarations. The other difference is implementation-related and can roughly be stated as follows — when trying to solve a subgoal several clauses may be tried in parallel. However, in order to be able to commit to a single clause, it may be necessary to bind variables in the call. Obviously these bindings should not be visible in the call's attempts to commit to other clauses. In theory this is not a very difficult problem but in a full-scale implementation it is nontrivial. In Concurrent Prolog this is handled by creating multiple environments for the calling subgoal. In PARLOG it is "solved" simply by disallowing such programs. Both approaches can be advocated but for different reasons. These problems have given rise to a subset of Concurrent Prolog called *Flat* Concurrent Prolog (FCP) [116] where these problems are easier to handle.

Guarded Horn Clauses (GHC) suggested by K. Ueda [167] is yet another language based on the same idea as PARLOG and Concurrent Prolog. It has emerged as a result of the Japanese Fifth Generation Project. In contrast to the previous two languages, GHC does not provide any explicit declarations for synchronization. Instead a subgoal suspends if it is not possible to commit to a clause without binding variables in the call. Like Concurrent Prolog implementation-problems motivated the restriction to a flat subset (FGHC) of the language.

Several other languages relying on concurrent execution models have been suggested. For instance, the language-scheme *CP* by V. Saraswat (see e.g. [144]), L. Pereira and R. Nasr's *Delta Prolog* [128] and R. Yang's *P-Prolog* [180]. Also, recently a new language called *ANDORRA Prolog* [70] has been proposed. The latter two are languages which combine both the don't know nondeterminism of

Prolog and the don't care nondeterminism of concurrent languages.

A large number of papers on concurrent logic programming languages are collected in [148]. For an excellent survey of most existing concurrent logic programming languages see [149].

**Equality:**  One of the clearest trends in research on logic programming has been the idea to combine logic programming with other computational paradigms. This includes both *object-oriented* and *functional* programming. The latter can be achieved in three basic ways:

- to integrate logic programming on top of some existing (functional) language, often Lisp (cf. LOGLISP [141], QLOG [88], POPLOG [115] and APPLOG [41]);

- to define a logic programming language able to call functions defined in arbitrary languages through a well-defined interface (cf. ALF [18,99]);

- to define a new language in which it is possible to define both logic and functional programs (cf. EQLOG [67], LEAF [11] and FUNLOG [164]).

All of these have their own merits depending on whether one is interested in efficiency or logical clarity. The first approach is usually the most efficient whereas the third is probably the most attractive from a logical point of view and also the one that is most closely related to what was said in Chapter 13.

The third approach usually consists of extending logic programming with equational theories. Operationally, it amounts to extending SLD-resolution with some form of equation solving — for instance, using different adaptations of *narrowing* [157]. For further reading see the work of J. M. Hullot [81], N. Dershowitz and D. Plaisted [51] or the excellent survey by G. Huet and D. Oppen [80]. However, as pointed out in Chapter 13, equation solving without restrictions is likely to end up in infinite loops. Much of the research is therefore directed towards finding more efficient methods and special cases when the technique is more likely to halt.

A survey of the area of integration of logic and functional programs is provided by M. Bellia and G. Levi [16]. Some of the papers cited above are collected in [48]. The generalization of model- and proof-theoretic semantics from definite programs into definite programs with equality is due to J. Jaffar, J-L. Lassez and M. Maher [84,85]. J. Gallier and S. Raatz [61] provide basic soundness and completeness results for SLD-resolution extended with $E$-unification.

A slightly different but very powerful approach to combining logic programming with functional programming can be obtained by exploiting higher-order unification of $\lambda$-terms [79,158]. This idea has been exploited in $\lambda$-Prolog developed at the University of Pennsylvania [117].

**Constraints:** The use of constraints (see [98,66]) in logic programming is closely related to the integration of logical and functional languages. In fact, most of the logic programming schemes are subsumed by the framework of J. Jaffar, J-L. Lassez and M. Maher described in [84,85] which is also the basis for constraint logic programming. Although Colmerauer's Prolog II [42] (now succeeded by Prolog III [44]) seems to be the first logic programming system which makes extensive use of constraints, the first formal *framework* for combining logic programming with constraint satisfaction (called $CLP(x)$ where $x$ may instantiated to alternative domains) was provided by J. Jaffar and J-L. Lassez [82]. An instance of the scheme called $CLP(\Re)$ (where $\Re$ stands for the domain of real numbers) was implemented at Monash University in Australia and is described in [72,86]. Several applications of the system have been demonstrated. For instance, in electrical engineering [71] and in option trading [97].

Several other constraint logic programming systems are reported recently. For instance, the Japanese language $CAL$ [3] which supports solving (non) linear algebraic polynomial equations, boolean equations and linear inequalities, the European language $CHIP$ [53,175] which solves equations involving finite domains, boolean and rational terms and the language $CLP(\Sigma^*)$ able to solve constraints over domains of regular sets [176].

# Appendix B

# Answers to Selected Exercises

1. The following is a possible solution (but not the only one):

$$\forall X \, (nat(X) \to \exists Y \, (eq(s(X), Y)))$$
$$\neg \, \exists X \, better(X, taking\_a\_nap)$$
$$\forall X \, (integer(X) \to \neg \, negative(X))$$
$$\forall X, Y \, (name(X, Y) \land innocent(X) \to changed(Y))$$
$$\forall X \, (area(X, computer\_science) \to important(logic, X)$$
$$\forall X, Y \, (\neg \, \exists Z \, solves(X, Z) \land intros\_in\_logic(Y) \to read\_one(X, Y))$$

2. The following is a possible solution (but not the only one):

$$better(bronze\_medal, nothing)$$
$$\neg \, \exists X \, better(X, gold\_medal)$$
$$better(bronze\_medal, gold\_medal)$$

3. Let $\text{MOD}(x)$ denote the set of all models of the formulas $x$. Then:

$$
\begin{array}{lll}
P \models F & \text{iff} & \text{MOD}(P) \subseteq \text{MOD}(F) \\
 & \text{iff} & \text{MOD}(P) \cap \text{MOD}(\neg F) = \varnothing \\
 & \text{iff} & \text{MOD}(P \cup \{\neg F\}) = \varnothing \\
 & \text{iff} & F \text{ is unsatisfiable}
\end{array}
$$

4. Take for instance, $F \to G \equiv \neg F \lor G$. Let $\mathfrak{I}$ and $\varphi$ be an arbitrary interpretation and valuation respectively. Then:

$$
\begin{array}{lll}
\models_{\mathfrak{I}}^{\varphi} F \to G & \text{iff} & \not\models_{\mathfrak{I}}^{\varphi} F \text{ or } \models_{\mathfrak{I}}^{\varphi} G \\
 & \text{iff} & \models_{\mathfrak{I}}^{\varphi} \neg F \text{ or } \models_{\mathfrak{I}}^{\varphi} G \\
 & \text{iff} & \models_{\mathfrak{I}}^{\varphi} \neg F \lor G
\end{array}
$$

7.  Let MOD($x$) denote the set of all models of the formula $x$. Then:

$$F \equiv G \quad \text{iff} \quad \text{MOD}(F) = \text{MOD}(G)$$
$$\text{iff} \quad \text{MOD}(F) \subseteq \text{MOD}(G) \text{ and } \text{MOD}(G) \subseteq \text{MOD}(F)$$
$$\text{iff} \quad \{F\} \models G \text{ and } \{G\} \models F$$

9.  *Hint*: Assume that there is a finite interpretation and establish a contradiction using the semantics of formulas.

13.  *Hints*:

$E(\theta\sigma) = (E\theta)\sigma$:    by the definition of application it suffices to consider the case when $E$ is a variable.

$(\theta\sigma)\gamma = \theta(\sigma\gamma)$:    it suffices to show that the two substitutions give the same result when applied to an arbitrary variable. The fact that $E(\theta\sigma) = (E\theta)\sigma$ can be used to complete the proof.

15.  Only the last one. (Look for counter-examples of the first two!)

16.      $p(X) \leftarrow q(X).$
         $p(X) \leftarrow q(X, Y), r(X).$
         $r(X) \leftarrow p(X), q(X).$
         $p(X) \leftarrow q(X), r(X).$

17.  Let:

$$U_0 = \{a, b\}$$
$$U_{i+1} = \{f(x) \mid x \in U_i\} \cup \{g(x) \mid x \in U_i\}$$

then:

$$U_P = \bigcup_{i=0}^{\infty} U_i$$

and $B_P = \{q(x, y) \mid x, y \in U_P\} \cup \{p(x) \mid x \in U_P\}$.

18.  $U_P = \{0, s(0), s(s(0)), \ldots\}$ and $B_P = \{p(x, y, z) \mid x, y, z \in U_P\}$.

19.  Formulas 2, 3 and 5. *Hint*: Consider ground instances of the formulas.

20.  Use the immediate consequence operator:

$$
\begin{aligned}
T_P \uparrow 0 &= \varnothing \\
T_P \uparrow 1 &= \{q(a, g(b)), q(b, g(b))\} \\
T_P \uparrow 2 &= \{p(f(b))\} \cup T_P \uparrow 1 \\
T_P \uparrow 3 &= T_P \uparrow 2
\end{aligned}
$$

That is, $M_P = T_P \uparrow 3$.

21. Use the immediate consequence operator:

$$
\begin{aligned}
T_P \uparrow 0 &= \varnothing \\
T_P \uparrow 1 &= \{p(0,0,0), p(0, s(0), s(0)), p(0, s(s(0)), s(s(0))), \ldots\} \\
T_P \uparrow 2 &= \{p(s(0), 0, s(0)), p(s(0), s(0), s(s(0))), \ldots\} \cup T_P \uparrow 1 \\
&\quad \vdots \\
T_P \uparrow \omega &= \{p(s^x(0), s^y(0), s^z(0)) \mid x + y = z\}
\end{aligned}
$$

23. *Hint*: Use induction on the number of recursive calls of the algorithm.

24. $\langle X; a \rangle$, $\langle g(a); Y \rangle$ and $\langle c; Z \rangle$.

25. $\{X/a, Y/a\}$, not unifiable, $\{X/f(a), Y/a, Z/a\}$ and the last pair is not unifiable because of occur-check.

26. For instance, $p(X, f(X))$ and $p(Y, Y)$.

27. Let $\sigma$ be a unifier of $s$ and $t$. By the definition of mgu there is a substitution $\delta$ such that $\sigma = \theta\delta$. Now since $\omega$ is a renaming it follows also that $\sigma = \theta\omega\omega^{-1}\delta$. Thus, for every unifier $\sigma$ of $s$ and $t$ there is a substitution $\omega^{-1}\delta$ such that $\sigma = (\theta\omega)(\omega^{-1}\delta)$.

28. $\{X/b\}$ is produced twice and $\{X/a\}$ once.

29. For instance, the program and goal:

$$
\begin{aligned}
&\leftarrow p(a). \\
&p(X) \leftarrow p(X), q(X).
\end{aligned}
$$

A "leftmost" computation rule produces an infinite tree whereas the "rightmost" computation rule gives a finitely failed tree.

32. *Hint*: Each clause of the form:

$$
p(t_1, \ldots, t_m) \leftarrow B
$$

in P gives rise to a formula of the form:

$$p(X_1, \ldots, X_m) \leftrightarrow \ldots \vee \exists \ldots (X_1 = t_1, \ldots, X_n = t_n, B) \vee \ldots$$

in comp(P). Use truth-preserving rewritings of this formula to obtain the program clause.

35. comp(P) consists of the formulas:

$$p(X_1) \leftrightarrow \exists X, Y \, (X_1 = Y, q(X, Y), r(X)) \vee \exists X \, (X_1 = X, r(X))$$
$$q(X_1, X_2) \leftrightarrow \exists X, Y \, (X_1 = f(X), X_2 = Y, q(X, Y))$$
$$r(X_1) \leftrightarrow X_1 = b$$

plus the appropriate instances of CET. To show that $\neg p(a)$ is a logical consequence of comp(P) it suffices to show that $\leftarrow p(a)$ is a finitely failed goal (of some rank).

36. *Hint*: Use structural induction on one of the two terms.

38. *Hint*: Use induction on $n$.

39. comp(P) consists of:

$$p(X_1) \leftrightarrow \exists X \, (X_1 = a, q(X)) \vee \exists X \, (X_1 = b, r(X))$$
$$r(X_1) \leftrightarrow X_1 = a \vee X_1 = b$$
$$q(X_1) \leftrightarrow \square$$

plus proper instances of CET.

41. For example, one which alternates between the leftmost and rightmost subgoal.

42. Only $P_1$ and $P_3$.

43. comp(P) consists of:

$$p(X_1) \leftrightarrow X_1 = a, \neg q(b)$$
$$q(X_1) \leftrightarrow \square$$

and some equalities including $a = a$ and $b = b$.

46. Without cut there are seven answers. Replacing $true(1)$ by cut eliminates the answers $X = e, Y = c$ and $X = e, Y = d$. Replacing $true(2)$ by cut eliminates in addition $X = b, Y = c$ and $X = b, Y = d$.

48. The goal without negation gives the answer $X = a$ while the other goal succeeds without binding $X$.

49. $var(X) \leftarrow not(not(X = a)), not(not(X = b)).$

51. $between(X, Z, Z) \leftarrow X \leq Z.$
$between(X, Y, Z) \leftarrow X < Z, W \text{ is } Z - 1, between(X, Y, W).$

52. For instance, since $(n + 1)^2 = n^2 + 2 * n + 1, n \geq 0$:

$sqr(0, 0).$
$sqr(s(X), s(Z)) \leftarrow sqr(X, Y), times(s(s(0)), X, W), plus(Y, W, Z).$

53. $gcd(X, 0, X) \leftarrow X > 0.$
$gcd(X, Y, Z) \leftarrow Y > 0, W \text{ is } X \text{ mod } Y, gcd(Y, W, Z).$

56. $grandchild(X, Z) \leftarrow parent(Y, X), parent(Z, Y).$

$sister(X, Y) \leftarrow female(X), parent(Z, X), parent(Z, Y), X \neq Y.$

$brother(X, Y) \leftarrow male(X), parent(Z, X), parent(Z, Y), X \neq Y.$

etc.

57. *Hint:* (1) Colours should be assigned to countries. Hence, represent the countries by variables. (2) Describe the map in the goal by saying which countries should be assigned different colours.

58. $and(1, 1, 1).$
$and(0, 1, 0).$
$and(1, 0, 0).$
$and(0, 0, 0).$

$inv(1, 0).$
$inv(0, 1).$

$circuit1(X, Y, Z) \leftarrow$
$\qquad and(X, Y, W), inv(W, Z).$

$circuit2(X, Y, Z, V, W) \leftarrow$
$\qquad and(X, Y, A), and(Z, V, B),$
$\qquad and(A, B, C), inv(C, W).$

59. $p(X, Y) \leftarrow husband(K, X), wife(K, Y).$

$q(X) \leftarrow parent(X, Y).$
$q(X) \leftarrow income(X, Y), Y \geq 20000.$

60.         $\pi_{X,Y}(Q(Y,X)) \cup \pi_{X,Y}(Q(X,Z) \bowtie R(Z,Y))$

61.         $compose(X,Z) \leftarrow r_1(X,Y), r_2(Y,Z).$

63.  Take the transitive closure of the *parent*/2-relation.

65.         $ingredients(tea, needs(water, needs(tea\_bag, nil))).$
            $ingredients(boiled\_egg, needs(water, needs(egg, nil))).$

            $available(water).$
            $available(tea\_bag).$

            $can\_cook(X) \leftarrow$
                    $ingredients(X, Ingr), all\_available(Ingr).$

            $all\_available(nil).$
            $all\_available(needs(X,Y)) \leftarrow$
                    $available(X), all\_available(Y).$

            $needs\_ingredient(X,Y) \leftarrow$
                    $ingredients(X, Ingr), among(Y, Ingr).$

            $among(X, needs(X,Y)).$
            $among(X, needs(Y,Z)) \leftarrow$
                    $among(X,Z).$

67.   - $.(a, .(b, []))$
      - $.(a, b)$
      - $.(a, .(.(b, .(c, [])), .(d, [])))$
      - $.(a, .(b, X))$

      - $.(a, .(b, .(c, [])))$
      - $.(a, .(b, []))$
      - $.([], [])$
      - $.(a, .(b, .(c, [])))$

70.         $length([], 0).$
            $length([X|Y], N) \leftarrow$
                    $length(Y, M), N \ is \ M + 1.$

71.         $lshift([X|Yz], Yzx) \leftarrow append(Yz, [X], Yzx).$

75.         $sublist(X,Y) \leftarrow$
                    $prefix(X,Y)$
            $sublist(X, [Y|Z]) \leftarrow$
                    $sublist(X, Z).$

78.    $msort([\,],[\,]).$
       $msort([X],[X]).$
       $msort(X,Y) \leftarrow$
                $split(X, Split1, Split2),$
                $msort(Split1, Sorted1),$
                $msort(Split2, Sorted2),$
                $merge(Sorted1, Sorted2, Y).$

       $split([X],[\,],[X]).$
       $split([X,Y|Z],[X|V],[Y|W]) \leftarrow$
                $split(Z, V, W).$

       $merge([\,],[\,],[\,]).$
       $merge([X|A],[Y|B],[X|C]) \leftarrow$
                $X < Y, merge(A, [Y|B], C).$
       $merge([X|A],[Y|B],[Y|C]) \leftarrow$
                $X \geq Y, merge([X|A], B, C).$

79.    $delta(1, 2, b).$
       $delta(2, 2, a).$
       $delta(2, 3, a).$
       $delta(3, 2, b).$

       $final(3).$

       $accept(State, [\,]) \leftarrow$
                $final(State).$
       $accept(State, [X|Y]) \leftarrow$
                $delta(State, NewState, X), accept(NewState, Y).$

83.    $palindrome(X) \leftarrow diff\_palin(X - [\,]).$

       $diff\_palin(X - X).$
       $diff\_palin([X|Y] - Y).$
       $diff\_palin([X|Y] - Z) \leftarrow diff\_palin(Y - [X|Z]).$

86. *Hint*: Represent the empty binary tree by the constant *empty* and the nonempty tree by $node(X, Left, Right)$ where $X$ is the label and *Left* and *Right* the two subtrees of the node.

90. The following program provides a starting point (the program finds all refutations but it does not terminate):

$$prove(Goal) \leftarrow$$
$$int(Depth), dfid(Goal, Depth, 0).$$

$$dfid(true, Depth, Depth).$$
$$dfid((X, Y), Depth, NewDepth) \leftarrow$$
$$dfid(X, Depth, TmpDepth),$$
$$dfid(Y, TmpDepth, NewDepth).$$
$$dfid(X, s(Depth), NewDepth) \leftarrow$$
$$clause(X, Y),$$
$$dfid(Y, Depth, NewDepth).$$

$$int(s(0)).$$
$$int(s(X)) \leftarrow$$
$$int(X).$$

91.  *Hint*: The fourth rule may be defined as:

$$d(X + Y, Dx + Dy) \leftarrow d(X, Dx), d(Y, Dy).$$

100.  DCG notation:

$$bleat --> [b], aaa.$$
$$aaa --> [a].$$
$$aaa --> [a], aaa.$$

Prolog program:

$$bleat(X_0, X_2) \leftarrow diff(X_0, X_1, [b]), aaa(X_1, X_2).$$
$$aaa(X_0, X_1) \leftarrow diff(X_0, X_1, [a]).$$
$$aaa(X_0, X_2) \leftarrow diff(X_0, X_1, [a]), aaa(X_1, X_2).$$
$$diff([X|Y], Y, X).$$

A refutation is obtained, for instance, by giving the goal $\leftarrow bleat([b, a, a], [])$.

101.  The DCG describes a language consisting only of the empty string. However, at the same time it defines the "concatenation"-relation among lists. That is, the nonterminal $x([a, b], [c, d], X)$ not only derives the empty string but also binds $X$ to $[a, b, c, d]$.

108.  The definition of *append*/3 and *member*/2 is left to the reader:

$$eq(T1, T2) \leftarrow$$
$$nodes(T1, N1),$$
$$nodes(T2, N2),$$
$$equal(N1?, N2?).$$

$nodes(empty, [\,])$.
$nodes(tree(X, T1, T2), [X|N]) \leftarrow$
        $nodes(T1, N1)$,
        $nodes(T2, N2)$,
        $append(N1?, N2?, N)$.

$equal(X, Y) \leftarrow$
        $subset(X, Y)$,
        $subset(Y, X)$.

$subset([\,], X)$.
$subset([X|Y], Z) \leftarrow$
        $member(X, Z)$,
        $subset(Y?, Z)$.

109. *Hint*: write a program which transposes the second matrix and then computes all inner products.

# Bibliography

[1] H. Abramson. Definite Clause Translation Grammars. In *Proc. 1984 Symposium on Logic Programming,* Atlantic City, pages 233–241, 1984.

[2] H. Abramson and M. H. Rogers, editors. *Meta-Programming in Logic Programming.* MIT Press, 1989.

[3] A. Aiba et. al. Constraint Logic Programming Language CAL. In *Proc. of International Conf. on Fifth Generation Computer Systems 88,* Tokyo, pages 263–276, 1988.

[4] K. Apt. *Efficient Computing of Least Fixpoints.* Report TR-88-33, Dept. of Computer Science, The University of Texas at Austin, 1988.

[5] K. Apt. *Introduction to Logic Programming.* Report TR-87-35, Dept. of Computer Science, The University of Texas at Austin, 1987. To appear in *Handbook of Theoretical Computer Science* (J. van Leeuwen, managing editor), North Holland.

[6] K. Apt, H. Blair, and A. Walker. Towards a Theory of Declarative Knowledge. In J. Minker, editor, *Foundations of Deductive Databases and Logic Programming,* pages 89–148, Morgan Kaufmann, Los Altos, 1988.

[7] K. Apt and M. van Emden. Contributions to the Theory of Logic Programming. *J. ACM,* 29(3):841–862, 1982.

[8] H. Bacha. Meta-Level Programming: A Compiled Approach. In *Proc. of Fourth International Conf. on Logic Programming,* Melbourne, pages 394–410, MIT Press, 1987.

[9] I. Balbin and K. Ramamohanarao. A Generalization of the Differential Approach to Recursive Query Evaluation. *J. of Logic Programming,* 4(3):259–262, 1987.

[10] F. Bancilhon et. al. Magic Sets and Other Strange Ways to Implement Logic Programs. In *Proc. of 5th ACM Symposium on Principles of Database Systems*, pages 1–15, 1986.

[11] R. Barbuti, M. Bellia, G. Levi, and M. Martelli. LEAF: A Language which Integrates Logic, Equations and Functions. In D. DeGroot and G. Lindstrom, editors, *Logic Programming, Functions, Relations and Equations*, pages 201–238, Prentice-Hall, 1986.

[12] R. Barbuti, D. Mancarella, D. Pedreschi, and F. Turini. A Transformational Approach to Negation in Logic Programming. *J. of Logic Programming*, 1989. To appear.

[13] R. Barbuti, D. Mancarella, D. Pedreschi, and F. Turini. Intensional Negation of Logic Programs: Examples and Implementation Techniques. In *Proc. of TAPSOFT '87*, LNCS 250, pages 96–110, Springer-Verlag, 1987.

[14] J. Beer. The Occur-Check Problem Revisited. *J. of Logic Programming*, 5(3):243–262, 1988.

[15] C. Beeri and R. Ramakrishnan. On the Power of Magic. In *Proc of 6th Symposium on Principles of Database Systems*, pages 269–283, 1987.

[16] M. Bellia and G. Levi. The Relation Between Logic and Functional Languages: A Survey. *J. of Logic Programming*, 3(3):217–236, 1985.

[17] D. Bjørner, A. Ershow, and N.D. Jones, editors. *Partial Evaluation and Mixed Computation*. North Holland, 1988.

[18] S. Bonnier and J. Małuszyński. Towards a Clean Amalgamation of Logic Programs with External Procedures. In *Proc. of Fifth International Conf/Symposium on Logic Programming*, Seattle, pages 311–326, MIT Press, 1988. Also in *Proc. of PLILP '88*, LNCS 348, Springer-Verlag, 1989.

[19] G. Boolos and R. Jeffrey. *Computability and Logic*. Cambridge University Press, 1980.

[20] K. Bowen. Meta-Level Programming and Knowledge Representation. *New Generation Computing*, 3(1):359–383, 1985.

[21] K. Bowen and R. Kowalski. Amalgamating Language and Metalanguage in Logic Programming. In K. Clark and S-Å. Tärnlund, editors, *Logic Programming*, pages 153–172, Academic Press, 1982.

[22] K. Bowen and T. Weinberg. A Meta-Level Extension of Prolog. In *Proc. 1985 Symposium on Logic Programming,* Boston, pages 48–53, 1985.

[23] I. Bratko. *Prolog Programming for Artificial Intelligence.* Addison-Wesley, 1986.

[24] A. Bruffaerts and E. Henin. Proof Trees for Negation as Failure: Yet Another Prolog Meta-interpreter. In *Proc. of Fifth International Conf/Symposium on Logic Programming,* Seattle, pages 343–358, MIT Press, 1988.

[25] L. Cavedon and J. Lloyd. A Completeness Theorem for SLDNF Resolution. *J. of Logic Programming,* 7(3):177–191, 1989.

[26] D. Chan. Constructive Negation based on the Completed Database. In *Proc. of Fifth International Conf/Symposium on Logic Programming,* Seattle, pages 111–125, MIT Press, 1988.

[27] A. Chandra. Theory of Database Queries. In *Proc of 7th Symposium on Principles of Database Systems,* 1988.

[28] A. Chandra and D. Harel. Horn Clause Queries and Generalizations. *J. of Logic Programming,* 2(1):1–16, 1985.

[29] C.L. Chang and R.C.T. Lee. *Symbolic Logic and Mechanical Theorem Proving.* Academic Press, New York, 1973.

[30] K. Clark. Negation as Failure. In H. Gallaire and J. Minker, editors, *Logic and Databases,* pages 293–322, Plenum Press, New York, 1978.

[31] K. Clark. *Predicate Logic as a Computational Formalism.* Report DOC 79/59, Dept. of Computing, Imperial College, 1979.

[32] K. Clark and S. Gregory. *A Relational Language for Parallel Programming.* Research Report DOC 81/16, Department of Computing, Imperial College, 1981.

[33] K. Clark and S. Gregory. Notes on the Implementation of PARLOG. *J. of Logic Programming,* 2(1):17–42, 1985.

[34] K. Clark and S. Gregory. PARLOG: Parallel Programming in Logic. *ACM TOPLAS,* 8(1):1–49, 1986.

[35] K. Clark and F. McCabe. Prolog: A Language for Implementing Expert Systems. In J.E. Hayes, D. Michie, and Y-H. Pao, editors, *Machine Intelligence 10*, pages 455–470, Ellis Horwood, 1982.

[36] K. Clark, F. McCabe, and S. Gregory. IC-Prolog Language Features. In K. Clark and S-Å. Tärnlund, editors, *Logic Programming*, pages 253–266, Academic Press, 1982.

[37] K. Clark and S-Å. Tärnlund. A First Order Theory of Data and Programs. In *Information Processing '77*, pages 939–944, North-Holland, 1977.

[38] W. Clocksin and C. Mellish. *Programming in Prolog*. Springer-Verlag, 1981.

[39] E. F. Codd. A Relational Model of Data for Large Shared Data Banks. *Communications of the ACM*, 13(6):377–387, 1970.

[40] J. Cohen and T. Hickey. Parsing and Compiling using Prolog. *ACM TOPLAS*, 9(2):125–163, 1987.

[41] S. Cohen. The APPLOG Language. In D. DeGroot and G. Lindstrom, editors, *Logic Programming, Functions, Relations and Equations*, pages 239–278, Prentice-Hall, 1986.

[42] A. Colmerauer. Equations and Inequations on Finite and Infinite Trees. In *Proc. of International Conf. on Fifth Generation Computer Systems 84*, Tokyo, pages 85–102, North-Holland, 1984.

[43] A. Colmerauer. Metamorphosis Grammars. In L. Bolc, editor, *Natural Language Communication with Computers*, pages 133–189, LNCS 63, Springer-Verlag, 1978.

[44] A. Colmerauer. Opening the Prolog III Universe. *BYTE Magazine*, 177–182, August 1987.

[45] A. Colmerauer et. al. *Un Système de Communication Homme-Machine en Francais*. Technical Report, Technical Report, Group d'Intelligence Artificielle, Marseille, 1973.

[46] V. Dahl and H. Abramson. *Logic Grammars*. Springer-Verlag, 1989.

[47] V. Dahl and H. Abramson. On Gapping Grammars. In *Proc. of Second International Conf. on Logic Programming*, Uppsala, pages 77–88, 1984.

[48] D. DeGroot and G. Lindstrom, editors. *Logic Programming, Functions, Relations and Equations.* Prentice-Hall, 1986.

[49] P. Deransart and J. Małuszyński. A Grammatical View of Logic Programming. In *Proc. of PLILP '88,* Orleans, France, pages 219–251, LNCS 348, Springer-Verlag, 1989.

[50] P. Deransart and J. Małuszyński. Relating Logic Programs and Attribute Grammars. *J. of Logic Programming,* 2(2):119–156, 1985.

[51] N. Dershowitz and D. Plaisted. Equational Programming. In J. E. Hayes, D. Michie, and J. Richards, editors, *Machine Intelligence 11,* pages 21–56, Oxford University Press, 1988.

[52] E. W. Dijkstra. *A Discipline of Programming.* Prentice-Hall, 1976.

[53] M. Dincbas et. al. The Constraint Logic Programming Language CHIP. In *Proc. of International Conf. on Fifth Generation Computer Systems 88,* Tokyo, pages 693–702, 1988.

[54] E. Eder. Properties of Substitutions and Unifications. *J. Symbolic Computation,* 1:31–46, 1985.

[55] A. P. Ershov et. al., editor. *Selected Papers from the Workshop on Partial Evaluation and Mixed Computation.* Special issue of New Generation Computing, 6(2-3), 1988.

[56] R. Fagin et. al. Updating Logical Databases. *Advances in Computer Research,* 3:1–18, 1986.

[57] M. Fitting and M. Ben-Jacob. Stratified and Three-valued Logic Programming Semantics. In *Proc. of Fifth International Conf/Symposium on Logic Programming,* Seattle, pages 1054–1069, MIT Press, 1988.

[58] T. Flannagan. The Consistency of Negation as Failure. *J. of Logic Programming,* 3(2):93–114, 1986.

[59] H. Gallaire and J. Minker, editors. *Logic and Databases.* Plenum Publishing Co, 1978.

[60] H. Gallaire, J. Minker, and J-M. Nicolas. Logic and Databases: A Deductive Approach. *Computing Surveys,* 16(2):153–185, 1984.

[61] J. Gallier and S. Raatz. SLD-Resolution Methods for Horn Clauses with Equality Based on *E*-Unification. In *Proc. 1986 Symposium on Logic Programming*, Salt Lake City, pages 168–179, 1986.

[62] G. Gazdar and C. Mellish. *Natural Language Processing in Prolog.* Addison-Wesley, 1989.

[63] M. Gelfond and V. Lifschitz. Compiling Circumscriptive Theories Into Logic Programming. In *Proc. of 2nd International Workshop on Non-Monotonic Reasoning,* Grassau, FRG, pages 74–99, LNCS 346, Springer-Verlag, 1989.

[64] M. Gelfond and V. Lifschitz. The Stable Model Semantics for Logic Programming. In *Proc. of Fifth International Conf/Symposium on Logic Programming,* Seattle, pages 1070–1080, MIT Press, 1988.

[65] M. Genesereth and N. Nilsson. *Logical Foundations of Artificial Intelligence.* Morgan Kaufmann, 1987.

[66] Steele G. L. *The Definition and Implementation of a Computer Programming Language based on Constraints.* PhD thesis, MIT AI–TR.595, 1980.

[67] J. Gougen and J. Meseguer. EQLOG: Equality, Types and Generic Modules for Logic Programming. In D. DeGroot and G. Lindstrom, editors, *Logic Programming, Functions, Relations and Equations*, pages 295–364, Prentice-Hall, 1986.

[68] S. Gregory. *Parallel Logic Programming in PARLOG.* Addison-Wesley, 1987.

[69] Å. Hansson and S-Å. Tärnlund. Program Transformation by Data Structure Mapping. In K. Clark and S-Å. Tärnlund, editors, *Logic Programming*, pages 117–122, Academic Press, 1981.

[70] S. Haridi and P. Brand. ANDORRA Prolog — An Integration of Prolog and Committed Choice Languages. In *Proc. of International Conf. on Fifth Generation Computer Systems 88,* Tokyo, pages 745–754, 1988.

[71] N. Heintze, S. Michaylov, and P. Stuckey. *CLP(ℜ)* and Some Electrical Engineering Problems. In *Proc. of Fourth International Conf. on Logic Programming,* Melbourne, pages 675–703, MIT Press, 1987.

[72] N. Heitze et. al. *The CLP(ℜ) Programmers Manual (version 2.0).* Technical Report, Dept. of Computer Science, Monash University, 1987.

[73] J. Herbrand. Investigations in Proof Theory. In J. van Heijenoort, editor, *From Frege to Gödel: A Source Book in Mathematical Logic, 1879–1931*, pages 525–581, Harvard University Press, 1967.

[74] P. Hill and J. Lloyd. *Analysis of Meta-Programs*. Report CS-88-08, Dept. of Computer Science, University of Bristol, 1988.

[75] P. Hill and J. Lloyd. *Meta-Programming for Dynamic Knowledge Bases*. Report CS-88-18, Dept. of Computer Science, University of Bristol, 1988.

[76] R. Hill. *LUSH-resolution and its Completeness*. DCL Memo 78, Dept. of Artificial Intelligence, University of Edinburgh, 1974.

[77] C. A. R. Hoare. *Communicating Sequential Processes*. Prentice-Hall, 1985.

[78] J. Hopcroft and J. Ullman. *Introduction to Automata Theory, Language, and Computation*. Addison Wesley, 1979.

[79] G. Huet. A Unification Algorithm for Typed $\lambda$-Calculas. *Theoretical Computer Science*, 1:27–57, 1975.

[80] G. Huet and D. Oppen. Equations and Rewrite Rules: A Survey. In R. Book, editor, *Formal Language Theory: Perspectives and Open Problems*, pages 349–405, Academic Press, 1980.

[81] J. M. Hullot. Canonical Forms and Unification. In *Proc. of 5th CADE*, Les Arcs, France, 1980.

[82] J. Jaffar and J-L. Lassez. Constraint Logic Programming. In *Conf. Record of 14th Annual ACM Symp. on POPL*, 1987.

[83] J. Jaffar, J-L. Lassez, and J. Lloyd. Completeness of the Negation as Failure Rule. In *Proc. of IJCAI-83*, pages 500–506, Karlruhe, 1983.

[84] J. Jaffar, J-L. Lassez, and M. Maher. A Theory of Complete Logic Programs with Equality. *J. of Logic Programming*, 1(3):211–223, 1984.

[85] J. Jaffar, J-L. Lassez, and M. Maher. Logic Programming Language Scheme. In D. DeGroot and G. Lindstrom, editors, *Logic Programming, Functions, Relations and Equations*, pages 441–467, Prentice-Hall, 1986.

[86] J. Jaffar and S. Michaylov. Methodology and Implementation of a CLP System. In *Proc. of Fourth International Conf. on Logic Programming*, Melbourne, pages 196–218, MIT Press, 1987.

[87] H. J. Komorowski. *A Specification of an Abstract Prolog Machine and its Application to Partial Evaluation*. PhD thesis, Linköping University, 1981.

[88] H. J. Komorowski. QLOG — The Programming Environment for Prolog in Lisp. In K. Clark and S-Å. Tärnlund, editors, *Logic Programming*, pages 315–324, Academic Press, 1982.

[89] R. Kowalski. Algorithm = Logic + Control. *Communications of the ACM*, 22(7):424–436, 1979.

[90] R. Kowalski. *Logic For Problem Solving*. Elsevier, North-Holland, New York, 1979.

[91] R. Kowalski. Predicate Logic as a Programming Language. In *Information Processing '74*, pages 569–574, North-Holland, 1974.

[92] R. Kowalski and D. Kuehner. Linear Resolution with Selection Function. *Artificial Intelligence*, 2:227–260, 1972.

[93] K. Kunen. Negation in Logic Programming. *J. of Logic Programming*, 4(4):289–308, 1987.

[94] K. Kunen. Signed Data Dependencies in Logic Programming. *J. of Logic Programming*, 7(3):231–245, 1989.

[95] A. Lakhotia and L. Sterling. *Development of a Prolog Tracer by Composing Interpreters*. Technical Report CES-88-03, Computer Engineering and Science, Case Western Reserve University, 1988.

[96] J-L. Lassez, M. Maher, and K. Marriott. Unification Revisited. In J. Minker, editor, *Foundations of Deductive Databases and Logic Programming*, pages 587–626, Morgan Kaufmann, Los Altos, 1988.

[97] K. Lassez, K. McAloon, and R. Yap. Constraint Logic Programming and Option Trading. *IEEE Expert*, Fall:42–50, 1987.

[98] W. Leler. *Constraint Programming Languages*. Addison Wesley, 1988.

[99] J. Leszczylowski, S. Bonnier, and J. Małuszyński. Logic Programming with External Procedures: Introducing S-Unification. *Information Processing Letters*, 27:159–165, 1988.

[100] V. Lifschitz. On the Declarative Semantics of Logic Programs with Negation. In J. Minker, editor, *Foundations of Deductive Databases and Logic Programming*, pages 177–192, Morgan Kaufmann, Los Altos, 1988.

[101] J. Lloyd, E. A. Sonenberg, and R. Topor. Integrity Constraint Checking in Stratified Databases. *J. of Logic Programming*, 4(4):331–344, 1987.

[102] J. Lloyd and R. Topor. A Basis for Deductive Database Systems. *J. of Logic Programming*, 2(2):93–110, 1985.

[103] J. Lloyd and R. Topor. A Basis for Deductive Database Systems II. *J. of Logic Programming*, 3(1):55–68, 1986.

[104] J. Lloyd and R. Topor. Making Prolog More Expressive. *J. of Logic Programming*, 1(3):225–240, 1984.

[105] J.W. Lloyd. *Foundations of Logic Programming*. Springer-Verlag, second edition, 1987.

[106] J. Małuszyński. Towards a Programming Language Based on the Notion of Two-Level Grammars. *Theoretical Computer Science*, 28:13–43, 1984.

[107] J. Małuszyński and T. Näslund. Fail Substitutions for Negation as Failure. In *Proc. of North American Conference on Logic Programming*, Cleveland, 1989.

[108] J. Małuszyński and J-F. Nilsson. A Comparison of the Logic Programming Language Prolog with Two-Level Grammars. In *Proc. of First International Conf. on Logic Programming*, Marseille, pages 193–199, 1982.

[109] K. Marriott and H. Søndergaard. On Prolog and the Occur Check Problem. *Sigplan Notices*, 24(5):76–82, 1989.

[110] K. Marriott and H. Søndergaard. *Prolog Program Transformation by Introduction of Difference-Lists*. Technical Report 88/14, Department of Computer Science, The University of Melbourne, 1988.

[111] A. Martelli and U. Montanari. An Efficient Unification Algorithm. *TOPLAS*, 4(2):258–282, 1982.

[112] Y. Matiyasevich. Diophantine Representation of Recursively Enumerable Predicates. In *Proc. of the Second Scandinavian Logic Symposium*, North-Holland, 1970.

[113] Y. Matsumoto et. al. BUP: A Bottom-Up Parser Embedded in Prolog. *New Generation Computing*, 1(1):145–158, 1983.

[114] M. McCord, J. Sowa, and W. Wilson. *Knowledge Systems and Prolog*. Addison-Wesley, 1987.

[115] C. Mellish and S. Hardy. Integrating Prolog in the Poplog Environment. In J. Campbell, editor, *Implementations of Prolog*, pages 147–162, Ellis Horwood, 1984.

[116] C. Mierowsky et. al. *The Design and Implementation of Flat Concurrent Prolog*. Technical Report CS85–09, Department of Applied Mathematics, Weizmann Institute of Science, Rehovot, 1985.

[117] D. Miller and G. Nadathur. Higher-Order Logic Programming. In E. Shapiro, editor, *Proc. of Third International Conf. on Logic Programming*, London, pages 448–462, LNCS 225, Springer-Verlag, 1986.

[118] J. Minker, editor. *Foundations of Deductive Databases and Logic Programming*. Morgan Kaufmann, Los Altos, 1988.

[119] J. Minker. Perspectives in Deductive Databases. *J. of Logic Programming*, 5(1):33–60, 1988.

[120] K. Morris et. al. YAWN! (Yet Another Window on NAIL!). Stanford University, Preprint, 1987.

[121] L. Naish. Automating Control for Logic Programs. *J. of Logic Programming*, 2(3):167–184, 1985.

[122] L. Naish. *Negation and Control in Prolog*. LNCS 225, Springer-Verlag, 1986.

[123] U. Nilsson. AID: An Alternative Implementation of DCGs. *New Generation Computing*, 4(4):383–399, 1986.

[124] R. O'Keefe. On the Treatment of Cuts in Prolog Source-Level Tools. In *Proc. 1985 Symposium on Logic Programming*, Boston, pages 68–72, 1985.

[125] M. Paterson and M. Wegman. Linear Unification. *J. Computer and System Sciences.*, 16(2):158–167, 1978.

[126] F. Pereira and S. Shieber. *Prolog and Natural-Language Analysis*. CSLI, 1987.

[127] F. Pereira and D.H.D. Warren. Definite Clause Grammars for Language Analysis—A Survey of the Formalism and a Comparison with Augmented Transision Networks. *Artificial Intelligence*, 13:231–278, 1980.

[128] L. Pereira and R. Nasr. Delta Prolog: A Distributed Logic Programming Language. In *Proc. of International Conf. on Fifth Generation Computer Systems 84*, Tokyo, pages 283–291, North-Holland, 1984.

[129] L. Pereira, F. Pereira, and D.H.D. Warren. *User's Guide to DECsystem-10 Prolog*. DAI. Occasional paper no. 15, Dept. of Artificial Intelligence, University of Edinburgh, 1979.

[130] D. Plaisted. The Occur-Check Problem in Prolog. In *Proc. 1984 Symposium on Logic Programming*, Atlantic City, pages 272–280, 1984.

[131] D. Prawitz. An Improved Proof Procedure. *Theoria*, 26:102–139, 1960.

[132] T. Przymusinski. On the Declarative Semantics of Logic Programs with Negation. In J. Minker, editor, *Foundations of Deductive Databases and Logic Programming*, pages 193–216, Morgan Kaufmann, Los Altos, 1988.

[133] T. Przymusinski. On the Relationship Between Logic Programming and Non-Monotonic Reasoning. In *Proc of AAAI-88*, St. Paul, pages 444–448, 1988.

[134] T. Przymusinski. Perfect Model Semantics. In *Proc. of Fifth International Conf/Symposium on Logic Programming*, Seattle, pages 1081–1096, MIT Press, 1988.

[135] T. Przymusinski. Three-valued Formalizations of Non-Monotonic Reasoning and Logic Programming. In *Proc. of Principles of Knowledge Representation and Reasoning*, Toronto, pages 341–348, Morgan Kaufmann, 1989.

[136] R. Ramakrishnan. Magic Templates: A Spellbounding Approach to Logic Programming. In *Proc. of Fifth International Conf/Symposium on Logic Programming*, Seattle, pages 140–159, MIT Press, 1988.

[137] R. Reiter. On Closed World Data Bases. In H. Gallaire and J. Minker, editors, *Logic and Databases*, pages 55–76, Plenum Press, New York, 1978.

[138] R. Reiter. Towards a Logical Reconstruction of Relational Database Theory. In M. Brodie et. al., editor, *On Conceptual Modelling: Perspectives from Artificial Intelligence, Databases and Programming Languages*, pages 191–233, Springer, 1984.

[139] J.A. Robinson. A Machine-Oriented Logic Based on the Resolution Principle. *J. ACM*, 12:23–41, 1965.

[140] J. A. Robinson. *Logic: Form and Function.* Edinburgh University Press, 1979.

[141] J. A. Robinson and E. Sibert. LOGLISP: Motivation, Design and Implementation. In K. Clark and S-Å. Tärnlund, editors, *Logic Programming*, pages 299–314, Academic Press, 1982.

[142] H. Rogers, Jr. *Theory of Recursive Functions and Effective Computability.* McGraw-Hill, 1967.

[143] P. Roussel. *Prolog: Manuel de Référence et d'Utilisation.* Technical Report, Group d'Intelligence Artificielle, Marseille, 1975.

[144] V. Saraswat. The Concurrent Logic Programming Language CP: Definition and Operational Semantics. In *Conf. Record of 14th Annual ACM Symp. on POPL*, pages 49–62, Munich, West Germany, 1987.

[145] D. Scott. Data Types as Lattices. *SIAM J. Comput.*, 5(3):522–587, 1976.

[146] E. Shapiro. *A Subset of Concurrent Prolog and Its Interpreter.* Technical Report TR–003, ICOT, 1983.

[147] E. Shapiro. Concurrent Prolog: A Progress Report. *IEEE Computer*, August:44–58, 1986.

[148] E. Shapiro, editor. *Concurrent Prolog: Collected Papers.* The MIT-Press, 1988.

[149] E. Shapiro. The Family of Concurrent Logic Programming Languages. *Computing Surveys*, 21(3):413–510, 1989.

[150] J. Shepherdson. Negation as Failure. *J. of Logic Programming*, 1(1):51–80, 1984.

[151] J. Shepherdson. Negation as Failure II. *J. of Logic Programming*, 2(3):185–202, 1985.

[152] J. Shepherdson. Negation in Logic Programming. In J. Minker, editor, *Foundations of Deductive Databases and Logic Programming*, pages 19–88, Morgan Kaufmann, Los Altos, 1988.

[153] J. Shoenfield. *Mathematical Logic.* Addison-Wesley, 1967.

[154] J. Siekmann. Universal Unification. In R. E. Shostak, editor, *Proc. of 7th CADE*, pages 1–42, 1984.

[155] J. Siekmann and G. Wrightson, editors. *Automation of Reasoning I.* Springer-Verlag, 1983.

[156] J. Siekmann and G. Wrightson, editors. *Automation of Reasoning II.* Springer-Verlag, 1983.

[157] J. R. Slagle. Automated Theorem-Proving for Theories with Simplifiers, Commutativity and Associativity. *J. ACM*, 28(3):622–642, 1974.

[158] W. Snyder and J. Gallier. Higher Order-Unification Revisited: Complete Sets of Transformations. Department of Computer and Information Science, University of Pennsylvania, 1988. Preprint.

[159] L. Sterling. A Meta-Level Architecture for Expert Systems. In P. Maes and D. Nardi, editors, *Meta-Level Architectures and Reflection*, pages 301–311, Elsevier Science Publishers B.V. (North-Holland), 1988.

[160] L. Sterling. *Incremental Flavor-Mixing of Meta-Interpreters for Expert System Construction.* Technical Report TR 103-86, Computer Engineering and Science, Case Western Reserve University, 1986.

[161] L. Sterling and A. Lakhotia. Composing Prolog Meta-Interpreters. In *Proc. of Fifth International Conf/Symposium on Logic Programming*, Seattle, pages 386–403, MIT Press, 1988.

[162] L. Sterling and M. Lalee. An Explanation Shell for Expert Systems. *Computational Intelligence*, 2:136–141, 1986.

[163] L. Sterling and E. Shapiro. *The Art of Prolog.* The MIT-Press, 1986.

[164] P. A. Subrahmanyam and J-H. You. FUNLOG: A Computational Model Integrating Logic Programming and Functional Programming. In D. DeGroot and G. Lindstrom, editors, *Logic Programming, Functions, Relations and Equations*, pages 157–198, Prentice-Hall, 1986.

[165] A. Tarski. A Lattice Theoretical Fixpoint Theorem and Its Applications. *Pacific J. Math*, 5:285–309, 1955.

[166] J. Thom and J. Zobel. *NU-Prolog Reference Manual.* Technical Report 86/10, Department of Computer Science, University of Melbourne, 1987. Revised May 1987.

[167] K. Ueda. *Guarded Horn Clauses.* Technical Report TR–103, ICOT, 1985.

[168] J. D. Ullman. Implementation of Logical Query Languages for Databases. *ACM Trans. Database Systems*, 10(3):289–321, 1985.

[169] J. D. Ullman. *Principles of Database and Knowledge-base Systems*. Volume I, Computer Science Press, 1988.

[170] J. D. Ullman. *Principles of Database and Knowledge-base Systems*. Volume II, Computer Science Press, 1989.

[171] D. Van Dalen. *Logic and Structure*. Springer-Verlag, second edition, 1983.

[172] M. van Emden and R. Kowalski. The Semantics of Predicate Logic as a Programming Language. *J. ACM*, 23(4):733–742, 1976.

[173] A. Van Gelder. Negation as Failure Using Tight Derivation for General Logic Programs. In J. Minker, editor, *Foundations of Deductive Databases and Logic Programming*, pages 149–176, Morgan Kaufmann, Los Altos, 1988.

[174] A. van Gelder, K. Ross, and J. Schlipf. *The Well-Founded Semantics for General Logic Programs*. Technical Report UCSC-CRL-88-16, Computer Research Laboratory, University of California, Santa Cruz, 1988.

[175] P. Van Hentenryck. *Constraint Satisfaction in Logic Programming*. The MIT-Press, 1989.

[176] C. Walinsky. CLP($\Sigma^*$): Constraint Logic Programming with Regular Sets. In *Proc. of Sixth International Conf. on Logic Programming*, Lisbon, pages 181–198, MIT Press, 1989.

[177] D. H. D. Warren. Higher-Order Extensions to Prolog: Are They Needed? In J.E. Hayes, D. Michie, and Y-H. Pao, editors, *Machine Intelligence 10*, pages 441–454, Ellis Horwood, 1982.

[178] D. S. Warren. Database Updates in Pure Prolog. In *Proc. of International Conf. on Fifth Generation Computer Systems 84*, Tokyo, pages 244–253, North-Holland, 1984.

[179] Ü. Yalçinalp and L. Sterling. An Integrated Interpreter for Explaining Prolog's Success and Failures. In *Preprints from the META88 workshop, Bristol*, 1988.

[180] R. Yang. *A Parallel Logic Programming Language and Its Implementation*. PhD thesis, Department of Electrical Engineering, Keio University, 1986.

[181] J. Zhang and P. W. Grant. An Automatic Difference-list Transformation Algorithm for Prolog. In *Proc. of ECAI'88*, pages 320–325, 1988.

# Index